8/35

MOUNTAIN
JOURNEYS

*Stories Of Climbers And
Their Climbs*

MOUNTAIN JOURNEYS

Stories Of Climbers And Their Climbs

EDITED BY
JAMES P. VERMEULEN

First published in 1989 by

The Overlook Press
Lewis Hollow Road
Woodstock, New York 12498

Library of Congress Cataloging-in-Publication Data

Mountain journeys.

   1. Mountaineering.   I. Vermeulen, James P., 1949–

GV200.M67   1989   796.5'22   88-43264
ISBN 0-87951-357-8 (cloth)
ISBN 0-87951-366-7 (paper)

CONTENTS

CONTENTS

For my father and all mountaineers

In our modern days, few things remain; night no longer exists, nor cold, nor wind, nor stars. All is neutralized. Where is the rhythm of life? Everything goes so quickly and makes so much noise. The hurried man is ignorant of the grass of the path, its color, its odor, its movement when the wind caresses it.

What a curious encounter then between a man and the high places of the planet, where he finds the silence of forgetfulness. A slope of snow steep as a pane of glass? He climbs it, signing his work with a curious trace. A rock as beautiful as an obelisk? He defies gravity and proves he can go anywhere.

Gaston Rébuffat

ILLUSTRATIONS

FOREWORD

Every mountain is a blank page.

Every blank page holds a frozen word waiting to be animated. Animated, every word leads to another word, until the thought is complete . . . the journey finished . . . the summit realized, even in turning one's back on it and roping down.

Climbing, like writing, depends upon imagination. Imagination depends upon risk. Collectively, climbers form a distinct tribe of risk-takers. Any "civilian" who has emerged from a gathering of mountainers can testify to their odd, group primitivism. They display a distinct body of laws, physical values, aesthetics, a humor that borders on black, desires that verge on the preposterous, and a highly refined technology barely tolerated by their fierce distaste for mechanism. All of this is fused to an extreme, dangerous activity. Above all, wherever two or more of them gather—clustered around a beer-stained table in Chamonix or mustering for an expedition in the courtyard of some Kathmandu hotel, gathered around a campfire or just sharing a tight bivouac—climbers exhibit their tribal bonds in one final, definitive way. They tell stories.

With an often bizarre language pregnant with codified terms and even hand signals, climbers will spend hours on end passing back and forth a richly textured folklore. Many of their tales are as familiar and meaningful to climbers as a bowline knot. Like any subculture's oral or written tradition, mountaineering stories instruct and entertain. The stories allow climbers to weather storms and outwit icy faces they have never encountered, to consider situations, learn tactics, and solve mountain riddles long before they ever start the actual climb. But more importantly, the word carries forward the mountain. Indeed, at the level of desire and imagination, the word *is* the mountain, and vice versa. Without their folklore, ascent would dissolve into brute, pointless labor.

To the nonclimber, mountaineering literature, like ascent itself, can seem forbidding and exclusionary, locked away in slang and radical geography. Happily, the stories in this paper feast were harvested with an eye to feeding everyone, for everyone's feast. They form a window upon a tribe that has spent generations listening to the mountains talk. Here, for all of us, is the mountaineer's blank page come alive.

Jeff Long

PREFACE

When climbers finally gain their hard-won summits, they are usually too cold, oxygen-starved, or exhausted to linger. A cursory panoramic gaze, a few quick photographs of the land falling away below, perhaps a private memento buried beneath the rocks or snow before hurriedly descending—to nonclimbers these fleeting moments hardly appear to justify the endless hours, days, and sometimes months of sacrifice and risk endured to achieve them. Not surprisingly, the question most asked about mountaineers is: Why?

If you query a randomly selected group of people, they will offer a variety of explanations for the behavior of mountain climbers. Some will say climbers are spiritual ascetics seeking a loftier communion through their high altitude, voluntary deprivations. Others will argue that mountaineers are latent artists who envision and "create" routes up alpine walls where flatlanders see only impassable cliffs, ice, and snow. You will also hear climbers labeled escapists and eccentric atavists who, unable to cope with complex modern life, then seek therapeutic simplicity in the mountains where they can climb "for the luxury of a concrete purpose, the summit." And there will always be the vocal percentage who dismiss climbers as merely fools.

Atavists, mystics, artists, fools. Mountaineers are certainly a hard lot to categorize. And if you ask mountaineers themselves, their responses range from Mallory's enigmatic and famous, "Because it is there" quote, to the defensive retort, "if you have to ask the question," to a simple, bemused silence. Normally bold mountaineers often shy away from admitting that they ascend again and again for reasons having to do with pleasure.

For the sheer fun of it. Such a rationale may at first seem incredulous because, to nonclimbers, mountaineering is only climbing—difficult, dangerous, exhausting climbing. Mountaineering, however, is much more. The sociologist Richard S. Mitchell has identified seven things that mountaineers *do* that mark them as mountaineers. Only one of those is climbing. Planning for ascents, amassing and maintaining gear, forming unique relationships with fellow climbers, speaking the eclectic language of mountaineering, training physically and mentally for difficult climbs, ascending, reminiscing about their climbs—these are, Mitchell explains, the complementary and continuous endeavors that pervade the daily lives of climbers and make mountaineering, in the final summation, pleasurable.

This book draws on a vast and rich reservoir of first-person climbing tales to illustrate that inclusive and cyclical nature of mountaineering. From idea to plan, from plan to ascent, and from summit homeward to the inevitable urge to do it all again—the arrangement of stories approximates the ceaseless evolution of climbs and demonstrates, I believe, why climbers never really "leave" their mountains. They wear their summit passions everywhere like familiar old parkas, proving that mountaineering occurs whenever the mind of the climber meets or imagines mountains.

I want to thank those who offered encouragement and timely suggestions during the compilation of this book: Barry Greer; Andrew Harvard; Mike Kennedy; George Hurley; Pat Fletcher; Deborah Baker; and especially Jeff Long, J. Peter Vermeulen, and Marsha Weissman—an invaluable trio of advisers and cheerleaders. For assistance in the selection and preparation of the manuscript, I also thank my generous friends and ropemates Michael Cross, Willard Moulton, and William Morris.

James P. Vermeulen
Editor

MOUNTAIN JOURNEYS

*Stories Of Climbers And
Their Climbs*

1
CHAPTER

BECAUSE IT WAS THERE:

The Call of the Mountains

The Mirage

FELICE BENUZZI

During World War II thousands of Italians stationed in eastern Africa were captured and imprisoned by British forces. Felice Benuzzi, an Italian Colonial Service officer and occasional mountaineer, was one of them. Separated from his wife and children, he was eventually interned near the town of Nanyuki, which lies at the base of 17,040-foot Mount Kenya. The deadly monotony of the changeless prison routines and the uncertain future began to drain Benuzzi of all hope until he hatched an audacious scheme, one that speaks in its own way of all climbers. The following excerpt is from Benuzzi's unique mountaineering account, No Picnic On Mount Kenya.

There came a day when we were transferred to 354 Camp, Nanyuki, at the foot of Mount Kenya. Our carriage—not a cattle truck this time—watched by sentries, remained from 5 A.M. till 11 A.M. in Nairobi station being shunted up and down in order, presumably, to comply with mysterious railway exigencies.

After about a year of incarceration we were able to see people living in freedom, coming and going as they liked. We gazed with fascinated eyes as though witnessing miracles.

A man stepped out of a train and bought a newspaper and a packet of cigarettes at the tobacconist's. He paid with clinking money and went off. Just like that! Soon we hear the sound of the engine of a car starting up. The very idea of steering a car gave me a dizzy feeling.

We saw women, young and good-looking, middle-aged, and

elderly. Among them were undoubtedly fiancées, wives, sisters and mothers, all real, alive, not mere phantoms as were ours in our dreams. We saw children, sweet little ones among them; one wanting to collect that empty red cigarette packet on the platform, another throwing his round arms about the neck of his Daddy who was just stepping out of a train. No doubt the few words they were able to stammer were spoken in English, but from a distance they might as well have been speaking in Italian. Their expressions, their gestures were the same as those of our own children, now interned in the camps of Ethiopia and Somaliland.

It was torture. One could have jumped out of the train for no other purpose than to mix for ten minutes with free people. I would bet that every one of us, looking from our carriage windows onto that crowded Nairobi platform, was busy with thoughts of escape, soon repressed.

The idea of escaping is a vital factor in the mind of every prisoner. On our arrival in East Africa I had as a matter of course carefully considered the chances of reaching the nearest neutral territory, Portuguese East Africa; but I had concluded that, for me at least, this would be impossible. The distances one had to cover were enormous, one needed a frightful lot of money, the opportunity of getting a car, knowledge of the country and of the main languages, and faked documents. Even if one reached Portuguese East Africa the problem of getting home from there presented still greater difficulties. As a matter of fact of all those who attempted to escape during our five years of captivity in order to reach Portuguese East Africa, only a group of four officers succeeded.

In the low barrack of tar-painted hessian, the night had closed in quickly. The wind whistled and rain thundered on the corrugated iron roof. Outside, throughout the camp the ground was a swamp. At every step one raised several pounds of sticky mud on one's shoes.

At a small makeshift table placed between two bunks sat four prisoners playing bridge around a flickering oil-lamp made of an empty meat tin.

"One down," remarked a player sadly putting down his last few cards.

"Of course," said his partner acidly, "if you insist on not drawing trumps . . ."

"But listen. Had I found the ten of spades on my left instead of on my right . . ."

The argument carried on endlessly. It's impossible for a bridge party in a prisoner-of-war camp not to degenerate into an argument.

On another bunk two men sat, wrapped in their blankets, sharing a single light while they read.

At the far end of the barrack a dead silence reigned. No lights showed there yet it was too early for anyone to have gone to sleep. People just lay on their bunks busy with their own thoughts.

On my bunk two men sat beside me, one of them playing chess with an opponent sitting on the opposite bunk, the chessboard on a stool between them.

A train whistled lamentably.

One of the chess players shook his head: "I'm going to lose the queen. I can see no remedy."

The other fellow sitting on my bunk bent over the chessboard, closing his book but keeping a finger between the pages.

"Let me see," he said, studying the strategic situation.

The train whistled again. The flame of the oil-lamp smoked and flickered.

From the bunk opposite the chess players Umberto, who I had thought to be asleep, called me and whispered: "I'm frightfully hungry."

"You're telling me!"

The next morning, May 13, I was shaken out of my sleep by Umberto: "Quick. Get up. Come and look at Mount Kenya!"

"What does it look like?"

"You shall see. The shape recalls Monviso viewed from Turin, but this is far more imposing."

Owing to the rainy season we had so far had no opportunity of seeing anything of the mountain but the huge forest-clad pedestal.

I was so anxious to see it now that I almost got entangled in my bootlaces while dressing.

"Hurry up," shouted Umberto from the door, "otherwise the peak will become covered with clouds again."

I emerged at last, stumbled a few steps in the mud and then I saw it: an ethereal mountain emerging from a tossing sea of clouds framed between two dark barracks—a massive blue-black tooth of sheer rock inlaid with azure glaciers, austere yet floating fairylike on the near horizon. It was the first 17,000-foot peak I had ever seen.

I stood gazing until the vision disappeared among the shifting cloud banks.

For hours afterward I remained spellbound.

I had definitely fallen in love.

Day followed weary day and the mountain remained blanketed under a pall mist and cloud. The one glimpse I had had of it days before seemed like a memory of a dream. Prison life fastened on me like a leaden chain. Future prospects were not even considered and only the present existed for us, dark and dismal.

For three months I had had no news of my family and to add to my anxiety there were rumors of a fatal epidemic of measles raging among the children in the evacuation camps of Ethiopia. Nerves were near the breaking point. The maddening worries about which one could do nothing, the passivity to which we were condemned, the deadly monotony of the rains and above all the communal life one was forced to lead in a small barrack with twenty-five or thirty similarly irritable people, seemed likely to drive one mad.

Never to be a moment alone was perhaps the worst thing for us in our state of nerves. Those with whom I shared a barrack were individually all nice lads, well bred and equitable by temperament, but how they racked one's nerves in the mass! Their most trivial activities, like knocking a nail into a pole on which to hang a towel or pulling aside a bunk in order to look for a missing clog, made one irritable.

Forced to endure the *milieu* we seemed most afraid of losing our individuality. Sometimes one felt a childish urge to assert one's personality in almost any manner, shouting nonsense, banging an empty tin, showing by every act that one was still able to do something other than to wait passively. I have seen normally calm people suddenly rise from their bunks and climb the roof-poles of the barrack, barking like monkeys. I felt I understood them and they had my sympathy.

On this particular evening even the last resource of the prisoner, a remnant of sense of humor, had left me and I felt only a dreadful emptiness, as if I had lost contact with the very ground under my feet.

The past was finished; there was nothing more to think about, to grasp. A normal life in the future seemed so far off, so impossible, that I did not even long for it any more. Only the present existed, unavoidable, overwhelming. For me, Time stood still. It was easy to understand how people go mad.

There was no oil left in the lamp and even if there had been I had no desire to read. I got up from my bunk and went slowly out of the barrack.

Umberto was on his bunk playing his thousandth game of patience. He raised his hand as he saw me:

"If this one comes out, we shall be free this year."

I could not even smile. I went out.

It had stopped raining and a chorus of crickets sang loud in the night. A prisoner walked with heavy steps toward the latrines and cursed the quaggy mud comprehensively.

I met another friend and accepted his invitation to play chess. I lost all three games and as I tramped toward my barrack in the darkness I was in no better mood than before, though normally I am not a bad loser. I was as tired as though I had marched for miles and miles. I did not even feel hungry.

As I approached my barrack I heard the noise of hammering. I wondered who was busy at that hour of the night and what he was doing. A strange sense of envy crept into my mind. That prisoner had set himself a task, whatever it was. For him the future existed because presumably he meant to finish his job. For the moment he had found a remedy against captivity.

The night sky was clear. There was a smell of good earth in the air such as I had seldom noticed in Africa. I was thinking, "The future exists if you know how to make it;" and "It's up to you," as I turned the corner of my barrack at the exact spot from which I had seen Mount Kenya for the first time, and from which I had always since then cast a look in the direction of the peak.

Now it was visible again and in the starlight it looked even more tantalizing than in daylight. The white glaciers gleamed with mysterious light and its superb summit towered against the sky. It was a challenge.

A thought crossed my numbed mind like a flash.

"What are you doing here?"
"I am waiting for midday. And you, what are you waiting for?"
"For the end of the war."

Nobody laughed at this sort of joke any more, because it had ceased to be a joke. It was a real expression of feeling. Time was no longer considered by the average prisoner as something of value to be exploited; time for them was an enemy, but for me this was no longer true.

I was already busy with a secret plan, which slowly took definite shape.

A prisoner of the last World War wrote in his memoirs: "At the front one takes risks, but one does not suffer; in captivity one does not take risks but one suffers."

In order to break the monotony of life one had only to start taking risks again, to try to get out of this Noah's Ark, which was preserving us from the risks of war but isolating us from the world, to get out into the deluge of life. If there is no means of escaping to a neutral country or of living under a false name in occupied Somalia as many have done, then, I thought, at least I shall stage a break in this awful travesty of life. I shall try to get out, climb Mount Kenya, and return here.

I realized from the start that I couldn't do this single-handed; I should have to find companions. As a proof that we had reached the summit—if ever we did—we should leave a flag there.

On page 108 of a torn copy of Steinbeck's *Grapes of Wrath* I found the following paragraph underlined:

> When I was in jail I never thought of the moment of liberation. I thought only of today, perhaps of the football match to be played on the following Saturday, never beyond. I took the days as they came.

An anonymous prisoner of war had written in the margin, "Good advice."

But, anonymous brother, have you ever thought of one difference between the conditions of a man sentenced to jail for an offense and those of a prisoner of war? The former, however long his sentence may be, has a precise knowledge of the date of his liberation; we on the other hand have not. No one can foretell how long this war will last, how long our sentence will last.

The more I considered the idea of escape, the more I realized the magnitude of the task I had set for myself. Should we be able to climb without a long period of acclimatization in the thin air of 17,000 feet? How should we make the actual climb? Whom should I ask to accompany me? How could we get out of the camp and in again? These and other problems kept my mind fully occupied. I found it fascinating to elaborate, in the utmost secrecy, the first details of my scheme.

Life took on another rhythm because it had a purpose.

Just a Small Mountain

JOE McGINNISS

The urge to climb, to ascend points higher than oneself, is often difficult to explain and sometimes impossible to justify. In 1975, Joe Mc-Ginniss accompanied several government employees on a twelve-day hike above the Arctic Circle in Alaska's Brooks Range. They were surveying a remote mountain region prior to its inclusion within the proposed Gates Of The Arctic National Park. Hoping to visit well-known Cockedhat Mountain, but tent-bound instead by several days of rainy weather, the bored men struck off one afternoon on separate hikes. Out of curiosity, McGinnis decided to ascend partway up a nameless peak near camp and, quite by accident, became an unwilling mountaineer. This neophyte's encounter with the high places is taken from McGinniss's book, Going To Extremes.

The morning was foggy and still. A solid low overcast blocked all view of anything more than fifty feet above the ground. We stayed in our tents much later than usual. There seemed nothing to get up for. Nothing to see; nothing to do. And we suffered from the extreme frustration of knowing that we had such a limited amount of time remaining to us. We could spend one more night here; possibly two. Then we would have to move on, further up the Itkillik Valley. Or down the valley. Up the map, anyway. Further north. Because there were other areas which John Kauffman wanted to reach on this trip.

So it seemed possible that, having come all this distance, we would never even see Cockedhat Mountain. Not that the trip would have then been deemed a failure. We had moved, not only beyond tree line, but beyond the standard definitions of concepts such as failure and success. Here, there would be a failure only if someone fell off a mountain or got mauled by a bear. Otherwise, just being there was a success. Still, to spend the remainder of the trip wandering creek beds in heavy mist would have been, at the least, a disappointment.

I lay in the tent, reading the one book I had brought with me, the Viking Portable Edition of Faulkner. I had never enjoyed Faulkner very much, but I thought that now, possibly, I would find myself in the mood for his novella *The Bear*.

Ray Bane lay next to me, filling page after page in a notebook. "I don't think a wilderness experience is complete," he said, "until it's been written about."

I wandered outside for a while and tossed a willow branch or two in the fire. I was getting into a mood as gloomy as the day. What a shame that we had, apparently, used up our quota of good weather on what had been, in terms of scenery and terrain, the least dramatic portion of the trip. And what an amazing contrast between one side of Oolah Pass and the other. That bright hot sun the first three days. And now three days of Arctic mist. Here we were, more than halfway up a valley, which, quite possibly, no one in modern times had viewed before, except by air. And now we weren't able to see it either. Well, only the bottom fifty feet. Even without John Kauffmann to tell us how dramatic Cockedhat Mountain looked, we could have guessed, just from studying the topographical maps, that something splendid and unusual lay at the valley's upper end. Just from the way all the little brown contour lines wriggled around. We had reached a point, however, where maps did not satisfy. We were hungry for the real thing. But we had absolutely no control over whether or not we would ever be able to see it, and absolutely no way of predicting what direction the weather pattern might take. Sometimes, Ray Bane said, weather like this blew off in a couple of days. Sometimes it settled in for weeks. The general rule, however, was that as August progressed, weather in the Arctic turned damp, as well as colder. We were right at the midline. Two weeks earlier, Ray said, he could have predicted with confidence that the sun would be shining within a couple of days. Two weeks later, he would have advised us to pack our things and move on. Right now, he could not guess. So we sat around the fire and tried to convince ourselves that the overcast was rising, or brightening, just a bit. But then new drizzle started and we all returned to our tents.

"Okay," Ray said. "I've had enough. Drastic measures are called for." He put down his notebook and unzipped the netting at the front of our tent. He stepped outside into the mist. I lay down my Faulkner and followed.

He began shouting, in an angry, guttural voice, at the sky. He was shouting something in Eskimo, repeating the same phrases several times.

"There," he said, "that ought to do it."

"What did you say?"

"I'm not sure I really ought to translate," he said. "It's pretty vulgar." But by then everyone else had come out of their tents, too, hearing the noise, and Ray had no choice. It was, he said, an old Eskimo chant, used to anger the sun; to provoke it into coming out from its hiding place behind the clouds. In translation it was: "Sun, Sun, your vagina smells horrible." Sometimes, Ray said, crude methods prove to be the most effective.

The weather did not improve, but by midday restlessness overcame our depression. We decided to split up and take day hikes in different directions. John Kauffmann and Boyd would go up the ravine in which we were camped. Ray said he would venture further up the main valley so that, if the weather did improve the next day, he would have an idea of the best route to Cockedhat. Ogden said his feet were bothering him and that he really rather welcomed a day off. He would spend the afternoon in camp.

I looked at the mountain just above us. Its lower slope began across the tributary stream, just on the other side of the ravine. The slope was composed mostly of scree and talus: loose rock debris. The upper, craggy, rocky section disappeared into the mist. On the map, the summit, which would be almost directly above our camp, across the ravine, seemed to be about 5,500 feet. I decided I would hike up the lower slope, until it became too difficult to go higher.

It was 1 P.M. when I began. I crossed the tributary and hiked up the east side of the ravine for about a mile. Then I began to cut diagonally up the slope, back in the direction from which I'd come. The higher I went, the steeper the side of the slope became, and when I looked down, after about forty-five minutes, I was surprised both by how far up I had come and by how sharply the slope dropped off beneath my feet. I was also surprised at the looseness of the scree. Ever time I stopped, for even a moment, I could feel the slope begin to give way beneath my boots, and start to slide. Therefore, I had to keep moving.

There was a rock ledge above me. I couldn't be sure how far, maybe another two hundred feet. I started toward it, thinking that, once there, I would at least be able to sit and rest. I began scrambling diagonally, on all fours, across the scree, which got looser the higher I went, and seemed ever more prone to start sliding. I was already so high by this time, and the mountainside below me so steep, that I decided I'd be better off continuing up. From that ledge above me, I could probably find an easier and safer route down. Now, if I could only reach the ledge before the whole damn mountain started to slide.

The scree was turning to powder now, and more and more was giving way beneath me with every step. I would start to slide downward, then claw my way back, always trying to move diagonally upward toward the ledge. Once a real slide started, it might not stop, and with nothing solid to cling to below the ledge, I might become part of the slide.

I was badly out of breath now, and getting worried, but I continued to scuttle, as best I could, gradually higher. The ledge appeared to be only fifty feet above me, but those fifty feet suddenly took on a new and more alarming degree of steepness. There was now almost a sheer wall of scree, and I scrambled up frantically, grabbing at any rock that looked larger than my hand. I could find nothing—neither handhold nor foothold—that would support me for more than seconds, until I reached the base of the ledge.

I wedged a boot into a crevice between two loose rocks, tested it with weight, and it held. I grabbed quickly at rocks that jutted out overhead, and found a couple of cracks into which I was able to squeeze my fingers. I clung to the side of the ledge, panting for breath. Then I made the mistake of looking down.

From below, it had seemed I could just continue to scramble up the scree all the way. I had not realized until too late that the last fifty feet were not a scree slope at all, but that they were, in fact, the side of a cliff.

I was stuck. I was hanging on to the cliff now, precariously, and there was no orderly, safe way to climb down. All I could have done was to let go, which, I realized, would have meant an unbroken fall of at least thirty feet to looser rocks below, and then probably an uncontrollable slide down the scree. A process that seemed quite certain to result in, if not loss of life, then loss of consciousness and, more than likely, broken bones. Not a cheery prospect deep in the Brooks Range.

Up was the only way to go. And I had to move fast, because this temporary hold I had was giving way. This was most definitely rock climbing now; not by any stretch of definition was it hiking. What was worse, it was climbing on extremely unsuitable rock, alone, with no equipment, no training, and absolutely no aptitude for the techniques.

I moved quickly. From both fatigue and fear. My legs, when I would find a jutting rock on which to support them, were trembling so hard I was afraid that the motion alone would dislodge the rock. My calf and thigh muscles had not been expecting this; nor had the muscles of my arms. I wasn't even wearing gloves, in fact—this was supposed to have been just a little walk on the lower slope— and my fingers were now scraped and bleeding.

I paused once more, looking up. I still could not see how far I had to go to reach the ledge. What if it had not really been a ledge? What if I had judged it incorrectly from below? I was going higher and higher now, up the crumbling rock face of a mountain, and with every new frantic scramble, the consequences were I to fall, grew more severe.

Once more I reached above me for something to cling to as I tried to push myself upward with my legs. I could feel rocks all around me giving way. This was an old decayed mountain. The whole face seemed about to collapse. Another handhold, and then another, and then—thank God!—I hoisted myself up over the ledge, onto a small plateau that was covered by a thin layer of tundra. I lay there, panting, in my no longer brand-new Camp Seven wind parka. I kissed the tundra. How magnificent it felt; how splendid it looked; how fine it was to feel living earth again.

The ledge was the size of about three or four double beds pushed together. Once my breath and composure had returned, I began to look around, trying to decide what to do next. I felt like a cat up a tree, but I was a long way from the nearest fire department.

Descending the way I had come up was out of the question. But in what other direction could I go? I had approached this ledge from the southwest, originally, cutting back toward the main valley after my hike of a mile or so up the ravine. The ledge was on the western, or ravine side, of the mountain. Just east of it, there was a long, sharp drop, and then the main mountain wall rose even higher. Looking up in that direction, I could see an old, dirty glacier about a hundred yards away. It was just a rim of ice, really; flanked by moraine. There was a ridge leading out from the rock wall to the left of this glacier, a long ridge that leveled out quickly and then proceeded in a northerly direction, rising, as it did, toward what I considered the front of the mountain—the aspect that overlooked the valley. It seemed that if I started out along the ridge that led north from the ledge I was on, I might at some point be able to cut across the scree side of a basin between the ridges and reach the second, longer ridge. From there, I might proceed to the northern face of the mountain, and, I hoped, find a way back down to the valley floor.

I was reluctant to leave the hard-won security of my little ledge, but a cold mist was now swirling around me, and a steady drizzle was starting to fall. It was already 4 P.M., and if I were not back in camp by dinnertime the others would worry, and eventually come looking for me. To cause them that inconvenience would have been a serious breach of hiking etiquette. Beside, my instinct for self-preservation had made me extremely eager to get back to the valley floor.

Amazing, how relative it all was: a week earlier, a campsite halfway up a nameless side valley that led from the Itkillik River to Cockedhat Mountain in the central Brooks Range, north of the Arctic Divide, would have seemed the ultimate in wildness and remoteness. It was still not exactly an urban ambience, but from 2,000 feet higher—from a tundra-covered perch two-thirds of the way up a nameless and unstable mountain—that camp seemed the essence of security and comfort.

Within a quarter mile, the ridge that my ledge opened onto began a steep climb to a rock wall of which I wanted no part. I dropped down from the ridge and tried to work my way around the scree rim of the basin, to the ridge that led down from the glacier. It was the same syndrome as before: scurrying along on all fours with slope sliding away beneath my feet. By now, though, I was familiar enough with the sensation to be merely worried, and not panic-stricken, and I already was sufficiently experienced in the technique to know enough not to stop. I made it to the new ridge, which was longer, wider, and more substantial than the one I had left. I was able to walk along it comfortably, heading north, toward what would be the front of the mountain. This ridge, too, sloped upward, at first gradually, then sharply, but here, instead of a sheer, unclimbable rock wall, there was a sharp slope of loose talus and patches of tundra, up which I was able to pick my way. I was once again on hands and knees—climbing, not hiking—and the larger rocks and boulders of the talus seemed scarcely more stable than the scree, but there were little veins of tundra threaded among them, and, by choosing my route carefully, I was able to work my way to the top without mishap.

I climbed over a final row of boulders, onto a ledge, looked around, and only then realized that I had, quite by accident, ascended to the summit of the mountain. To the front summit, at least. Whether or not it was the true summit depended on where one considered that one mountain ended and another began, for a mile or so further back, above the glacier, this ridge, and the rock wall it led to, climbed to an even higher point. But where I was now standing was what had appeared as the summit of this mountain from below, from our camp, and without having had the slightest intention of doing so, I had reached it.

Across the ravine, there was a 6,800-foot peak about a mile and half back to the southwest. It was a craggy, barren mountain, as was the one I was on, and its summit was enshrouded by fog. My own altitude seemed to be about 5,500 feet.

Looking due west, I could see to the upper end of the valley, to where the front walls of the Cockedhat Mountain mass began to rise. They appeared made of dark gray, almost slate-colored stone, but it was hard to tell much about them because even the lower slopes were quickly hidden by drifting mist.

To the east, I could look all the way down the valley, to the Itkillik Valley and, where clouds permitted, to the Oolah Mountain Sector that lay beyond.

But it was the view directly across the side valley, the view of the weird, unearthly, jumbled, tilted, platelike, scaly, multilayered valley wall, that held my eye.

We had experienced some sense of it yesterday, from the head of the valley, but from here, looking straight across, from this higher altitude, the scene was much more astonishing.

I had no idea what sort of geologic activity had formed these mountains, or why they were—in angle, shape, and texture—so unlike any other mountains I'd ever seen, but looking at them through the mist, from my hard-won mini-summit, was like being given a unique glimpse into prehistoric times.

It was as if a giant had been sleeping in this valley and had rolled to one side, pressing back the northern valley wall. Then another image came to mind: the angle at which those mountain walls sloped back from the valley floor seemed the same as that angle at which human figures in certain Renaissance paintings recoiled from the image of the newly risen Christ.

I stepped forward to the front of the ledge and looked down, through the mist, to the bottom of the valley. A rainbow arched toward the lower end. Looking just below me, and slightly to the left, across the ravine, I could also see, very faintly, through my monocular, and through the mist, the specks of bright color that were our tents.

Foolishly, and in a hurry, I decided to work my way straight down the front of the ledge, instead of descending to the east, on a more gradual slope that led back down the valley, away from the camp. I had to come down chimney fashion, my back wedged against one side of a little rock chute, my feet against the other, with rocks and boulders, loosened by my passage, beginning to tumble down behind me. I clung to the sides, fighting for handholds and footholds, just as I had done coming up, but here, with the rocks even bigger, though just as loose, the situation was, in a way, even more precarious. Several times the rolling rocks, and the smaller stones and loose scree that fell behind them, almost carried me away, and at this angle it would not have been a slide that resulted in only cuts and bruises, it would have meant, once again, a fall, of undetermined distance, the consequences of which I much preferred not to imagine.

Tired and trembling, both from exhaustion and from the aftermath of fear, I slid back into camp at 6 P.M. The others were already there. Ogden, in fact, had spotted me, through binoculars, about halfway down, and had followed my progress the rest of the way.

"Jolly good show," he remarked. "Thought you might have been in for a bit of a tumble."

Freeze-dried stew and freeze-dried rice in the damp and chilly fog and it was the best meal of the trip. I kept looking up at where I had been; not really sure I had done it, and wondering whether I had intended to all along. It was, actually, an ordinary-looking mountain, and the front summit, I determined from the map, was not much more than 1,500 feet above our camp. But I knew how deceiving appearances were. I had been up there. And it was very different from down here.

Alone on Bear Creek Spire

GALEN ROWELL

The traditional mountaineer is essentially an explorer, one for whom the joys of discovery often supersede the satisfactions of a victorious ascent. Testing one's skills and resources over unknown or unclimbed terrain is, for many climbers, the highest expression of their sport. In 1971, the well-known climber, writer, and photographer, Galen Rowell, made the first ascent of Bear Creek Spire's south face—alone. The description of that adventurous climb is from his collection of essays and stories, High And Wild.

On a Friday evening in 1971 I drove two hundred miles east from Berkeley, California, on a road as familiar to me as my home street. It led to Yosemite Valley, where I had been climbing on weekends for a decade. As the winding road enters the national park, it parallels the Merced River through a deep gorge, and the canyon broadens into a flat valley surrounded by cliffs that rise to the stars.

Even to those who have been there hundreds of times, the first glimpse of Yosemite is overwhelming. As a child I imagined that the valley at night looked like a movie set. Moonlight reflected from the massive granite forms made them appear too stark and simple to be big; the valley seemed like a small model of itself. I felt I could almost reach out and touch the tops of cliffs 3,000 feet overhead.

I stopped at Yosemite Lodge, where I met a group of climbers who gathered there every weekend. Within minutes I was invited to join friends on a route I had done many times before. Though I had intended to climb in Yosemite, I felt a sudden urge to change that plan and suggested an alternative—the south face of Bear Creek Spire in the John Muir Wilderness adjoining Yosemite National. No interest. I might as well have suggested Patagonia.

I sat and thought for a while about why I had lost enthusiasm for a Yosemite climb, and soon realized that I felt a need to escape the security Yosemite represented. It was home—familiar walls, faces, sounds, smells—and I was already part of an earlier generation, from a time when climbers knew the wonder of gazing at great cliffs still untouched by the hand of man. When I first climbed in Yosemite in 1957, none of the big walls had been ascended. Since that time, all of Yosemite's major cliffs had been climbed by at least one route; El Capitan now had eleven; the front face of Half Dome, four. The simple joys of exploration were on the wane; in their place was a trend to count and compare experiences with those of others who had climbed the same routes. I had no doubt that many Yosemite climbs demanded greater skill than the hardest routes of the highest ranges, but a big red flag went up when I saw climbers far more talented than myself unwilling to test in the nearby wilderness the skills acquired in the fair-weather womb. There was little I could do personally to reverse what I considered an unfortunate trend, except to bow out of it. I decided to go to Bear Creek Spire, alone. The decision to solo did not come from any high motive; quite simply, no one would go with me.

I slept fitfully in a crowded campground before driving at dawn toward Tioga Pass, on the park's eastern boundary. The pass, at almost 10,000 feet, was just below timberline; and though summer was nearly over, the meadows were still lush. My climb would begin in just this sort of terrain, but farther south, where not a single road crossed the rugged Sierra crest for two hundred miles. To reach my starting point I drove another hundred miles, first dropping thousands of feet to the desert floor of the Mono Basin, then along the base of the mountains until a dead-end side road brought me back up to 10,400 feet.

Here I locked my ten-speed bicycle to a tree in the woods not far from the roadhead. My plan was to drive on to another trailhead farther south, walk eight miles in and 5000 feet up to the base of Bear Creek Spire, climb it, traverse the north side to pick up my bicycle, and ride forty miles back to my car.

From where I cached my bike, I could see Bear Creek Spire about ten miles away, and before turning around to continue south, I took a long look at it. I had once wondered why this undistinguished 13,713-foot peak, which had been climbed from the west by a moderate scramble in 1923, was named a spire. The answer was clear when I first saw its south face from the ridge of another mountain. The face is a pointed blade of granite, which to the best of my knowledge had never been attempted.

I drove on into America's deepest valley, the Owens Valley, created by a massive fault block between the 14,000-foot summits of the High Sierra and the White Mountains twenty miles to the east. An earthquake greater than the one that almost destroyed San Francisco in 1906 dropped the valley twenty feet in 1872. I took a side road up Pine Creek to the largest tungsten mine in North America. Outwardly it looks like a normal mining operation in a mountain valley; actually, it is upside-down. Shafts climb from the tunnel up into the mountains, and one penetrates Bear Creek Spire, four air miles away.

I left my car and began hiking away from the creaks and whines of the milling operation. I soon came upon what looked like a natural marble quarry: glacial polish had combined with frost-heaving to segment white aplite into piles of burnished blocks that gleamed against the surrounding granite. By noon I left the last whitebark pines below and set out across a barren moraine composed of loose granite blocks. When I saw the vivid green of a tiny lake set amid the glacial debris, I knew that ice somewhere beneath the surface was still carving the landscape. Glacially scoured rock dust—"glacier milk"—accounted for the water's tint.

My memory of how impressive the south face appeared from a distance had been tempered somewhat by a recent look at the contour map, which showed the wall to be about eight hundred feet high and not particularly steep. Now, at close range, my original impression returned; the face was fully 1200 feet high, without a single large ledge. The situation gave me pause. It was two o'clock in the afternoon, and I was carrying only minimal equipment: a three-eighth-inch rope, one quart of water, some food, a short, half sleeping bag, and a handful of pitons and carabiners. I foresaw a demanding afternoon on the face under a hot sun, but nothing to make me seriously consider giving up the ascent.

The climbing began with deceptive ease. I didn't even rope up for several hundred feet, because cracks and handholds kept appearing in just the right places. A squeeze chimney at nearly 13,000 feet left me panting, however; and I used rope and pitons for safety on the steep face above. I made steady progress until I reached a small pedestal and discovered a smooth headwall above; I tried to free-climb it with the rope for safety, but failed. The only crack I could spot was separated from better terrain above by about eight feet of blank overhanging rock.

Dropping back to the top of the pedestal, I drank the last of my water and thought about Yosemite. My bright idea of a remote climb was losing its luster rapidly. I could picture my friends in the Valley, who had probably come down from their routes before the afternoon heat, and were now sitting in the restaurant with a drink or cavorting in Camp Four, the Yosemite climbers' camp. I, on the other hand, contemplated a cold night at 13,000 feet and an arduous descent in the morning.

After a brief rest, I clipped a sling into my highest piton and stood on it. The overhanging wall pushed me out, and after a futile effort to surmount it, I descended again. The sun was about to leave the face, and I knew that my best chance was to give it everything I had while the rock was still warm. This time I put the shortest possible loop into the piton so I could stand a bit higher than before. The headwall had a shallow vertical groove; and I worked, with elbow pointed skyward, to secure an arm lock between my inverted palm and shoulder. When I tried to move my free leg, I felt completely helpless, but I made one final attempt. Dangling from the overhang by the arm lock, I pulled my foot away from the security of the loop and up onto the eye of the piton. The extra inches let me move the arm lock higher. I was now out of balance, but very near a wide crack, and a desperate lunge took me high enough to jam a fist into the bottom of the crack. Relief surged through me, as though a gun aimed at my head had just misfired. The danger was not entirely over, however; I knew that my adrenalin-stimulated strength would be short-lived. I continued up, fist-jamming thirty feet to a narrow ledge, and panted there for long minutes. The ledge traversed the steep headwall for a hundred feet and then connected with a chimney system. It was a lucky break; I wouldn't need to bivouac on the cliff if I could move efficiently in the minutes remaining before dark.

The day's harsh sunlight gave way to dusk, and in the indirect light I could see into the shadowy north faces of an endless sea of peaks. It was a more rugged Sierra vista than I had ever known in summer. At my feet were alpine flowers; this very contrast of life and barren rock had let John Muir to call the range "the gentle wilderness."

All along the ledge yellow hulsea and purple poplemoniun were still in bloom. Sierra bighorn sheep depend on them as an important part of their summer diet. In Muir's day, the flowers might have been nibbled down to the roots. Weathered horns and ancient Indian hunting blinds attest to the fact that the bighorn, now a threatened species, once ranged as high as the very tops of most mountains along the crest. I could imagine a ram profiled on the summit ramparts only a hundred feet above me as I hurried along the ledge below.

Having reached the chimney, I climbed steadily with the pack suspended below me, and within minutes I was standing on the summit in the last rays of the sun. I would have liked to linger, but it was late. I scrambled toward the shadows of the north side, heading down the broken face toward a tiny meadow with a stream. An hour later, in the dark, I bent down for my first drink in many hours.

I had planned to stop by the stream for only a minute, then descend in the moonlight to the forest below, but after eating a package of freeze-dried hash mixed with cold water, I realized that my legs didn't want to support my body any longer. Without standing up again, I crawled into my half-bag. Though extremely fatigued, I lay sleepless for hours, still carried along by the forced awareness the day had demanded. I felt lucky to have made the climb and to have gotten safely down. I no longer envied the climbers loafing around the Yosemite campground. I was content where I was, alone under the stars on a clear night. . . .

The North Face of the Drus

GASTON RÉBUFFAT

Gaston Rébuffat, the famous French mountain guide, was one of those few for whom climbing approached a spiritual practice. The variant moods of mountain light, storms, the smell of alpine rock—he held a deep and abiding appreciation for all aspects of mountaineering. The following translation from Rébuffat's book, Stars And Storms, *describes his ascent of a well-known peak in the European Alps.*

The Montenvers train moves off slowly, engages its rack, begins to climb, jolting its cargo of chattering or sleeping tourists, plunges into a tunnel, then another, arrives in Caileet and stops: the engine needs water.

The wind from the height begins to blow.

The train departs again; shortly after, in a curve, a spire appears: it's the Drus . . . within a stone's throw.

The tourists rush to look and then sit down again.

The mountain climbers look fondly; the Drus have always been the first summits to which the train brings them. They know these peaks well, they wait for them, and rediscover them as they would an old friend. At the train station platform, next to the tired engine, the guide announces, "Before you are the Drus, where the drama of 'First On The Rope' took place; on the left, in profile, the northern wall with its niche, this enormous hole half way up. Opposite is the western wall with a barrier of overhangs. On the right is the ridge of the Flammes de Pierre. . . ."

* * *

The name of Franz Lochmatter remains associated with this northern face. Since 1904, with his brother Josef and Captain V.J.E.
Ryan, he dared to attack this wall; the three climbers succeeded in
climbing as far as 70 meters from the niche; a remarkable feat for
the period.

In 1930, Félix Batier and Arthur Ravanel climbed a third of the
wall. Two years later, during an attempt, the German climbers
Krinner and Kofler fell to their deaths, approximately one hundred
meters above the bergschrund. Their comrades Bratschko and Schrei-
ner, who had seen them fall, turned back.

A few days later, on July 21 and 22, 1932, two Swiss climbers
Robert Gréloz and André Roch, who had climbed the ordinary route
[the easier standard route up another side of the mountain], made
the first and only descent of the wall; a dizzy journey with a series
of unending rappels.

In 1935, Dupont, Gotch, Lamert, and Mussard from Geneva,
succeeded in climbing 50 meters above the niche, but then were
forced to give up. Three days later, on July 31 and August 1, Pierre
Allain and Raymond Leininger succeeded in the ascent. A great
first!

The guide is on the mountains each day with different companions. The weather has been good for two weeks and I have been
climbing nonstop. But this afternoon, while we descended the Aig-
uilles du Diable, the sun slowly dissolved and drowned in a confusion
of clouds streaking the west. My companion, Michel del Campo,
was almost joyful with this bad weather which announced the end
of vacation and fewer regrets on leaving Chamonix. But I was thinking about René Mailleux; with him I had to bivouac tomorrow at
the foot of the north face of the Drus in order to climb the next
day, August 14. To delay the journey was impossible. The Festival
of the Guides was on August 15 and I had to be there. Good or
bad weather, the Mont Blanc chain is deserted: the guides of Chamonix and of Courmayeur would be in the valley for their annual

festival; there, as at home, the same rule and the same tradition exist.

In the evening, on La Poste square, I met René. As usual, we wandered through Chamonix doing the tour of the barometers; but in all mountain centers, these scientific instruments are always suspect for promising clear skies even when the west releases its reserve of clouds.

The next day, it was raining. René was heart-broken; I knew that for years he wanted to climb this northern face.

In the afternoon, there was a clearing and the sun was shining slightly; you could even see the summits. Luckily, it had not snowed high up. We were sorry that we had not left, but, shortly later, the sky became cloudy again and this time, the barometer dropped. We went from pastry shop to pastry shop and from Guides' office to the café opposite. An idea kept going through my head but I didn't dare put it into words. Finally, I asked René:

"Are you in shape? Could you climb quickly?"

"Very quickly, if necessary." He hesitated a moment and then added, "Why?"

"There is a solution to try. If the weather is good tomorrow, let's take the first train to Montenvers, at 8:30, and try to do the climb in the afternoon."

There are some moments of intense joy: I watched René's face light up with a smile; the climb had begun. Our happiness overshadowed the evidence of the heavy evening sky.

"Until tomorrow morning at 8:15 at the Montenvers stations."

Then we left each other.

But since I was alone, the heavy sky seemed hopeless to me; not a single star.

I had dinner with Michel, and, later some friends took me to the Outa, where they were going to celebrate their departure. At two in the morning when we left, a few stars were winking. At 7:30, when my alarm clock rang, the weather was really good. René would be at the train.

I prepared my bag, jumped on my bike, and raced to the train station of Montenvers. René was there, happy and impatient.

I had breakfast on the train, reading a newspaper that a tourist loaned me, and wondering if we were really going to the north face of the Drus.

At a curve after Caillet, the Drus appeared more beautiful than usual; they already belonged a little to us.

At 9:15, we were at Montenvers. The guide was beginning his convincing speech. The spivs were going to wait for the tourists at the end of the path. We crossed the Mer de Glace in a hurry. At 12:30, we had a picnic on the grass of the last terraces. Forty-five minutes later, we roped up and passed the bergschrund: the long awaited climb began . . .

Nature is only traditions: the turning of seasons, of day and night, of sun and of storm. Mountain climbing is the same: the difficult awakening, the glance at the sky through the window of shelter, breakfast swallowed without appetite, the departure by lantern, the thousand and one things about the climb, the return toward noon, the wandering on the sheltered terrace . . .

Today, at the hour in which peaceful people were having coffee, at the hour in which climbers usually finished their climb, I felt a certain uneasiness to be beginning: a kind of fear, like the fear that must trouble men in the ages when mountains were made only for demons and gods.

But the good weather returned like a gift, and it was necessary to take it. There we were, in shirt sleeves, at an outrageous hour, on the north face of the Drus. The weather was fine that August afternoon! The wall was in the shade, but an encompassing mildness breathed cheerfulness instead of the severity and the cold of the early morning. A strange charm broke free: surely the mountain was going to confide secrets to us; this afternoon had the beauty of autumn.

We climbed quickly, very quickly indeed for we had to! To-morrow morning, I had to be in Chamonix for the Festival of the Guides. That brought a zest to our climb. To go quickly for the sake of going quickly often seemed stupid to us, but today was a different story: we only had a few hours to climb the eight hundred meters of the wall. René had not exaggerated when he told me that he was capable of moving fast: he was constantly on my heels. Around three o'clock, we arrived at the Niche, this giant thumb-print in the clay of our mountain. We stopped to look at it, and also the west face which rose like a stone waterspout of moraines as far as the sky.

"Ten years from now, that will be climbed," I said to René.

We ate a few dates, some dried currants, an orange—the fruits of the sun in the fresh air of the north face—then we started the climb again. We climbed with pleasure and ease. Our movements were linked together without sudden jolts and flowed like water from a spring. It is the characteristic of all the skills of a well-trained body to suppress the difficulty and to obtain only the joy of work well-done and well-prepared. As children, we used to climb trees; perhaps we knew how to maintain that instinct. It seemed to me that if we were suddenly stopped and asked the inevitable question: "Why do you climb mountains?" today we would at once answer: "We are made for it."

Instinct, love of rocks, skill . . . we climb without being overcome by the problems of climbing. Thus, everything was a benefit: watching the climb, the joyous spirit could wander. What a delightful afternoon!

During this agreeable climb, there were no incidences nor accidents.

The air was fresh, kind, brotherly. The sun hidden behind the west face spared us its overpowering heat, but to be there, nearby, it spread serenity. Down below, the Montenvers train continued to pick at the rail, the torrent to flow, the glacier to advance imperceptibly, the waterfall to tear its sheet of water in a disorderly fringe. . . . Nearby, the rock had the good rock odor, and these innumerable grains of granite continued to become encrusted in our fingers and in our rubber soles. All of that was good, reassuring, like the shade of an oak tree. The world was made for us. We were at peace in this corner of the planet.

I climbed first because it was my job, but René was as much tied to the rope as I. We climbed together most of the time: to climb more quickly and because confidence was reciprocal.

When, six months before, I had gone to Brussels to give a lecture to the members of the Belgian Alpine Club at the request of its vice-president, René Mallieux, I guessed his old desire: to climb the north face of the Drus. Older than I, René was in Chamonix in 1935, the year of the first climb. Since then, the idea of climbing the face was formulated. The war came and he had to set aside this desire; winter passed, I re-awoke this somnolent desire.

The moments which create happiness and friendship are so simple and quiet, so natural they are not obvious.

Now, we were on the face and for a moment, while we climbed, something delighted me. What? I could not define it. At first, I thought that it came from the climb, but this song from within me came from something else. There were all these small shudderings from the atmosphere and from the planet that we received with trust, this taste of air, the gold of the sun around our mountain.

But all that was only perfume. We were two men in a land of stone and we walked toward the same star. René's joy was to carry out this nine-year old plan, mine was to help him do it. I was happy to be on the Drus, but here as elsewhere, my happiness was to lead a companion. What would a guide be without someone to lead? Good weather, bad weather, easy, difficult, I needed to sing the same tune as he. That was the best gift of our mountains. Climbing to the summit, one man does his job, another is on vacation and the luxury of their efforts is friendship.

Now, we were seated next to each other on the granite terrace. It was snowing lightly. It was dark. While we had been finishing the climb, the storm had broken. We passed under the summit along the quartz edge to rejoin the ordinary route and to begin the descent. But after two rappels, we had to pull on our bivouac hoods and stop. That snow thwarted our plans but was not overly unpleasant. Rain is disagreeable; but snow is as much a part of the mountain as sun and clear skies. Clouds were not very thick. It wasn't completely dark; we were bathed in a delicate patch of light; behind the clouds there was, as we well knew, a full moon.

Around ten o'clock, the cold started. Like the shroud of clouds above rivers when the morning sun dissolves them, the layer of clouds stretched out, then filled the valley of Chamonix and separated us from the world. The blond moon appeared in the black sky; under its light, the fresh snow glittered like stardust. Now, it was very cold. Curled up seated next to each other, in our down jackets, the "bones of the earth" made a cradle for us. In our hearts, we held the whole sky; we followed the path of the innumerable stars. A light breeze arose. We thought about the first man who had climbed the mountains. Eighteen hundred meters below, on the glacier edge, the small lakes of Tacul shone like precious stones. On our right, in the valley, the sea of clouds, shivering in the wind, covered the sleeping Chamonix.

The next morning, when we arrived in the valley, the ceremony at the cemetery and the blessing of the ice-axes had already taken place; I would be fined for being late.

In the afternoon, I climbed on the Gaillands for the climbing demonstration of the Festival of the Guides.

A Perilous Night on Shasta's Summit

JOHN MUIR

The mountaineer's deep affinity for the alpine environment is often revealed by the way he or she revels in the elements. John Muir delighted in mountain storms and often went out of his way to fully experience them. The following excerpt from Mountaineering Essays *actually consists of two ascents of California's Mount Shasta by Muir, the first in October 1874 and the second in late April 1875.*

Toward the end of summer, after a light, open winter, one may reach the summit of Mount Shasta without passing over much snow, by keeping on the crest of a long narrow ridge, mostly bare, that extends from near the campground at the timberline. But on my first excursion to the summit the whole mountain, down to its low swelling base, was smoothly laden with loose fresh snow, presenting a most glorious mass of winter mountain scenery, in the midst of which I scrambled and reveled or lay snugly snowbound, enjoying the fertile clouds and the snow bloom in all their growing, drifting grandeur.

I had walked from Redding, sauntering leisurely from station to station along the old Oregon stage road, the better to see the rocks and plants, birds and people, by the way, tracing the rushing Sacramento to its fountains around icy Shasta. The first rains had fallen on the lowlands, and the first snows on the mountains, and everything was fresh and bracing, while an abundance of balmy sunshine filled all the noonday hours. It was the calm afterglow that usually succeeds the first storm of the winter. I met many of the birds that had reared their young and spent their summer in the Shasta woods and chaparral. They were then on their way south to their winter homes, leading their young full-fledged and about as large and strong as the parents. Squirrels, dry and elastic after the storms, were busy about their stores of pine nuts, and the latest goldenrods were still in bloom, though it was now past the middle of October. The grand color glow—the autumnal jubilee of ripe leaves—was past prime, but, freshened by the rain, was still making a fine show along the banks of the river and in the ravines and the dells of the smaller streams.

At the salmon-hatching establishment on the McCloud River I halted a week to examine the limestone belt, grandly developed there, to learn what I could of the inhabitants of the river and its banks, and to give time for the fresh snow that I knew had fallen on the mountain to settle somewhat, with a view to making the ascent. A pedestrian on these mountain roads, especially so late in the year, is sure to excite curiosity, and many were the interrogations concerning my ramble. When I said that I was simply taking a walk, and that icy Shasta was my mark, I was invariably admonished that I had come on a dangerous quest. The time was far too late, the snow was too loose and deep to climb, and I should be lost in drifts and slides. When I hinted that new snow was beautiful and storms not so bad as they were called, my advisers shook their heads in token of superior knowledge and declared the ascent of "Shasta Butte" through loose snow impossible. Nevertheless, before noon of the second of November I was in the frosty azure of the utmost summit.

When I arrived at Sisson's everything was quiet. The last of the summer visitors had flitted long before, and the deer and bears also were beginning to seek their winter homes. My barometer and the sighing winds and filmy, half-transparent clouds that dimmed the sunshine gave notice of the approach of another storm, and I was in haste to be off and get myself established somewhere in the midst of it, whether the summit was to be attained or not. Sisson, who is a mountaineer, speedily fitted me out for storm as only a mountaineer could, with warm blankets and a week's provisions so generous in quantity and kind that they easily might have been made to last a month in case of my being closely snowbound. Well I knew the weariness of snow-climbing, and the frosts, and the dangers of mountaineering so late in the year; therefore I could not ask a guide to go with me, even had one been willing. All I wanted was to have blankets and provisions deposited as far up in the timber as the snow would permit a pack animal to go. There I could build a storm nest and lie warm, and make raids up and around the mountain in accordance with the weather.

Setting out on the afternoon of November first, with Jerome Fay, mountaineer and guide, in charge of the animals, I was soon plodding wearily upward through the muffled winter woods, the snow of course growing steadily deeper and looser, so that we had to break a trail. The animals began to get discouraged, and after night and darkness came on, they became entangled in a bed of rough lava, where, breaking through four or five feet of mealy snow, their feet were caught between angular boulders. Here they were in danger of being lost, but after we had removed packs and saddles and assisted their efforts with ropes, they all escaped to the side of a ridge about a thousand feet below the timberline.

To go farther was out of the question, so we were compelled to camp as best we could. A pitch-pine fire speedily changed the temperature and shed a blaze of light on the wild lava slope and the straggling stormbent pines around us. Melted snow answered for coffee, and we had plenty of venison to roast. Toward midnight I rolled myself in my blankets, slept an hour and a half, arose and ate more venison, tied two days' provisions to my belt, and set out for the summit, hoping to reach it ere the coming storm should fall. Jerome accompanied me a little distance above camp and indicated the way as well as he could in the darkness. He seemed loathe to leave me, but, being reassured that I was at home and required no care, he bade me good-bye and returned to camp, ready to lead his animals down the mountain at daybreak.

After I was above the dwarf pines, it was fine practice pushing up the broad unbroken slopes of snow, alone in the solemn silence of the night. Half the sky was clouded; in the other half the stars sparkled icily in the keen, frosty air; while everywhere the glorious wealth of snow fell away from the summit of the cone in flowing folds, more extensive and continuous than any I had ever seen before. When day dawned the clouds were crawling slowly and becoming more massive, but gave no intimation of immediate danger, and I pushed on faithfully, though holding myself well in hand, ready to return to the timber; for it was easy to see that the storm was not far off. The mountain rises ten thousand feet above the general level of the country, in blank exposure to the deep upper currents of the sky, and no labyrinth of peaks and cañons I had ever been in seemed to me so dangerous as these immense slopes, bare against the sky.

The frost was intense, and drifting snow dust made breathing at times rather difficult. The snow was as dry as meal, and the finer particles drifted freely, rising high in the air, while the larger portions of the crystals rolled like sand. I frequently sank to my armpits between buried blocks of loose lava, but generally only to my knees. When tired with walking I still wallowed slowly upward on all fours. The steepness of the slope—thirty-five degrees in some places—made any kind of progress fatiguing, while small avalanches were being constantly set in motion in the steepest places. But the bracing air and the sublime beauty of the snowy expanse thrilled every nerve and made absolute exhaustion impossible. I seemed to be walking and wallowing in a cloud; but, holding steadily onward, by half-past ten o'clock I had gained the highest summit.

I held my commanding foothold in the sky for two hours, gazing on the glorious landscapes spread maplike around the immense horizon, and tracing the outlines of the ancient lava streams extending far into the surrounding plains, and the pathways of vanished glaciers of which Shasta had been the center. But, as I had left my coat in camp for the sake of having my limbs free in climbing, I soon was cold. The wind increased in violence, raising the snow in magnificent drifts that were drawn out in the form of wavering banners glowing in the sun. Toward the end of my stay a succession of small clouds struck against the summit rocks like drifting icebergs, darkening the air as they passed, and producing a chill as definite and sudden as if ice water had been dashed in my face. This is the kind of cloud in which snow flowers grow, and I turned and fled.

Finding that I was not closely pursued, I ventured to take time on the way down for a visit to the head of the Whitney Glacier and the "Crater Butte." After I reached the end of the main summit ridge the descent was but little more than one continuous soft, mealy, muffled slide, most luxurious and rapid, though the hissing, swishing speed attained was obscured in great part by flying snow dust—in marked contrast to the boring seal-wallowing upward struggle. I reached camp about an hour before dusk, hollowed a strip of loose ground in the lee of a large block of red lava, where firewood was abundant, rolled myself in my blankets, and went to sleep.

Next morning, having slept little the night before the ascent and being weary with climbing after the excitement was over, I slept late. Then, awaking suddenly, my eyes opened on one of the most beautiful and sublime scenes I ever enjoyed. A boundless wilderness of storm clouds of different degrees of ripeness were congregated over all the lower landscape for thousands of square miles, colored gray, and purple, and pearl, and deep-glowing white, amid which I seemed to be floating; while the great white cone of the mountain above was all aglow in the free, blazing sunshine. It seemed not so much an ocean as a *land* of clouds—undulating hill and dale, smooth purple plains, and silvery mountains of cumuli, range over range, diversified with peak and dome and hollow fully brought out in light and shade.

I gazed enchanted, but cold gray masses, drifting like dust on a windswept plain, began to shut out the light, forerunners of the coming storm I had been so anxiously watching. I made haste to gather as much wood as possible, snugging it as a shelter around my bed. The storm side of my blankets was fastened down with stakes to reduce as much as possible the sifting-in of drift and the danger of being blown away. The precious bread sack was placed safely as a pillow, and when at length the first flakes fell I was exultingly ready to welcome them. Most of my firewood was more than half resin and would blaze in the face of the fiercest drifting; the winds could not demolish my bed, and my bread could be made to last indefinitely; while in case of need I had the means of making snowshoes and could retreat or hold my ground as I pleased.

Presently the storm broke forth into full snowy bloom, and the thronging crystals darkened the air. The wind swept past in hissing floods, grinding the snow into meal and sweeping down into the hollows in enormous drifts all the heavier particles, while the finer dust was sifted through the sky, increasing the icy gloom. But my fire glowed bravely as if in glad defiance of the drift to quench it, and, notwithstanding but little trace of my nest could be seen after the snow had leveled and buried it, I was snug and warm, and the passionate uproar produced a glad excitement.

Day after day the storm continued, piling snow on snow in weariless abundance. There were short periods of quiet, when the sun would seem to look eagerly down through rents in the clouds, as if to know how the work was advancing. During these calm intervals I replenished my fire—sometimes without leaving the nest, for fire and woodpile were so near this could easily be done—or busied myself with my notebook, watching the gestures of the trees in taking the snow, examining separate crystals under a lens, and learning the methods of their deposition as an enduring fountain for the streams. Several times, when the storm ceased for a few minutes, a Douglas squirrel came frisking from the foot of a clump of dwarf pines, moving in sudden interrupted spurts over the bossy snow; then, without any apparent guidance, he would dig rapidly into the drift where were buried some grains of barley that the horses had left. The Douglas squirrel does not strictly belong to these upper woods, and I was surprised to see him out in such weather. The mountain sheep also, quite a large flock of them, came to my camp and took shelter beside a clump of matted dwarf pines a little above my nest.

The storm lasted about a week, but before it was ended Sisson became alarmed and sent up the guide with animals to see what had become of me and recover the camp outfit. The news spread that "there was a man on the mountain," and he must surely have perished, and Sisson was blamed for allowing any one to attempt climbing in such weather; while I was as safe as anybody in the lowlands, lying like a squirrel in a warm, fluffy nest, busied about my own affairs and wishing only to be let alone. Later, however, a trail could not have been broken for a horse, and some of the camp furniture would have had to be abandoned. On the fifth day I returned to Sisson's, and from that comfortable base made excursions, as the weather permitted, to Black Butte, to the foot of the Whitney Glacier, around the base of the mountain, to Rhett and Klamath lakes, to the Modoc region and elsewhere, developing many interesting scenes and experiences.

But the next spring, on the other side of this eventful winter, I saw and felt still more of the Shasta snow. For then it was my fortune to get into the very heart of a storm, and to be held in it for a long time.

On the 28th of April [1875] I led a party up the mountain for the purpose of making a survey of the summit with reference to the location of the Geodetic monument. On the 30th, accompanied by Jerome Fay, I made another ascent to make some barometrical observations, the day intervening between the two ascents being devoted to establishing a camp on the extreme edge of the timberline. Here, on our red trachyte bed, we obtained two hours of shallow sleep broken for occasional glimpses of the keen, starry night. At two o'clock we rose, breakfasted on a warmed tin-cupful of coffee and a piece of frozen venison broiled on the coals, and started for the summit. Up to this time there was nothing in sight that betokened the approach of a storm; but on gaining the summit, we saw toward Lassen's Butte hundreds of square miles of white cumuli boiling dreamily in the sunshine far beneath us, and causing no alarm.

The slight weariness of the ascent was soon rested away, and our glorious morning in the sky promised nothing but enjoyment. At 9 A.M. the dry thermometer stood at 34° in the shade and rose steadily until at 1 P.M. it stood at 50°, probably influenced somewhat by radiation from the sun-warmed cliffs. A common bumblebee, not at all benumbed, zigzagged vigorously about our heads for a few moments, as if unconscious of the fact that the nearest honey flower was a mile beneath him.

In the mean time clouds were growing down in Shasta Valley—massive swelling cumuli, displaying delicious tones of purple and gray in the hollows of their sun-beaten bosses. Extending gradually southward around on both sides of Shasta, these at length united with the older field towards Lassen's Butte, thus encircling Mount Shasta in one continuous cloud-zone. Rhett and Kalmath lakes were eclipsed beneath clouds scarcely less brilliant than their own silvery disks. The Modoc Lava Beds, many a snow-laden peak far north in Oregon, the Scott and Trinity and Siskiyou Mountains, the peaks of the Sierra, the blue Coast Range, Shasta Valley, the dark forests filling the valley of the Sacramento, all in turn were obscured or buried, leaving the lofty cone on which we stood solitary in the sunshine between two skies—a sky of spotless blue above, a sky of glittering cloud beneath. The creative sun shone glorious on the vast expanse of cloudland; hill and dale, mountain and valley springing into existence responsive to his rays and steadily developing in beauty and individuality. One huge mountain-cone of cloud, corresponding to Mount Shasta in these newborn cloud-ranges, rose close alongside with a visible motion, its firm, polished bosses seeming so near and substantial that we almost fancied we might leap down upon them from where we stood and make our way to the lowlands. No hint was given, by anything in their appearance, of the fleeting character of these sublime and beautiful cloud mountains. On the contrary they impressed one as being lasting additions to the landscape.

The weather of the springtime and summer, throughout the Sierra in general, is usually varied by slight local rains and dustings of snow, most of which are obviously far too joyous and life-giving to be regarded as storms—single clouds growing in the sunny sky, ripening in an hour, showering the heated landscape, and passing away like a thought, leaving no visible bodily remains to stain the sky. Snowstorms of the same gentle kind abound among the high peaks, but in spring they not unfrequently attain larger proportions, assuming a violence and energy of expression scarcely surpassed by those bred in the depths of winter. Such was the storm now gathering about us.

It began to declare itself shortly after noon, suggesting to us the idea of at once seeking our safe camp in the timber and abandoning the purpose of making an observation of the barometer at 3 P.M. —two having already been made, at 9 A.M., and 12 noon, while simultaneous observations were made at Strawberry Valley. Jerome peered at short intervals over the ridge, contemplating the rising clouds with anxious gestures in the rough wind, and at length declared that if we did not make speedy escape we should be compelled to pass the rest of the day and night on the mountain. But anxiety to complete my observations stifled my own instinctive promptings to retreat, and held me to my work. No inexperienced person was depending on me, and I told Jerome that we two mountaineers should be able to make our way down through any storm likely to fall.

Presently thin, fibrous films of cloud began to blow directly over the summit from north to south, drawn out in long fairy webs like carded wool, forming and dissolving as if by magic. The wind twisted them into ringlets and whirled them in a succession of graceful convolutions like the outside sprays of Yosemite Falls in floodtime; then, sailing out into the thin azure over the precipitous brink of the ridge they were drifted together like wreaths of foam on a river. These higher and finer cloud fabrics were evidently produced by the chilling of the air from its own expansion caused by the upward deflection of the wind against the slopes of the mountain. They steadily increased on the north rim of the cone, forming at length a thick, opaque, ill-defined embankment from the icy meshes of which snowflowers began to fall, alternating with hail. The sky speedily darkened, and just as I had completed my last observation and boxed my instruments ready for the descent, the storm began in serious earnest. At first the cliffs were beaten with hail, every stone of which, as far as I could see, was regular in form, six-sided pyramids with rounded base, rich and sumptuous-looking, and fashioned with loving care, yet seemingly thrown away on those desolate crags down which they went rolling, falling, sliding in a network of curious streams.

After we had forced our way down the ridge and past the group of hissing fumaroles, the storm became inconceivably violent. The thermometer fell 22° in a few minutes, and soon dropped below zero. The hail gave place to snow, and darkness came on like night. The wind, rising to the highest pitch of violence, boomed and surged amid the desolate crags; lightning flashes in quick succession cut the gloomy darkness; and the thunders, the most tremendously loud and appalling I ever heard, made an almost continuous roar, stroke following stroke in quick, passionate succession, as though the mountain were being rent to its foundations and the fires of the old volcano were breaking forth again.

Could we at once have begun to descent the snow slopes leading to the timber, we might have made good our escape, however dark and wild the storm. As it was, we had first to make our way along a dangerous ridge nearly a mile and a half long, flanked in many places by steep ice slopes at the head of the Whitney Glacier on one side and by shattered precipices on the other. Apprehensive of this coming darkness, I had taken the precaution, when the storm began, to make the most dangerous points clear to my mind, and to mark their relations with reference to the direction of the wind. When, therefore, the darkness came on, and the bewildering drift, I felt confident that we could force our way through it with no other guidance. After passing the "Hot Springs" I halted in the lee of a lava block to let Jerome, who had fallen a little behind, come up. Here he opened a council in which, under circumstances sufficiently exciting but without evincing any bewilderment, he maintained, in opposition to my views, that it was impossible to proceed. He firmly refused to make the venture to find the camp, while I, aware of the dangers that would necessarily attend our efforts, and conscious of being the cause of his present peril, decided not to leave him.

Our discussions ended, Jerome made a dash from the shelter of the lava block and began forcing his way back against the wind to the "Hot Springs," wavering and struggling to resist being carried away, as if he were fording a rapid stream. After waiting and watching in vain for some flaw in the storm that might be urged as a new argument in favor of attempting the descent, I was compelled to follow. "Here," said Jerome, as we shivered in the midst of the hissing, sputtering fumaroles, "we shall be safe from frost." "Yes," said I, "we can lie in this mud and steam and sludge, warm at least on one side; but how can we protect our lungs from the acid gases, and how, after our clothing is saturated, shall we be able to reach camp without freezing, even after the storm is over? We shall have to wait for sunshine, and when will it come?"

The tempered area to which we had committed ourselves extended over about one fourth of an acre; but it was only about an eight of an inch in thickness, for the scalding gas jets were shorn off close to the ground by the oversweeping flood of frosty wind. And how lavishly the snow fell only mountaineers may know. The crisp crystal flowers seemed to touch one another and fairly thicken the tremendous blast that carried them. This was the bloom time, the summer of the cloud, and never before have I seen even a mountain cloud flowering so profusely.

When the bloom of the Shasta chaparral is falling, the ground is sometimes covered for hundreds of square miles to a depth of half an inch. But the bloom of this fertile snowcloud grew and matured and fell to a depth of two feet in a few hours. Some crystals landed with their rays almost perfect, but most of them were worn and broken by striking against one another, or by rolling on the ground. The touch of these snow flowers in calm weather is infinitely gentle—glinting, swaying, settling silently in the dry mountain air, or massed in flakes soft and downy. To lie out alone in the mountains of a still night and be touched by the first of these small silent messengers from the sky is a memorable experience, and the fineness of that touch none will forget. But the storm blast laden with crisp, sharp snow seems to crush and bruise and stupefy with its multitude of stings, and compels the bravest to turn and flee.

The snow fell without abatement until an hour or two after what seemed to be the natural darkness of the night. Up to the time the storm first broke on the summit its development was remarkably gentle. There was a deliberate growth of clouds, a weaving of translucent tissue above, then the roar of the wind and the thunder, and the darkening flight of snow. Its subsidence was not less sudden. The clouds broke and vanished, not a crystal was left in the sky, and the stars shone out with pure and tranquil radiance.

During the storm we lay on our backs so as to present as little surface as possible to the wind, as to let the drift pass over us. The mealy snow sifted into the folds of our clothing and in many places reached the skin. We were glad at first to see the snow packing about us, hoping it would deaden the force of the wind, but it soon froze into a stiff, crusty heap as the temperature fell, rather augmenting our novel misery.

When the heat became unendurable, on some spot where steam was escaping through the sludge, we tried to stop it with snow and mud, or shifted a little at a time by shoving with our heels; for to stand in blank exposure to the fearful wind in our frozen-and-broiled condition seemed certain death. The acrid incrustations sublimed from the escaping gases frequently gave way, opening new vents to scald us; and, fearing that if at any time the wind should fall, carbonic acid, which often formed a considerable portion of the gaseous exhalations of volcanoes, might collect in sufficient quantities to cause sleep and death, I warned Jerome against forgetting himself for a single moment, even should his sufferings admit of such a thing.

Accordingly, when during the long, dreary watches of the night we roused from a state of half-consciousness, we called each other by name in a frightened, startled way, each fearing the other might be benumbed or dead. The ordinary sensations of cold give but a faint conception of that which comes on after hard climbing with want of food and sleep in such exposure as this. Life is then seen to be a fire, that now smoulders, now brightens, and may be easily quenched. The weary hours wore away like dim half-forgotten years, so long and eventful they seemed, though we did nothing but suffer. Still the pain was not always of that bitter, intense kind that precludes thought and takes away all capacity for enjoyment. A sort of dreamy stupor came on at times in which we fancied we saw dry, resinous logs suitable for campfires, just as after going days without food men fancy they see bread.

Frozen, blistered, famished, benumbed, our bodies seemed lost to us at times—all dead but the eyes. For the duller and fainter we became the clearer was our vision, though only in momentary glimpses. Then, after the sky cleared, we gazed at the stars, blessed immortals of light, shining with marvelous brightness with long lance rays, near-looking and new-looking, as if never seen before. Again they would look familiar and remind us of stargazing at home. Oftentimes imagination coming into play would present charming pictures of the warm zone below, mingled with others near and far. Then the bitter wind and the drift would break the blissful vision and dreary pains cover us like clouds. "Are you suffering much?" Jerome would inquire with pitiful faintness. "Yes," I would say, striving to keep my voice brave, "frozen and burned; but never mind, Jerome, the night will wear away at last, and tomorrow we go a-Maying, and what campfires we will make, and what sunbaths we will take!"

The frost grew more and more intense, and we became icy and covered over with a crust of frozen snow, as if we had lain cast away in the drift all winter. In about thirteen hours—very like a year—day began to dawn, but it was long ere the summit's rocks were touched by the sun. No clouds were visible from where we lay, yet the morning was dull and blue, and bitterly frosty; and hour after hour passed by while we eagerly watched the pale light stealing down the ridge to the hollow where we lay. But there was not a trace of that warm, flushing sunrise splendor we so long had hoped for.

As the time drew near to make an effort to reach camp, we became concerned to know what strength was left us, and whether or no we could walk; for we had lain flat all this time without once rising to our feet. Mountaineers, however, always find in themselves a reserve of power after great exhaustion. It is a kind of second life, available only in emergencies like this; and, having proved its existence, I had no great fear that either of us would fail, though one of my arms was already benumbed and hung powerless.

At length, after the temperature was somewhat mitigated on this first day of May, we arose and began to struggle homeward. Our frozen trousers could scarcely be made to bend at the knee, and we waded the snow with difficulty. The summit ridge was fortunately windswept and nearly bare, so we were not compelled to lift our feet high, and on reaching the long home slopes laden with loose snow we made rapid progress, sliding and shuffling and pitching headlong, our feebleness accelerating rather than diminishing our speed. When we had descended some three thousand feet the sunshine warmed our backs and we began to revive. At 10 A.M. we reached the timber and were safe.

Half an hour later we heard Sisson shouting down among the firs, coming with horses to take us to the hotel. After breaking a trail through the snow as far as possible he had tied his animals and walked up. We had been so long without food that we cared but little about eating, but we eagerly drank the coffee he prepared for us. Our feet were frozen, and thawing them was painful, and had to be done very slowly by keeping them buried in soft snow for several hours, which avoided permanent damage. [This practice is no longer medically recommended.] Five thousand feet below the summit we found only three inches of new snow, and at the base of the mountain only a slight shower or rain had fallen, showing how local our storm had been, notwithstanding its terrific fury. Our feet were wrapped in sacking, and we were soon mounted and on our way down into the thick sunshine—"God's Country," as Sisson calls the Chaparral Zone. In two hours' ride the last snowbank was left behind. Violets appeared along the edges of the trail, and the chaparral was coming into bloom, with young lilies and larkspurs about the open places in rich profusion. How beautiful seemed the golden sunbeams streaming through the woods between the warm brown boles of the cedars and pines! All my friends among the birds and plants seemed like *old* friends, and we felt like speaking to every one of them as we passed, as if we had been a long time away in some far, strange country.

In the afternoon we reached the Strawberry Valley and fell asleep. Next morning we seemed to have risen from the dead. My bedroom was flooded with sunshine, and from the window I saw the great white Shasta cone clad in forests and clouds and bearing them loftily in the sky. Everything seemed full and radiant with the freshness and beauty and enthusiasm of youth. Sisson's children came in with flowers and covered my bed, and the storm on the mountaintop vanished like a dream.

CHAPTER 2

UP, DOWN AND TOWARD

Get It to the Port on Time

NICHOLAS CLINCH

Climbs on the major mountains of the world require enormous amounts of preparation and coordination, and most mountaineers who have conducted expeditions to the Andes of South America, the Alaksan ranges or the Himalayas will admit that enjoying the "freedom of the hills" is usually preceded by the oppression of planning and organizing deadlines. Food, equipment, team membership, medical supplies, and a myriad of other essential items must be arranged before the journey begins. When the 1958 American Karakoram Expedition unexpectedly received permission from the Pakistani government to attempt Hidden Peak, the group was more a hope in Nicholas Clinch's heart than an organized entity. In a few months time, however, Clinch proceeded to do the seemingly impossible: organize and finance a team that would become the only Americans to make a first ascent of an 8,000-meter peak. This he accomplished while finishing a hitch in the Air Force and preparing for a lawyer's bar examination. Clinch's wry portrayal of preparatory hassles is taken from his book, A Walk In The Sky.

The granting of permission by the Pakistani government was not an unmixed blessing. If our request had been denied we could have relaxed and consoled ourselves with the thought that we had tried. Now we had our long desired opportunity and little else.

Like all expeditions to the Himalaya our schedule was determined by weather and climatic conditions. Mountaineers have argued for years over whether the monsoon ever penetrates the Karakoram. It is evident that prolonged bad weather does strike the region and although certain experts say it cannot be the monsoon, it suspiciously resembles that phenomenon. Regardless of nomenclature, a long storm can be disastrous to any party caught high on an Eight Thousander. Accounts of prior expeditions to the Karakoram and neighboring Nanga Parbat indicated that summit attempts should be made before the middle of July, as the weather tends to deteriorate after that time. In some years there were unsettled conditions early in the summer that eventually improved, while in other years the weather remained fair throughout. However, June and early July seemed to offer the greatest chance of good weather.

In order to be in a position to make the summit assault on Hidden Peak during the first week of July, we should reach Base Camp no later than the end of May. Calculating back from that date, and allowing sufficient time for the 135-mile approach march from Skardu and the delays inherent in shipping supplies halfway around the world, we learned that our equipment would have to be at the port of New York no later than the middle of March. We had exactly three and a half months to raise the money, enlist personnel, order equipment, and get everything to the dock properly crated.

Not only did we lack funds, but the entire party also had to be reorganized. We had not heard from the Pakistani army concerning our two Pakistani mountaineers. Dr. Nello Pace, Dr. Bruce Meyer, and Felix Knauth definitely could not participate. Gary Driggs was practically out, Gil Roberts and Dick Irwin were doubtful, and Andy Kauffman, though eager, was hesitant. Only Bob Swift and I were certain that we would go. Swift had had a special clause inserted into his teaching contract that permitted him to leave his duties early if our expedition became a reality. The principal of the Half Moon Bay Union High School had agreed to this only after Swift assured him that the chances of the expedition taking place were extremely remote. Swift had told him the absolute truth, although I doubt that the principal ever believed it. I was not confronted with such difficulties. I was out of the Air Force and unemployed.

Upon learning that we had received permission, I dispatched telegrams to all members of the expedition, to John Oberlin, president of the American Alpine Club, and to Lawrence Coveney. Also, as I suspected that Jurg Marmet, a very practical Swiss, would wait a while to see what developed before ordering our oxygen, I sent him a cablegram saying that permission had been received and requested him to increase our oxygen order to twenty-nine bottles and five regulators.

Next, Roberts, Swift, and I held an emergency conference in Roberts's apartment in San Francisco. The general tenor of the meeting was aptly summed up by Swift's comment, "That's good news. Now what do we do with it?" The response among non-mountaineers was even less enthusiastic. One person who was told about the permission remarked, "Wonderful. How much can you sell it for?" Any illusions about our expedition suddenly becoming a popular crusade were quickly dispelled.

At the annual meeting of the American Alpine Club I told the members of the council that we would put at least a small party into the field, without bothering them with minor details such as just how small the party was going to be. I was not fooling anyone, but the club was completely behind the project and lent us their entire expedition fund of $6,000. Although the reputation of the club was at stake, during the critical months that followed, the council gave us complete control in the organization and execution of the expedition, a demonstration of trust that greatly increased our confidence. Frequently we had to ask the impossible from the club and its individual members and somehow they always fulfilled our requests.

I now was studying for the California bar examination that was to be given for three days early in March. I still lived in an alley a block and a half from the Pacific Ocean in Long Beach in the same small house that I had rented primarily because the nearby beach was an inconspicuous place for me to run in an effort to get into physical condition. My portable typewriter could not make sufficient carbon copies of the weekly bulletin I had to send to all concerned informing them of the expedition's lack of progress, so I made a deal with my former Air Force boss. In exchange for having access to the legal office and its electric typewriter, I spent several hours a day helping process claims.

By December 1957, Dick Irvin, despite his experiences on Rakaposhi, was eager to return to the Karakoram, and in one fourteen-hour effort he compiled two tentative food and equipment lists for a four-month expedition. One list was for an optimum budget of $45,000 and the other was for the probable budget of $25,000.

Despite the general lack of interest in mountaineering in the United States, there is one source of support that all American Himalayan expeditions have relied upon for the last ten years—*The Saturday Evening Post*. I contacted Martin Sommers, the foreign editor, and by return mail I received a much-needed option for the story of the trip. Jokes such as "John, will you please fall into the next crevasse for the benefit of our *Post* article?" are a constant source of amusement to American mountaineers, but mountaineers are very thankful for this one bright spot in an otherwise dismal picture. With the receipt of the *Post* option, our project started to become respectable. Then at the end of December the bottom fell out.

First, Gary Driggs wrote that he definitely could not go. This was a terrific blow, not only because he is an extremely fine mountaineer and I was counting heavily upon his ability and strength, but also because he is a close friend with whom I have done some of my finest climbs. I have absolute confidence in him. Next, the Austrians announced that they had received permission from the Pakistani government to attempt Hidden Peak. Their expedition was under the leadership of Fritz Moravec, who had climbed Gasherbrum II, and was supposed to leave Austria in February for the Karakoram. This seemed incredible, as one reason official permission is required is to prevent two parties from engaging in a race up the same mountain. While I found this difficult to believe, in 1956 a French and a British party were climbing the Muztagh Tower simultaneously from opposite sides, so anything was possible. The Austrian announcement meant that our expedition could not approach prospective backers by saying we had exclusive permission to attempt Hidden Peak, since if the Austrians also had permission they would beat us to the mountains as they were closer and had the necessary money. I immediately sent letters to the American embassy in Karachi and to General Hayaud-Din in Washington requesting them to check into this situation. Six weeks later the American embassy learned that the Austrians did not have permission after all, but by then it was too late for us to obtain outside backing.

Finally, I received from the French company that was making our oxygen regulators a letter stating that the firm manufacturing the oxygen bottles could not produce them until the end of March, which would be too late for our expedition. There has been much discussion about the ethics of using oxygen to climb high mountains and no prior American expedition had ever used it except for medical purposes. The use of oxygen is the same as the use of pitons for safety. It has been proved that Eight Thousanders can be climbed without oxygen. However, the use of oxygen not only increases the chance for success but also definitely protects the health of mountaineers who use it. Parties that systematically use oxygen above 23,000 feet almost always return without permanent injury. Expeditions that do not use oxygen often suffer severely from frostbite. Thus, while the loss of our oxygen equipment would not necessarily doom us to failure, it would greatly increase the risk of someone's getting hurt. I knew exactly one French and one Swiss mountaineer, but Jean Couzy and Jurg Marmet happened to be the oxygen experts for the French Alpine Club and the Swiss Foundation for Alpine Research, and I wrote them pleading letters requesting that they do everything in their power to try to speed up the production of our bottles. Also, I phoned Andy Kauffman at the American embassy in Paris. We had one of those garbled connections in which I could hear Kauffman's voice clear as a bell saying over and over again, "I can't understand you." Later during the long evenings of the approach march, Kauffman would regale us with imitations of the squawks and gurgles at his end of that ill-fated phone call. This was the nadir of the expedition: no oxygen, no party, and the Austrians were going to climb the mountain.

By the middle of January the situation began to improve. Jean

Couzy and Jurg Marmet simultaneously jumped on the bottle manufacturer in the name of French and Swiss mountaineering and the impossible deadline was moved up to the end of February, which gave us sufficient time to have the bottles filled and shipped to Pakistan. Several members of the American Alpine Club offered to donate enough money to the expedition that, combined with the loan from the club and the assets of the members of the party, would permit us to operate a trip on a budget of about $25,000, which was adequate but did not allow such luxuries as mail runners.

On January 25, 1958, Swift, Irvin, and I met to thrash out more details. Both Irvin and Gil Roberts could not be in the main party. Irvin cold not leave his teaching duties and Roberts could not leave medical school early. At this point we invited Tom McCormack to join the expedition. McCormack accepted our invitation and the 1958 American Karakoram Expedition consisted of four climbers: Swift, Kauffman, McCormack, and me.

Meanwhile Jurg Marmet wrote that the Bally Shoe Company would furnish us with the same type of handmade climbing boots and high-altitude reindeer boots that the 1956 Swiss Everest Expedition had used. It would take eight weeks to make the boots; therefore the fifteenth of February, which was the last day the Bally company could receive the foot outlines and still make the boots in time for the trip, was the deadline for having a definite party. With this deadline only two and a half weeks away, we still needed another climber and a climbing doctor. By now I had an impressive file of letters from the most distinguished mountaineers and climbing doctors in the United States who could not participate in the expedition. I began to call various physicians long distance. Once I heard myself callously saying, "My heartiest congratulations on your first son, Fred, and when you return to the hospital to see your wife, tell her you want to go to the Karakoram. I'll call you back Sunday." Needless to say, Dr. Fred Dunn could not go.

Dunn suggested Dr. Tom Nevison. It is amazing how one can overlook the obvious. I had first met Nevision in 1952 when he came to Stanford University for advanced study after graduating from Harvard University. He had been the president of the Harvard

Mountaineering Club and had participated in an expedition to the Windy Range of the Northern Selkirks in British Columbia. In the spring of 1952 while on a ski tour to Ostrander Lake in Yosemite National Park, I miscalculated the snow texture and broke my left leg. It took my friends and the park rangers twenty-four hours to haul me out. Nevison participated in the rescue and he remained in Yosemite Valley bolstering my morale by soundly beating me at various card games until I was in condition to return to Stanford. I had not seen Nevison since that spring, and while I was going to law school he was attending Harvard Medical School. My invitation to join the expedition caught him by surprise. "Isn't it a bit late to be asking me?" he responded. But Tom is a strong man and an eager mountaineer, and I was not going to let him get away that easily. "Look," I repeated, "we've got the permission and we will never get another opportunity." "Okay, I'll see if I can get away and then I'll let you know," he replied. "While you're checking send me an outline of your feet with two pairs of heavy wool socks on," I added. Nevison became the medical officer.

In the summer of 1957 when it became apparent that our expedition would need more men, I conducted a letter poll of the members for suggestions as to whom we should invite to join us. The first choice of every member was identical—Pete Schoening, a thirty-one-year-old chemical engineer from Seattle, Washington. In 1952 Schoening had led a highly successful expedition to King Peak near Mount Logan in the Yukon. He had been a member of the 1953 American expedition to K2 and it was his belay that held five falling men above 25,000 feet during the retreat off that mountain. In response to our invitation Schoening said that he could not go. In December, when I saw him at the annual meeting of the American Alpine Club and again tried to persuade him to join us, he still insisted that it was impossible for him to break away. For the next two months I kept putting pressure on him but he still had other commitments. Finally in one of his letters I detected slight signs that he was beginning to waver and I bombarded him with special-delivery letters and long distance phone calls. With the boot deadline only a few days away he reluctantly agreed to join the expedition.

The leader of an expedition should always be the man whom other mountaineers will blame for the results of the trip regardless of whether he is in a position of authority. By unanimous consent of the members of the party, Pete Schoening was elected leader.

Just before Schoening agreed to go I received a letter from the Sports Control Committee of the Pakistani army stating that Lieutenant Mohd Akram and Captain N. A. Soofi would be our Pakistani mountaineers. Enclosed in the letter were the officers' measurements and the precious foot outlines. We had our team.

With the exception of Pete Schoening, it was our first try at an Eight Thousander so we relied upon the experience of recent European expeditions. A pattern of success over these mountains had been established, which we intended to follow closely. As we could not count on contributions of equipment and would have to pay for almost everything, we decided to use the finest equipment in the world, regardless of its source. The foot outlines were rushed to Bally. Jurg Marmet and the extremely efficient Swiss Foundation for Alpine Research went to work to obtain our oxygen masks, helmets, and breathing tubes, as well as less exotic equipment such as ice-axes, crampons, snow glasses, silk gloves, and countless other articles. In Paris, Andy Kauffman, assisted by Guido Magnone and Raymond Leininger, ordered butane-gas stoves and the equipment for our high-altitude porters. Kauffman also monitored the progress of our oxygen bottles. Schoening contacted the Weyerhaeuser Timber Company and they agreed to furnish plywood for the porters' boxes we needed to carry our equipment during the approach march. Nevison obtained radios and medical supplies. We also received a transistor shortwave receiver from the Zenith Radio Corporation to pick up weather broadcasts, and Bradford Washburn, director of the Museum of Science in Boston and veteran Alaskan mountaineer, lent us three walkie-talkie radios for intercamp communication.

Almost every night I stayed up until three in the morning typing coordination bulletins, letters, and appeals for help on the indispensable electric typewriter. There were so many faint carbon copies of the bulletin that most of the recipients were unable to tell exactly what was happening. I had a strict priority system for determining who got legible copies. John Oberlin got the original by virtue of being president of the American Alpine Club. I kept the first carbon and distributed the other copies in accordance with the importance of each person's task in that particular bulletin. Nevison began to flood the mail with medical bulletins and Lawrence Coveney, who had been head of the New York office of an international trading company before he retired, sent out numerous reports concerning the impending shipping deadlines. At the bottom of my copy of one bulletin in which he pleaded with everyone to hurry up and get the supplies to the transfer company in New York, Coveney scrawled, "Do you really think that it is all going to get here on time?"

Already it was too late to order our food in the United States and still have it packaged into approach march, base camp, and high-altitude rations. I remembered Len Frank, a book dealer and member of the Alpine Club, whom I had met when I went through England in 1956. I had been overweight for the plane flight back to Iceland and he graciously shipped my pitons and other hardware to me without any facetious remarks about the decadence of the younger generation. Len readily agreed to help procure our food as well as our air mattresses and wind suits. Originally I had hoped that the firm that had furnished the food for the British Everest and Kangch-enjunga expedition would handle our order, as both those expedi-tions had been eminently successful and I had never heard any violent complaints about the food. However, Len Frank and I quickly learned that once a company has gone through the ordeal of fur-nishing and packaging food for a three-month trip, it never wants to do it again. Len was getting desperate when his wife woke him up in the middle of the night and said, "Why not try Hudson Brothers?" Hudson Brothers referred him to its subsidiary firm, Peter Keevil & Sons, which did not realize what it was getting into and agreed to handle the order.

The previously hectic pace became more frenzied as the shipping deadlines approached. Crisis after crisis broke over us in ever in-creasing waves as this phase of the expeditionary tide swelled toward its crest, sweeping all of us before it. The bar examination began to descend upon me like the blade of a guillotine. Every expedition member was instructed as to what items he should beg, borrow, or, as a last resort, buy; and in the United States, England, France, and Switzerland lamps burned late into the night. Schoening took charge of the remaining details of the United States shipment and he and Coveney nipped at the heels of our supplier like a couple of hungry wolves after a herd of deer. Gerry Cunningham shipped his eight high-altitude tents at the last minute. Allen Steck of the Ski Hut in Berkeley barely managed to get our rucksacks to the port. The Eddie Bauer Company in Seattle put our sleeping bags and down clothing on a fast truck heading east. Swift checked into our order of mountain pants and wrote, "They mailed them yesterday, which is fortunate. You should have seen their faces when they found out that we aren't being sponsored by the government. I suggest you pay them as soon as we get some money." Drugs, film, pitons, rappel pickets, pliers, and other small but indispensable items poured into the transfer warehouse to be crated for immediate overseas shipment. Despite Coveney's premonition of disaster, when the *S.S. Flying Enterprise II* sailed from New York, all of our equipment from the United States was on board.

In London Len Frank was having trouble getting our food properly packaged in time to make the early boat, the *S.S. Kallada*. With my bar examination a week away we exchanged daily cablegrams. Finally I instructed him to ship the food in bulk. They could dump it down the hatch, as long as the food got on board. On Monday morning, March 11, the day before the examination began, I received another cablegram, which read, "All well, food will be on Kallada, Len." I breathed a sigh of relief, picked up some law outlines, and began to cram furiously. Then workmen from the city street department began to tear up the alley with jackhammers.

When I returned to my house from the bar examination, there was just a small stack of letters and telegrams to add to the twenty pounds of paper piled on top of my letter that began, "Dear Dr. Houston . . ."

I put thirty-five crates of mountaineering books and one record player into storage and began the long trip to Orosi, San Francisco,

Dallas, and points east. I was to be the vanguard of the expedition. After checking on our shipments from England, France, and Switzerland and learning from Jurg Marmet how to use the oxygen equipment, I was supposed to arrive in Karachi sufficiently ahead of the rest of the party to get our equipment out of customs and sent to Rawalpindi. Perhaps with a little luck I could even get the equipment flown to Skardu before May 13, when the rest of the party was scheduled to reach Pakistan.

Although Dick Irvin and Gil Roberts could not leave the United States until June 6, we had been promised a special contribution for the specific purpose of having them come in later to reinforce us. First we had to find out if they would be allowed to make a separate approach march. On March 22, when I visited Irvin in Orosi, California, he and I agreed that I would send him a cablegram from Karachi if it was all right for the two of them to join the main party.

That night I left Irvin's house and drove to Swift's cottage in Moss Beach. On the way I stopped for gasoline at a service station near Fresno. I have been in the mountains since I was nine years old and although I once broke my leg skiing, I have never been injured climbing. Reentering my car I was completely preoccupied with the problems of the expedition and failed to open the door wide enough, with the result that I gashed my forehead against the edge of the window and had to have the wound sewed up at the local hospital. As I drove on to Swift's house I suddenly realized how dangerous Himalayan expeditions are. Already I had three stitches in my head and I was still in the United States!

When I got to Dallas there was the usual pile of correspondence. Andy Kauffman wanted to know how many butane-gas stoves we could afford to buy. I instructed him to get as many stoves as he thought necessary and Kauffman promptly got the stoves, oxygen bottles, and other equipment shipped out of France. The Pakistan Army Sports Control committee wrote that Captain Soofi could not participate but that Captain S.T.H. Rizvi, who had been with the 1957 Manchester Himalayan Expedition that attempted Masherbrum (25,660 feet) would take his place. Rizvi had climbed to

22,500 feet on that mountain and knew the region extremely well. His measurements were the same as Captain Soofi's, except that his feet were a size larger. It was impossible to change the order for our boots so it seemed that Rizvi was going to get sore feet. Also there was a personal letter from Rizvi, which contained much useful information. His most important advice was that we should have two persons who could use the expedition's letter of credit. The treasurer of his prior expedition had died of pneumonia.

I established an expedition bank account and had all the members of the party sign waivers of liability in the event of an accident. Also everyone agreed that if by a miracle the expedition made a profit it would go to the expedition fund of the American Alpine club.

There was one more problem. Every major Himalayan expedition has to have a treasurer who stays behind to handle the accounts and stall off the creditors. There were no volunteers for this job, so I gave it to my long-suffering father. Like most responsible citizens, my parents are unenthusiastic about mountaineering. However, they learned years ago that I was going to climb anyway so they have tried to make my various trips successful. Besides, I could always end my father's occasional remonstrances by reminding him that at the age of seventeen he had run off and joined the French army as an ambulance driver in World War I. After presenting the expedition files to my father, I was ready to leave for Pakistan.

A Walk in the Sun

ERIC NEWBY

Take two adventuresome English lads, infuse them with the dream of finding and climbing a remote, little-known mountain deep in Afghanistan, deprive them (unlike major expeditions) of adequate resources to conduct their odyssey and then send them off overland through strange lands and in unreliable vehicles. This recipe for adventure proved successful as Eric Newby and Hugh Carless attempted to ascend Mir Samir in 1959. Along the way, they endured enough mishaps and surprises to last a lifetime, and they proved that, in climbing, the journey sometimes surpasses the mountain. This chapter from Newby's A Short Walk In The Hindu Kush, *picks up their trip as they begin the on-foot stage toward the dangerous Afghan mountain region of Nuristan.*

I woke the following morning to find Abdul Ghiyas regarding me at close range with his large haggard eyes. I had the sensation that he had been doing this for some time, perhaps trying to make up his mind by a close inspection what defects I possessed. Partly in order to reassure him, I went to swim in the river. The water was like ice. I emerged from it with chattering teeth to find that Ghulam Naabi had made tea and that the other drivers [men with horses who are contracted to transport goods] had already arrived.

While drinking our tea Hugh and I regarded them covertly. Our first reactions were not altogether favorable; judging by the hostile glances they shot at us from time to time, neither were theirs. Both of them were about our own age. One was thin, with a small foxy moustache. He wore a striped jacket that was part of a Western suit, loose *shalvar* trousers, a huge, floppy turban, and shoes with curly points. He looked cunning, intelligent, and the antithesis of the faithful retainer. The other had a broad, stupid face, like an old-fashioned prize-fighter, with a thick, trunklike nose and a deeply lined forehead with a wart on it. On the back of his head he wore a little pillbox. He looked as hard as nails.

They were crouching with Abdul Ghiyas over a wooden bowl containing curds and talking with great animation while they scraped the bottom of the bowl with great hunks of bread; occasionally they would interrupt their conversation to look at us with sinister emphasis. There was no question of our accepting or rejecting them. It was Abdul Ghiyas who was hiring them.

Outside the garden, on a small strip of green by the river, the three horses were picketed to iron pins driven into the ground. I knew little enough about horses but these seemed very small horses.

"Surely mules would be better. Why don't we take mules?"

"There aren't any mules in Afghanistan. At least I've never seen any."

It seemed extraordinary that, after a century of guerrilla warfare on the northwest frontier, no one had succeeded in capturing any mules from the British, but whatever the reason I never saw a mule in Afghanistan.

Now all our gear was brought out and stacked around us in the garden; coils of rope, boxes of rations, bags of flour, damp things that had already squashed and our *crampons*, those metal frames covered with sharp spikes that defied all efforts to pack them.

The driver from the embassy prepared to leave. From an inside pocket Ghulam Naabi produced a letter addressed to Hugh, which he handed to him. His face wore an expression of masklike innocence. The letter was short but to the point. It was from his employer, the Australian.

Sir,

    I understand from my servant, Ghulam Naabi, that you are proposing to relieve me of his services for a month, leaving me with a sick wife, several children, and no cook. I write to inform you that Ghulam Naabi is *not* accompanying you on your expedition. He will return to Kabul immediately.

There was nothing to say to this. It was the sort of letter I should have written myself in similar circumstances. With some show of emotion Ghulam Naabi transferred his few belongings to the station wagon. They were so few that it was obvious that the contents of the letter had already been communicated to him before he had left Kabul. Soon he was gone in a cloud of dust.

My worst fears were realized. I was now alone in Asia with a companion whose attitude to food was one of undisguised contempt and whose ideas were almost as austere as those of the followers who surrounded us.

"I can't understand that Australian," said Hugh. "It's a most extraordinary attitude. Never mind, we shall probably get on much better without Ghulam Naabi. Be able to travel faster. Less of a problem."

"Yes."

"Of course, it means doing the cooking ourselves."

"Yes."

"Still, it's all in tins."

"I know."

"You're unusually quiet."

"Yes."

"Hope you're feeling all right. Nothing wrong inside?"

"Nothing like that. I just feel as though I've been sentenced to death."

There seemed little hope of leaving that day. It was not due to lack of preparation. There was little to prepare. It was simply that the first day of a caravan was like being under starter's orders on a racecourse—only there was no starter.

Bloated with mulberries and slightly sticky, I lay on my stomach on the river bank, looking into the water. Occasionally a shaft of sunlight filtering down through the upper branches would illuminate a small fish, no more than six inches long, darting among the roots of the willows where the earth had been washed away. Out in midstream in the midday sun the river bubbled and surged past, the color of jade rippled with dazzling silver. On the far bank sheep and goats browsed in a deep—water meadow; birds Abdul Ghiyas called *parastu*, brown banded bank swallows, flew over the shingle without ever alighting; above the valley the mighty screes with small sunbaked patches of grass on them swept up and up; beyond the road the house simmered in the heat, its brown mud walls baking harder and harder. There was no sign of Abdul Ghiyas or the other drivers.

I was joined by Hugh. He buried his head in the river and drank. "Is that a good thing?" I asked.

"Excellent water. Comes from the high glaciers. You shouldn't drink it when you're hot, of course."

Remembering the affair of the icecream that had all but destroyed my wife [Newby's wife, who had accompanied them partway, had been stricken by a bad ice cream cone bought en route.], and the *qanat* water in north Persia, I was suspicious. The water certainly looked delicious; besides, there was so much of it. Surely such a volume would nullify all but the most urban germs.

"What about the villages higher?"

"There's nothing large enough to infect it," he said. "Besides you have to accustom yourself to this kind of thing. The most important thing is never to drink unless you absolutely have to. I never do," he added.

So I drank some too.

By three-thirty in the afternoon all hope of leaving seemed to have gone. Drivers and animals were locked in lassitude and indifference. Neither wanted to leave at the fag-end of the day—and they were right; to venture into the ovenlike landscape beyond the garden seemed to them suicide. Only by shouting at them and appealing to Abdul Ghiyas were the drivers finally prevailed upon to load their horses.

It was a long job. All the stuff had to be slung in nets made from a special reed and hooked to the pack saddles. Soon everything was ungettable: the rations in their fiber boxes, everything else in sacks as a protection against the battering it would receive from the rocks. It was obvious that unless one started the day with the gear one required, one would never see it till evening.

Unwisely, we decided to carry loaded rucksacks. "To toughen ourselves," as we optimistically put it.

"About forty pounds should be enough," Hugh said, "so that we can press on."

Our drivers were aghast. It was difficult to persuade Abdul Ghiyas that we were not out of our minds. With the temperature around 110°, carrying our forty-pound loads and twirling our ice axes, we set off from Jangalak.

It was good to be on the road; it stretched ahead of us full of ruts, following the river. On both sides the mountains rose steeply. Looking back we could see Abdul Ghiyas in the orchard at Jangalak where he was making the last adjustments, putting off his departure to the last possible moment.

At first we congratulated ourselves on seeing more of the countryside on foot. What we had not taken into account was the diminished social status that was accorded to a couple of Europeans plodding through Asia with heavy loads on their backs. It was after a long mile, when we met two wild-looking crop-headed mountaineers coming down from above by a rough track, that we first realized that nobody admired us for what we were doing. They themselves were carrying immense loads of rock salt in conical baskets. We waved cheerfully but they uttered such angry cries and made such threatening gestures that we passed hurriedly on. They turned to shout after us. It was always the same word.

"What's a *sag*?"

"It's a dog."

"Is it rude in Persian?"

"Very, they think we should be on horseback."

The road followed the west bank of the river through mulberry orchards and fields of wheat and Indian corn. At this time of day all were deserted. After two miles we reached the village of Mala

Asp. From here the road became impassable for vehicles. At the stop beyond the village the evening bus stood up to its axles in a deep puddle. That we should have walked here heavily laden when we might quite easily have traveled by bus seemed to make us even more ludicrous figures. As we left, a nasty old man screamed at us from the top of a rock, "Xar, Xar, Donkeys! Why don't you ride?"

To which we replied, in fury, "--- off!"

The two miles we had covered since Jangalak had wrought great changes in us. We no longer chatted gaily. In the cool garden it had been difficult to realize how hot it really was. Soon we were suffering all the agonies of heat, thirst, and fatigue, accelerated by poor condition. Our legs felt like melting butter.

So that Hugh could give me a piece of chewing gum, we halted for a moment in the shade of a solitary tree. Already our mouths were full of a thick, elastic scum, which with the chewing gum became like a gigantic gobstopper. Our rucksacks with their forty-pound loads seemed to weigh a hundredweight; nevertheless we both agreed that whatever else happened we should carry them for today. I was wearing a new pair of Italian boots that had been specially constructed for me in Italy. In the whole of England I had not been able to find, in the short time at my disposal, a pair of climbing boots that would fit me (my old boots had collapsed during a visit to Wales). As the Italian bootmaker at Brescia said, with a simplicity that robbed his words of offense:

"Signore, non sono piedi d'uomo, sono piedi di scimmia." [Sir, these are not the feet of a man, but of a monkey.]

The boots had arrived by air in Tehran on the morning we left for Meshed and, apart from our short outing on Legation Hill, I had not tried them. Now, in the hot afternoon, they became agonizing. Apart from a pair of gym shoes they were the only foot covering I possessed, my walking shoes having failed to arrive from England, where they too had had to be made.

We were now traveling what, before the motor road had been constructed over the Hindu Kush by the Shibar Pass, had been the main caravan route to Northern Afghanistan, Badakshan, and the crossing of the Oxus. Coming down toward us we met a variety of travelers. First a band of Tajiks mounted on donkeys who were on their way from Jurm in Dadakshan more than 150 miles to the northeast to buy teapots and tea at Gulbahar; they had been twelve days on the road and the skin around their eyes was all shriveled by the sun. Then there were some Pathan camel drivers who had come over from Andarab with wheat, their beasts swaying down like great galleons under a press of sail. Going up were caravans of donkeys with cotton goods from the mill at Gulbahar. All the people we met who were traveling the road were more friendly than the householders we had so far encountered.

"How is your condition?" "Are you well?" "Are you strong?" "Where are you going?" To which we replied, invariably, "Up," or "Parian mirim," [to Parian]—the upper part of the Panjshir Valley; vague enough, yet it seemed to satisfy them. All soon became a bore. For our part we did not speak to one another; we had no moisture to spare.

At six o'clock, when the heat had gone, we reached a place where the road passed close to the river at its junction with a torrent coming from a big valley to the east. This was the Darra Hazara, where some 400 families of Hazaras live who have become Sunnites as the price of living in peace among the Tajiks.

It was an eerie place. Behind us the sun was lost in clouds of yellow dust raised by the wind that had got up suddenly, howling across the valley as the sun went down and lashing the river so that it smoked.

On the left of the track, already in cold shadow, were a number of tombs on a hillock; piles of stones decked with tattered flags that fluttered sadly in the wind and ibex horns decorated with twists of colored paper. According to Hugh it was a *ziarat*, a shrine, and the tomb decorated with ibex horns that of a *mirgun*—a matchlock man, or master hunter.

On the Hazara side there was a fort. Marz Robat, the Fort of the Frontier. It was about a hundred feet square, built of mud brick and defended at the four corners by towers that tapered thickly to their bases.

"One way into Nuristan," Hugh said as we plodded past the

Darra Hazara. "Two days over the pass and you'd be on the head-waters of the Alishang River, but you'd still only be on the outskirts of Nuristan. You'd have to cross the Alishang Pass into the Alingar Valley and then you'd only be in the lower part. I want to get to the upper part."

It sounded very complicated.

As we covered the last awful mile into the village that takes its name from the fort but is called by the locals Omarz, two fit-looking men came steaming up behind us. The taller of the two, a fine-looking fellow with a black beard, turned out to be of the same profession as the one under the pile of stones, a *mirgun*.

I was too far gone to really care what a *mirgun* was but Hugh, with a perversity that I had already remarked in him, proceeded to tell me at great length, translating, sentence by sentence, as the man spoke.

From beneath an immense *chapan* the *mirgun* produced a muzzle-loading rifle fired by a percussion cap. It looked quite new. Every-thing this man had about him was robust and strongly constructed for the hard life he lived on the mountainside.

"From *Enlestan*," he said. "I have not had it long."

While I was trying to imagine some small factory in Birmingham still turning out muzzle-loaders for *mirgun*, he added, "I have buried my other in an orchard. When I killed a thousand ibex I became a *mirgun*. Then I buried the gun with which I slew them. It is the custom. I buried it secretly in my orchard. Then the young men for the village came to seek for it. He who finds it can buy the gun."

"Why should he wish to do so?"

"Because with it he too will slay a thousand ibex and himself in turn become *mirgun*."

At six-thirty we arrived at the village of Marz Robat itself. We had been on the road for three hours and during this time had covered perhaps ten miles; nevertheless, I felt utterly exhausted. By the look on Hugh's face he was experiencing somewhat similar sensations.

Outstripped by the *mirgun* and his companion, whose opinions of our powers of locomotion were plain enough, we followed them into a narrow enclosure on the right of the road and sank down on the scruffy grass.

"You know," said Hugh, "I feel rather done up, I can't think why."

"It must be the change of air."

We were in a little garden high above the river, on the outskirts of the village, which belonged to a *chaie khana* across the road. The *chaie khana* was really only a hole in a wall with a sagging roof of dead vegetation strung on some long poles. Standing in a wooden cradle, looking like a medieval siege mortar and equally defunct, was a Russian samovar made of copper and decorated with the imperial eagles. It was splendid but unfortunately it was not working. Deciding that it would take a long time to get up a head of steam in a thing of this size, I closed my eyes in a coma of fatigue.

When I next opened them I was covered with a thick blanket of flies. They were somnolent in the cool of the evening and, when I thumped myself, squashing dozens of them, they simply rose a foot in the air and fell back on me with an audible "plop," closing the ranks left by the slaughtered like well-drilled infantry.

Now the samovar was belching steam, jumping up and down on its wooden cradle in its eagerness to deliver the goods. It no longer resembled a cannon; it was more like an engine emerging from its shed anxious to be off up the line and away.

Bending over us was the proprietor, a curious-looking giant in a long brown cloak reaching to his feet, which stuck out coyly from under it. He was an object of nightmare but he brought with him all the apparatus of tea.

My teeth were chattering like castanets and without a word the giant took off his verminous cloak and wrapped me in it, leaving himself in a thin cotton shift. Another cloak was brought for Hugh. Here, when the sun went down, it was cold.

Regarding us silently from the walls of the little garden there was an immense audience. The male population of Marz Robat, all but the bedridden, come to view these extraordinary beings who to them must have had all the strangeness of visitors from outer space. To appreciate their point of view one would to imagine a Tajik stretched out in a garden in Wimbledon.

It was green tea and delicious but the cups were small; pretty things of fine porcelain. After we had each drunk two entire pots we still had need of more liquid. Ours was not a thirst that preceded from dry throats but a deep internal need to replace what had been sucked out of us in our unfit state by the power of the sun.

"I shouldn't do that," Hugh croaked, as I demanded water. "You'll be sorry."

My powers of restraint, never great, had been broken. Now our roles were reversed.

"I thought you wanted me to drink it."

"Not when you're tired. It's too cold."

He was too late; the giant had already sent down to the river for a *chatti* of water. Somewhere I had read that salt was the thing for a person suffering from dehydration, so I called for salt too; a rock of it was produced and I put it in the pot, sluiced it round and drank deep. It was a nasty mixture but at least I felt that in some way I was justifying my lack of self-control.

All this time the crowd had been quietly slipping down off the wall and closing in on us; now they were all round us gorging with their eyes. We were the cynosure. Hugh was the first to crack.

"----!" He got up and stalked to the far end of the garden, tripping over his *chapan*. The crowd followed him but he barked at them so violently that they sheared off and settled on me.

With the intention of splitting them, I made for the only available corner (the other was occupied by the *mirgun* and his friend), but as soon as I started to walk I found that there was something very wrong with my feet inside the Italian boots. It was as if a tram had gone over them. I sat down hastily, took the boots off and found that my socks were full of blood.

It seemed impossible that such damage could have been done in the space of three hours and some ten miles. My feet looked as though they had been flayed, as indeed they had.

How it had happened was a mystery; the boots were not tight, rather there was an excess of living room inside them. The real trouble was that they were slightly pointed, whether because pointed shoes were the current Italian fashion and the designers thought that the appearance was improved or whether to facilitate rock climbing was not clear. What was certain was that for me pointed boots were excruciatingly painful.

Hugh tottered over to look and the villagers made little whistling sounds when they saw the extent of the damage. All of them knew the value of feet in the Hindu Kush. For some time Hugh said nothing. There was nothing to say and nothing to be done until Abdul Ghiyas arrived with the horses and the medicine chest.

"They're bad," he said at last. "What do you want to do, go back to Kabul?"

To return to Kabul was useless; yet to go on seemed madness.

There was no question of my feet healing, the daily quota of miles would ensure that. I thought of all the difficulties we had overcome to get even as far as Marz Robat: the children uprooted from school; our flat let; my job gone; the money that Hugh and myself had expended; his own dotty dream of climbing Mir Samir to be frustrated at the last moment; my own dream, equally balmy, of becoming an explorer in the same way going up in smoke. I thought of the old inhabitant at Kabul. "They're always setting off," he had chuckled. "That's as far as they get." Were we to join this select body who had traveled only in their cups? There seemed to be no alternative but to go on. The fact that there was none rallied me considerably.

"We might be able to get you a horse," Hugh said.

He could not have said anything better. I am completely ignorant of horses. The last time I had attempted to mount one I faced the wrong way when putting my foot in the stirrup and found myself in the saddle facing the creature's tail. Worse, being nervous of horses, I emanate a smell of death when close to them so that, sniffing it, they take fright themselves and attempt to destroy me. A horse would certainly have destroyed me on the road we had traversed that afternoon. At some places it had been only a couple of feet wide with a sheer drop to the river below.

"I think I'll carry on as I am. Another horse means another driver."

"It would be *your* horse. We wouldn't need another driver."

"If I walk they may harden up." It was a phrase that I was to use constantly from now on.

It was fortunate that Abdul Ghiyas chose this moment to arrive with the rest of the party. Drivers and horses came lurching into the garden, all our gear banging against the stone walls in an alarming way. If this was what had been happening all along the road at the narrow places, most of it must have been shattered long ago.

All three were in a filthy temper, having been uprooted from their afternoon siesta and made to travel in the heat of the day. In an instant they cleared the garden of the crowds that milled about us and began to unload the horses, banging the boxes down like disgruntled housemaids and mumbling to themselves with averted eyes. It was not a propitious beginning to our life together.

"Are they always like this?" Watching this display of temperament I expressed my fears to Hugh.

"We haven't discussed terms with them yet. They're building themselves up for a good set-to about how much they're going to be paid. Then they'll quiet down a lot."

"They're rather like *vendeuses*. Can't we put them out of their misery?"

"You can't hurry things in this part of the world. They'll do it in their own way. Besides we don't want an audience. Wait until it gets dark. I should get on with dressing your feet."

As it grew dark Abdul Ghiyas moved all the equipment of the expedition close-in around us, hedging us with boxes and bundles so that we resembled ambushed settlers making a last stand. "For fear of robbers," as he put it. Within this enclosure we ate stewed apricots with lots of sugar, the only food that we could stomach in our debilitated condition. Almost at once, as Hugh had prophesied, we started to wrangle over wages.

"For the journey we offer thirty Afghanis a day. Also we will provide you the food for your horses." Hugh managed to make the part about the food sound like a benediction. At the bazaar rate of exchange thirty Afghanis is about four shillings.

The larger of the two drivers, whose name is Shir Muhammad, a surly-looking brute, said nothing but spat on the ground. To dispose of him at this delicate moment in the negotiations Hugh sent him to get sugar.

"Sugar, what do you want with sugar? If you come to our country why don't you live like us?" he mumbled, throwing the bag down in an ungracious way. "This is a country of poor men."

"What a noble animal is the horse," said Abdul Ghiyas, striving to inject a more lofty note into a conversation that was in imminent danger of degenerating into an affair of mutual recrimination. "The way is stony and hard for our horses. No man will take you to this mountain for thirty Afghanis a day." ". . . and food for the men," said Hugh.

"That is the custom. Besides, who knows what perils careless *Seb* will lead us into. Where will he take us after the mountain? Mir Samir is very close to Nuristan."

"Thirty-five Afghanis." Abdul Ghiyas had struck a subject that neither of us wanted to discuss at this stage. It was a shrewd thrust.

The silence that followed was as long that I began to think the discussion had lapsed completely.

"The horse is the friend of man," he said at last. "The road is a difficult one. There are many perils on it, robbers and evil men. We are all married men. I am married, Shir Muhammad is married, Badar Khan is married . . ." He indicated the smaller driver, the one with a thin moustache, who began to giggle.

"He looks like a pansy to me," said Hugh in English. "Forty Afghanis. Not one more."

"Our children are numerous," Shir Muhammad leered horribly. "Who is to look after them when we are gone?"

"This is your own country. Surely you're not afraid of Tajiks?"

"There are Hazaras, heathen Shias . . ."

"But the Hazaras of the Darra Hazara are your brothers, Sunnites."
This was one up to Hugh but Abdul Ghiyas ignored it.

"I have heard from the *mullah* at Jangalak," he went on, "that
only two days ago a Nuristani going to Kabul to stay with his
brother in the army was robbed of everything, his cloak too, by the
Gujaras."

I asked who the Gujaras were.

"Hill shepherds; partly nomad, for the Frontier, originally from
the Punjab. There are some in Nuristan. They're semicriminal—
forty-five Afghanis."

Finally, we settle for fifty Afghanis. Hugh grumbled a lot, "Don't
know what the country's coming to," but to me it seemed remarkable
that we had secured the services of three able-bodied men and their
wiry little horses for the equivalent of six and eightpence each.

Now that all was concluded satisfactorily, the water pipe was
circulated and Shir Muhammad heaped the fire with the fuel that
the horses were producing at a greater rate than it could be con-
sumed, an unusual experience for anyone used to living in Britain.

All night I was racked with pains in the stomach, the result of
drinking water that was both ice cold and dirty. Hugh, of course,
was completely unaffected. Each time I got up I encountered Abdul
Ghiyas. He was not asleep but squatting in the moonlight, ghostly
in his white *chapan*, brooding over the kit, listening to the roar of
the river.

A Short Walk with Whillans

TOM PATEY

No climb is more firmly embedded in mountaineering lore than one in the Swiss Alps. Mention the North Face of the Eiger and climbers worldwide who have never touched its dark visage will spin gruesome tales of the nationalistic race for its first ascent and will name its well-known features, each steeped with climbing history: the Hinterstoisser Traverse; the Death Bivouac; the Traverse of the Gods; the White Spider. In 1963, two human legends sauntered to the Eiger's base, intent of climbing it. The Britisher, Don Whillans, had been there several times without success. The Scot, Tom Patey, a ribald and respected mountaineer, was eager to attempt the face and enjoy the company of his taciturn ropemate. Patey's humorous recollection of this unique encounter of three legends is taken from a collection of his writings, One Man's Mountains.

"Did you spot that great long streak of blood on the road over from Chamonix? Twenty yards long, I'd say."

The speaker was Don Whillans. We were seated in the little inn at Alpiglen and Don's aggressive profile was framed against an awe-inspiring backdrop of the Eiger-Norwand. I reflected that the conversation had become attuned to the environment.

"Probably some unfortunate animal," I ventured without much conviction.

Whillans's eyes narrowed. "Human blood," he said. "Remember—lass?" (appealing to his wife Audrey), "I told you to stop the car for a better look. Really turned her stomach, it did. Just when she was getting over the funeral."

I felt an urge to inquire whose funeral they had attended. There had been several. Every time we went up on the Montenvers train we passed a corpse going down. I let the question go. It seemed irrelevant, possibly even irreverent.

"Ay, it's a good life," he mused, "providing you don't weaken."

"What happens if you do?"

"They bury you," he growled, and finished his pint.

Don has that rarest of gifts, the ability to condense a whole paragraph into a single, terse, uncompromising sentence. But there are also occasions when he can become almost lyrical in a macabre sort of way. It depends on the environment.

We occupied a window table in the inn. There were several other tables, and hunched round each of these were groups of shadowy men draped in black cagoules—lean-jawed, grim, uncommunicative characters who spoke in guttural monosyllables and gazed steadfastly towards the window. You only had to glimpse their earnest faces to realize that these men were Eiger Candidates—martyrs for the "Mordwand" [literally "murder wall"].

"Look at the big black bastard up there," Whillans chuckled dryly, gesturing with his thumb. "Just waiting to get its claws into you. And think of all the young lads who've sat just where you're sitting now, and come back all tied up in sacks. It makes you think."

It certainly did. I was beginning to wish I had stayed at Chamonix, funerals or no funerals.

"Take that young blond over there," he pointed toward the sturdy Aryan barmaid, who had just replenished his glass. "I wonder how many dead men she's danced with? All the same," he concluded after a minute's reflection, "t'wouldn't be a bad way to spend your last night."

I licked my lips nervously. Don's philosophic discourses are not for the fainthearted.

One of the Eiger Candidates detached himself from a neighboring group and approached us with obvious intent. He was red-haired, small, and compact and he looked like a Neanderthal man. This likeness derived from his hunched shoulders, and the way he craned his head forward like a man who had been struck repeatedly on the crown by a heavy hammer, and through time developed a protective overgrowth of skull. His name proved to be Eckhart, and he was a German. Most of them still are.

The odd thing about him was his laugh. It had an uncanny hollow quality. He laughed quite a lot without generating a great deal of warmth, and he wore a twisted grin which seemed to be permanently frozen onto his face. Even Whillans was moved.

"You—going—up?" he inquired.

"Nein," said Eckhart. "Nix gutt! . . . You wait here little time, I think. . . . Now there is much vatter." He turned up his coat collar ruefully and laughed. "Many, many stein fall. . . . All day, all night. . . . Stein, stein." He tapped his head significantly and laughed uproariously. "Two nights we wait at *Tod Bivouac* ['death bivouac']." He repeated the name as if relishing its sinister undertones. ("It means Dead Man," I said to Whillans in a hushed whisper.) "Always it is nix gutt. . . . Vatter, stein. . . . Stein, vatter. . . . So we go down. It is very funny."

We nodded sympathetically. It was all a huge joke.

"Our two Kameraden, they go on. They are saying at the telescopes, one man he had fallen fifty meters. Me? I do not believe this." (Loud and prolonged laughter from the company.)

"You have looked through the telescope?" I inquired anxiously.

"Nein," he grinned, "Not necessary . . . tonight they gain summit . . . tomorrow they descend. And now we will have another beer."

Eckhart was nineteen. He had already accounted for the North Face of the Matterhorn as a training climb and he intended to camp at the foot of the Eigerwand until the right conditions prevailed. If necessary, he could wait until October. Like most of his countrymen he was nothing if not thorough, and finding his bivouac-tent did not measure up to his expectations he had hitchhiked all the way back to Munich to secure another one. As a result of this, he had missed the settled spell of weather that had allowed several rivals to complete the route, including the second successful British

76

team, Baillie and Haston, and also the lone Swiss climber, Darbellay, who had thus made the first solo ascent.

"Made of the right stuff, that youngster," observed Don.

"If you ask me I think he was trying to scare us off," I suggested. "Psychological warfare that's all it is."

"Wait till we got on the face tomorrow," said Whillans. "We'll hear your piece then."

Shortly after noon the next day we left Audrey behind at Alpiglen, and the two of us set off up the green meadows which girdle the foot of the Eigerwand. Before leaving, Don had disposed of his Last Will and Testament. "You've got the carkey, lass, and you know where to find the housekey. That's all you need to know. Ta, for now."

Audrey smiled wanly. She had my profound sympathy.

The heat was oppressive, the atmosphere heavy with menace. How many Munich Bergsteigers had trod this very turf on their upward path never to return to their native Klettergarten? I was humming Wagner's Valkyrie theme music as we reached the lowest rocks of the face.

Then a most unexpected thing happened. From an alcove in the wall emerged a very ordinary Swiss tourist, followed by his very ordinary wife, five small children and a poodle dog. I stopped humming immediately. I had read of tearful farewells with wives and sweethearts calling plaintively, but this was ridiculous. What an undignified send-off! The five children accompanied us up the first snow slope scrambling happily in our wake, and prodding our rucksacks with inquisitive fingers. "Go away," said Whillans irritably, but ineffectively. We were quite relieved when, ultimately, they were recalled to base and we stopped playing Pied Pipers. The dog held on a bit longer until some well directed stones sent it on its way. "Charming, I must say," remarked Don. I wondered whether Hermann Buhl [a postwar German climber best known for his first ascent of the Himalayan peak, Nanga Parbat] would have given up on the spot—a most irregular start to an Eiger Epic and probably a bad omen.

We started climbing up the left side of the shattered pillar, a variant of the normal route, which had been perfected by Don in the course of several earlier attempts. He was well on his way to becoming the Grand Old Man of Grindelwald, though not through any fault of his own. This was his fourth attempt at the climb and on every previous occasion he had been turned back by bad weather or by having to rescue his rivals. As a result of this he must have spent more hours on the face than any other British climber.

Don's preparations for the Eiger—meticulous in every other respect—had not included unnecessary physical exertion. While I dragged my weary muscles from Brueil to Zermatt via the Matterhorn he whiled away the days at Chamonix sunbathing at the Plage until opening time. At the Bar Nationale he nightly sank five or six pints of "heavy," smoked forty cigarettes, persuaded other layabouts to feed the juke box with their last few francs and amassed a considerable reputation as an exponent of "Baby Foot," the table football game that is the national sport of France. One day the heat had been sufficiently intense to cause a rush of blood to the head because he had walked four miles up to the Montenvers following the railway track, and had acquired such enormous blisters that he had to make the return journey by train. He was nevertheless just as fit as he wanted to be, or indeed needed to be.

First impressions of the Eigerwand belied its evil reputation. This was good climbing rock with excellent friction and lots of small incuts. We climbed unroped, making height rapidly. In fact I was just starting to enjoy myself, when I found the boot. . . .

"Somebody's left a boot here," I shouted to Don.

He pricked up his ears. "Look and see if there's a foot in it," he said.

I had picked it up: I put it down again hurriedly.

"Ha! Here's something else—a torn rucksack," he hissed. "And here's his waterbottle—squashed flat."

I had lost my new-found enthusiasm and decided to ignore future foreign bodies. (I even ignored the pun.)

"You might as well start getting used to them now," advised

Whillans. "This is where they usually glance off, before they hit the bottom."

He's a cheery character I thought to myself. To Don, a spade is just a spade—a simple trenching tool used by gravediggers.

At the the the top of the Pillar we donned our safety helmets. "One thing to remember on the Eiger," said Don, "never look up, or you may need a plastic surgeon."

His advice seemed superfluous that evening, as we did not hear a single ricochet. We climbed on up, past the Second Pillar and roped up for the traverse across to the Difficult Crack. At this late hour the Crack was streaming with water so we decided to bivouac while we were still dry. There was an excellent bivouac cave near the foot of the crack.

"I'll have one of your cigarettes," said Don. "I've only brought Gauloises." This was a statement of fact, not a question. There is something about Don's proverbial bluntness that arouses one's admiration. Of such stuff are generals made. We had a short discussion about bivouacking, but eventually I had to agree with his arguments and occupy the outer berth. It would be less likely to induce claustrophobia, or so I gathered.

I was even more aware of the sudden fall in temperature. My ultra-warm Terray *duvet* failed by a single critical inch to meet the convertible bivvy-rucksack I had borrowed from Joe Brown. It had been designed, so the manufacturers announced, to Joe's personal specifications, and as far as I could judge, to his personal dimensions as well.

Insidiously and from nowhere it seemed, a mighty thunderstorm built up in the valley less than a mile away. Flashes of lightning lit up the whole face and gray tentacles of mist crept out of the dusk threatening to envelop our lofty eyrie.

"The girl in the Tourist Office said that a ridge of high pressure occupying the whole of central Europe would last for at least another three days."

"Charming," growled Whillans. "I could give you a better forecast without raising my head."

"We should be singing Bavarian drinking songs to keep our spirits up," I suggested. "How about some Austrian yodeling."

"They're too fond of dipping in glacier streams . . . that's what does it," he muttered sleepily.

"Does what?"

"Makes them yodel. All the same, these bloody Austrians."

The day dawned clear. For once it seemed that a miracle had happened and a major thunderstorm had cleared the Eiger, without lodging on the face. Don remained inscrutable and cautious as ever. Although we were sheltered from any prevailing wind we would have no advance warning of the weather, as our horizons were limited by the face itself.

There was still a trickle of water coming down the Difficult Crack as Don launched himself stiffly at the first obstacle. Because of our uncertainty about the weather and an argument about who should make breakfast, we had started late. It was 6:30 A.M. and we would have to hurry. He made a bad start by clipping both strands of the double rope to each of the three pitons he found in position. The rope jammed continuously and this was even more disconcerting for me, when I followed carrying both rucksacks. Hanging down the middle of the pitch was an old frayed rope, said to have been abandoned by Mlle Loulou Bolaz, and this kept getting entangled with the ice-axes. By the time I had joined Don at this stance I was breathing heavily and more than usually irritated. We used the excuse to unrope and get back into normal rhythm before tackling the Hinterstoisser [so-named for a blank passage that once ascended couldn't be reversed]. It was easy to find the route hereabouts: you merely followed the pitons. They were planted everywhere with rotting rope loops (apparently used for *abseils*) attached to most of them. It is a significant insight into human psychology that nobody ever stops to remove superfluous pegs on the Eiger. If nothing else they help to alleviate the sense of utter isolation that fills this vast face, but they also act as constant reminders of man's ultimate destiny and the pageant of history written into the rock. Other reminders were there in plenty—gloves, socks, ropes, crampons, and boots. None of them appeared to have been abandoned with the owners' consent.

The Hinterstoisser Traverse, despite the illustrations of prewar heroes traversing "a la Dulfer," is nothing to get excited about. With two fixed ropes of unknown vintage as an emergency handrail, you can walk across it in three minutes. Stripped of scaffolding, it would probably qualify as Severe by contemporary British standards. The fixed ropes continued without a break as far as the Swallow's Nest—another bivouac site hallowed by tradition. Thus far I could well have been climbing the Italian Ridge of the Matterhorn.

We skirted the first ice field on the right, scrambling up easy rubble where we had expected to find black ice. It was certainly abnormally warm, but if the weather held we had definite grounds for assuming that we could complete the climb in one day—our original intention. The Ice Hose, which breaches the rocky barrier between the First and Second Ice fields, no longer merited the name because the ice had all gone. It seemed to offer an easy alley but Don preferred to stick to known alternatives and advanced upon an improbably looking wall some distance across to the left. By the time I had confirmed our position on Hiebeler's route description, he had completed the pitch and was shouting for me to come on. He was well into his stride but still did not seem to share my optimism.

His doubts were well founded. Ten minutes later, we were crossing the waterworn slabs leading on to the Second Ice Field when we saw the first falling stones. To be exact we did not see the stones, but merely the puff of smoke each one left behind at the point of impact. They did not come bouncing down the cliff with a noisy clatter as stones usually do. In fact they were only audible after they had gone past—WROUFF!—a nasty sort of sound half-way between a suck and a blow.

"It's the small ones that make that sort of noise," explained Whillans, "Wait till you hear the really big ones!"

The blueprint for a successful Eiger ascent seems to involve being at the right place at the right time. According to our calculations the face should have been immune to stonefall at this hour of the morning.

Unfortunately the Eiger makes its own rules. An enormous black cloud had taken shape out of what ought to have been a clear blue sky, and had come to rest on the summit ice field. It reminded me of a gigantic black vulture spreading its wings before dropping like lightning on unsuspecting prey.

Down there at the foot of the Second Ice Field, it was suddenly very cold and lonely. Away across to the left was the Ramp; a possible hideaway to sit out the storm. It seemed little more than a stone's throw, but I knew as well as Don did, that we had almost 1,500 feet of steep snow-ice to cross before we could get any sort of shelter from stones.

There was no question of finding adequate cover in the immediate vicinity. On either side of us steep ice slopes, peppered with fallen debris, dropped away into the void. Simultaneously with Whillans's arrival at the stance the first flash of lightening struck the White Spider [a convergence of several ice gullies high on the Eiger face].

"That settles it," said he, clipping the spare rope through my belay karabiner.

"What's going on?" I demanded, finding it hard to credit that such a crucial decision could be reached on the spur of the moment.

"I'm going down," he said, "That's what's going on."

"Wait a minute! Let's discuss the whole situation calmly." I stretched out one hand to flick the ash off my cigarette. Then a most unusual thing happened. There was a higher pitched "WROUFF" than usual and the end of my cigarette disappeared! It was the sort of subtle touch that Hollywood film directors dream about.

"I see what you mean," I said. "I'm going down, too."

I cannot recall coming off a climb so quickly. As a result of a long acquaintance Don knew the location of every *abseil* point and this enabled us to bypass the complete section of the climb, which includes the Hinterstoisser Traverse and the Chimney leading up to the Swallow's Nest. To do this, you merely *rappel* directly downward from the last *abseil* point above the Swallow's Nest and so reach a key piton at the top of the wall overlooking the start of the Hinterstoisser Traverse. From here a straightforward *rappel* of 140 feet goes vertically down the wall to the large ledge at the start of the traverse. If Hinterstoisser had realized that he would probably not now have a Traverse named after him, and the Eigerwand would not enjoy one half its present notoriety. The idea of a "Point of No Return" always captures the imagination, and until very recent times, it was still the fashion to abandon a fixed rope at the Hinterstoisser in order to safeguard a possible retreat.

The unrelenting bombardment, which had kept us hopping from one *abseil* to the next like demented fleas, began to slacken off as we came into the lee of the "Rote Fluh." The weather had obviously broken down completely and it was raining heavily. We followed separate ways down the easy lower section of the face, sending down volleys of loose scree in front of us. Every now and again we heard strange noises, like a series of muffled yelps, but since we appeared to have the mountain to ourselves, this did not provoke comment. Whillans had just disappeared round a nearby corner when I heard a loud ejaculation.

"God Almighty," he said (or words to that effect) "Japs! Come and see for yourself!"

Sure enough, there they were. Two identical little men in identical climbing uniforms, sitting side by side underneath an overhang. They had been crouching there for an hour, waiting for the bombardment to slacken. I estimated that we must have scored several near misses.

"You—Japs?" grunted Don. It seemed an unnecessary question.

"Yes, yes," they grinned happily, displaying a full set of teeth. We are Japanese."

"Going—up?" queried Whillans. He pointed meaningfully at the gray holocaust sweeping down from the White Spider.

"Yes, yes," they chorused in unison. "Up. Always upward. First Japanese Ascent."

"You-may-be-going-up-Mate," said Whillans, giving every syllable unnecessary emphasis, "but-a-lot-'igher-than-you-think!"

They did not know what to make of this, so they wrung his hand several times, and thanked him profusely for the advice.

"'Appy little pair!" said Don. "I don't imagine we'll ever see them again."

He was mistaken. They came back seven days later after several feet of new snow had fallen. They had survived a full-scale Eiger blizzard and had reached our highest point on the Second Ice Field. If they did not receive a medal for valor they had certainly earned one. They were the forerunners of the climbing elite of Japan, whose members now climb Mount Everest for the purpose of skiing back down again.

We got back to the Alpiglen in time for late lunch. The telescope stood forlorn and deserted in the rain. The Eiger had retired into its misty oblivion, as Don Whillans retired to his favorite corner seat by the window.

The Final Attack

ELIZABETH KNOWLTON

The 1932 German-American Expedition to Nanga Parbat, a 26,620-foot Himalayan peak, was the first in a series of determined struggles by the Germans to obtain its virgin summit. Just as unclimbed Everest was always considered a "British mountain," so did Nanga Parbat become known as the German Mountain of the East. The 1932 venture was led by Willi Merkl and included the Americans Rand Herron, Fritz Wiessner, and Elizabeth Knowlton. Inexperience with the Himalaya caused the expedition to squander several weeks of stable weather, and their first serious assault on the summit was defeated by storm and deep snow. Discouraged, several members left the expedition to return home. From Base Camp, Merkl, Weissner and Herron left with twelve porters to reoccupy their upper camps on the mountain and mount a last attempt on the summit. Knowlton remained in Base Camp. She describes in this chapter from her book, The Naked Mountain, *the progress of the men and their dreams of victory.*

> *Let him who seeks the monarch of our quest*
> *Challenge their wakened might,*
> *. . . summits crowned with summer light.*
> *Not his to tempt their rest*
> *When winter rigors and cold snows encumber:-*
> *The sleeping ones have but to stir in slumber,*
> *And he shall sleep with them.*
>
> Geoffrey Winthrop Young

I

On the morning of August 28th, the climbers set out for the final attack on the mountain.

"A fine day!" Merkl had shouted, and had awakened the camp to preparation soon after dawn. It was glorious autumn weather again—cool and crystal clear. The sky was without clouds. The porters' rations of chappatis were cooked—enough for ten days. The loads were ready. Things seemed auspicious at last.

At about half past eight, they left—Merkl, Herron, Weissner, and twelve porters. It had taken a long time to give final directions and get started. At the very end, there was a lineup for a snapshot. The twelve porters stood in an impressive row in the rear, with Merkl, Herron, and Weissner kneeling in front. Sahibs and coolies, they all smiled cheerily into the camera. But I do not believe I was the only one to whom the thought came that for some of those smiling men this might prove to be their last picture. I brushed the thought aside, like a troublesome fly. Our brief farewell words were only of good luck, with strong hopes of victory. The climbers shook hands with me. They bent to the ascent, and started up the steepness of the Moraine Hill.

It made a fine-looking procession, crawling up the autumn-brown slopes, the largest, the fittest, the most completely equipped caravan that had ever left the base camp. The Jemadar and the rest of the coolies stood about, watching with interest. Suddenly a call came down: the porters had forgotten some essential. The base camp coolies ran over to their encampment, retrieved it, and hurried on, to hand it to one who was lagging part way down the hillside. Now they were really off. . . .

Slowly the procession mounted, scattering a little as it bent to the steep slopes. The dun figures grew smaller and higher, hardly visible on the brown autumn grass or the gray summit rocks, only occasionally silhouetted as moving dots against the skyline. Then they vanished.

II

I had decided to follow, the hour or two's climb to the top of the Moraine Hill, and watch them start up the glacier. From its summit, I could see that there was a great delay about getting on to the ice from the final rocks. Where our earlier path had gone, was now a complete network of vicious crevasses. As these had been opening, more and more of them, wider and wider, during the summer, slowly the route had been pushed farther and farther to the right, beneath the threatening, avalanching north face. Now it was proving necessary for the men to work their way to the very end of the moraine rocks, at the extreme right. I saw a long line at last emerge on to the glacier, already far behind the normal time schedule, directly under that terrible fourteen thousand feet of precipices.

They moved along the snow very slowly, fifteen black dots, in four groups—three, three, five, and four. Herron and Wiessner, with a coolie between them, were the three black dots of the first rope. They were taking turns in going first, for the difficult work of breaking trail Merkl led the second rope. The others were made up entirely of coolies. The long line gradually moved on, leaving a little dark thread of footprints behind. Even so early in the morning, they were finding the snow soft and tiring, for after the last storm it had not melted and frozen solid in customary summer style. It was winter snow conditions that they were meeting now. Already, on the comparative level of the beginning of the glacial basin, the coolies were going badly, and resting often and long. It seemed to me, watching, that they were taking an interminable time to get on. The string of dots crawled, and halted, and crawled again, close under Nanga Parbat's great north face. Surely never had they progressed so slowly before.

Finally, they began to mount the steep rise. Now, they were beyond the special avalanche danger: I could breathe easily again, at last. They stopped, as they so frequently did, to rest. Fifteen little dots sitting along the white slopes, they looked for all the world like a row of black crows, perched there.

Suddenly above me on the right I heard a roar, the familiar roar of an avalanche. It was such a big one that I quickly located its giant waterfall of powder snow, starting down from almost the very top of the wall. Remorselessly it poured down, falling over precipices with snow dust rising like spray, tumbling in cataracts from cliff to cliff, gathering volume on intervening snow slopes, roaring louder and louder. It was a perceptible moment from the time it started, before it finally spread its weight of snow over the glacial basin. The cloud of snow dust around it hid the men from my sight; it billowed higher and higher; it filled the whole basin with a solid whiteness; it rolled out, and piled itself up and up, until it concealed even the side of Camp Two, on the skyline three or four thousand feet above the basin. In all that summer of avalanches, this was the most tremendous and magnificent avalanche I had seen.

Gradually the cloud settled. The black crows were still perched unmoved, safe on their high slopes. Before the three cameras had got filled with snow dust, they had managed to take some fine snapshots of the avalanche.

As the air cleared, I noticed how for hundreds of feet it had buried deep under its crumbled snow mass the little dark line of footprints which had been made not twenty minutes before. . . .

I turned back to the base camp—to find myself again in the idyll. Bright autumn days, nights of warm, safe sleep, good food.

But for the men—

III

As they went on, the going grew continually softer and more difficult. Now that the crevasses of the summer had opened, they had continually to find new ways among the great ice towers. At one place, they must creep crouching under overhanging walls of ice, and then climb almost straight up a snow wall. There was a long rest for the coolies, in the middle of these evolutions. The distance between Camp One and Camp Two had never seemed longer or steeper. As the rise steepened, Herron and Wiessner, leading, found that the layer of soft fresh snow slipped away underfoot at every step, from the frozen surface beneath. It was like walking up a treadmill. Frequently the first man had to clear off all the new-fallen snow, and cut steps in the ice below. The coolie between Herron and Wiessner, whose boots were badly nailed, must several times be pulled up, by main strength, on the rope.

The coolies were growing steadily slower, and more sulky, and the sahibs were putting all of themselves into it. Morally as well as physically, they must drag the porters up the mountain, with the force of their own unbreakable will and purpose. It was back-breaking work, for shoulders only a little less heavily loaded than the coolies', fighting and tramping a way up the rise, through that deep soft snow; but, worse than that, it was heart-breaking work. The physical energy used was nothing to the nervous energy. Merkl's voice was pleasantly commanding; Herron spent himself in earnest friendliness; Wiessner went through prodigies of bluff good humor: all of them continually urging on those twelve flagging men.

They reached Camp Two at seven o'clock—ten and a half hours, wading through deep snow, instead of the customary easy five to six.

Everything seemed to be making difficulties, little things as well as big. After their day's long battle with bad snow and coolies, they found now that one of the tents would not stay upright. They worked with it a long time, bracing it as best they could with ice-axes. Still its eaves flapped too low for comfort. To keep the coolies as healthy and good-natured as possible was the vital thing. So the three sahibs took the undesirable tent, themselves. Between the physical discomfort of it, their nervous fatigue, and the keen excitement of hope, they did not sleep a great deal that night.

When snow conditions were proving so bad, it might have seemed natural to begin to think of the possibility of giving up. But the idea did not occur to any of them. They rose next morning, and went on.

And the route to Camp Three was another day—sinking kneedeep in soft snow at every step on the level, slipping and stepcutting on the slopes, with weakening coolies always. As they went higher, their feet, continually in the chill of the deep snow, numbed and froze very quickly. At least every half hour the men must stop and take off their boots, and rub them. It was a grim business.

They thought of the long-ago days at the beginning of July, when they had first come up the mountain. Then they had not been acclimated, as they were now. They could never have fought through such going as this. But how longed for that hard-frozen morning snow! As they looked back to that earlier time, it was like remembering childhood—something bright and far away, before disillusionment began. Yet, in spite of everything, today was better. They felt strong, and ready for the coming fight. Now, at last, they were about to reap the reward of all those months of effort and of waiting. They plodded on and on.

Seven hours it took, of the hardest work, to reach Camp Three, that short stage. The only variety of their heavy journey was furnished by Shukar-Ali the Astori, on Merkl's rope, who broke through a snowbridge into a crevasse. Which, on this route, was not even news.

At Camp Three, another restless night for the climbers, pulled taut between exhaustion and hope.

The snow was steadily deepening as they went higher—ominously reminiscent of the powder of the Mulde [A vast avalanche-swept hollow on Nanga Parbat through which the climbers' route up the mountain passed]. Above Camp Three they forged along thigh-deep, and in one place they sank to their breasts. At two o'clock that afternoon, in the midst of a driving snow scud, still going strongly after three days, they stepped across the last crevasse, breasted the last steep little pitch, and drew breath on the familiar rolling white plateau where Camp Four stood.

Even this was not the end of their work. Here, too, the storm had brought trouble. The three little tents sagged, almost buried under the snowfall, and the two ice caves were lost completely, their entrances filled up level. The sleeping ice cave was abandoned for good, but the kitchen, with its stove, provisions, and dishes, must be dug out—to locate and unearth the stove.

But finally everything was finished. Housekeeping could begin again in the same old spot; only with a Hunza coolie, Azil, acting as cook, since Ramana had bad feet and had not come up. And this time the stay was to be only a very temporary affair—a rest of one day. Then they would start, actually start on the final attack. This grinding pull to Camp Four had been just the inevitable preliminary, the familiar route and thoroughfare to the familiar settlement. Beyond, began the real work; at last, at long last, they would be off; above, waited the summit!

IV

They lay about luxuriously in the dim brownish light of the tent, thoroughly enjoying their day of rest. For breakfast, for lunch, and for dinner they regaled themselves on the leg of mutton and potatoes they had brought from the base camp. This fresh food of civilization possessed rare charms in the wild snowy wastes of Camp Four. Between meals, Wiessner looked over for the nth time Frier's old London *Weekly Times*. Merkl, with occasional consultations with the others, jotted down in his DAHE book memoranda about the carrying down of equipment, complete with figures of weight and division into loads, for use on the way back from the final push. Herron composed a poem, "La Cresta dei Dementi," and smiled good-humoredly when the others made fun of his unmanly occupation. Everything was going well at last. "Tomorrow we will start," said the poem. Or he happily noted down for my newspapers all the favoring circumstances of the situation. "As far as health, and adaptation to altitude, we find ourselves much better and stronger, even after the strenuous ascent to here and sleepless night, than before descending. . . . Extraordinary as it may seem, I notice no difference in breathing (speed or irregularity) from that in the base camp. . . . We arrived yesterday in a snowstorm, while we could see now and again that higher on Nanga Parbat the finest weather was reigning. In the evening it cleared up beautifully here. . . . No coolie has got sick so far, though most of them had frozen feet upon arriving here, and they seem in pleasant humor."

During the day the men walked a few steps up the plateau, to see if the snow there had settled and frozen any better than on the way up. Regretfully, they found it had not. They sank in, a foot or more, at every step. There would be real work ahead. No easy promenade to the summit. But for all that they were ready, keyed up to fighting pitch. It was even a tremendous relief to look forward to, after over a month of the nerve strain of enforced inactivity. It was a cheerful day, a day full of rising exaltation, with hopes so long deferred now at last about to be realized.

> *Tomorrow we will start*
> *And we will return*
> *With the ridge conquered,*
> *And perhaps the mountain . . .*

V

Toward the end of the that afternoon, the brightness of sure victory began to dim. The weather was going back on them; clouds were gathering in the west. And mournful coolies came drifting, in ones and twos, to the sahibs' tent. "Bima! Bima! (Sick! Sick!)"—that most familiar music of Camp Four, they whined.

By evening, Herron was noting: "Things again look black. The weather seems turning and, and nine (nine!) coolies declare themselves ill."

When the climbers opened their eyes the next morning, the tent was still in dark twilight. It was snowing!

The snow must have been falling all night, it had piled so high already outside the tent. The great accumulation of the long storm seemed nothing, to what had come in just this one night. Still through the day it kept falling. They watched it, hour after hour, by the gap in the tent flaps—hurrying down through the thick air, and heaping higher and higher. . . . Every moment of it seemed to bury more deeply their chances of success.

Never had the men seen snow collect so fast. It was weird, uncanny, like some horrible portent, outside the ordinary course of nature. They had worked and hoped for so long, they had fought through so many things. Now, they said, it seemed to them in their discouragement as if the mountain itself were punishing them for their striving.

During that day, September 1st, "The situation looks hopeless," Herron wrote. But not yet did they give up. They decided to fight it through. Their wills had been clenched so long on this one thing. It would be almost impossible to let go.

The nine coolies did not get any better. The three others came to declare that they too would not go on. They were tired of the mountain and everything concerned with the mountain. The snow kept on falling.

That evening there was a brief discussion. Events had conquered. The refusal of the coolies was the final argument. "Push on! push on!" said the climbers' feelings. But to push on, without coolies, through new snow, snow which even if they should wait, still in these winter conditions would never harden. The discussion was brief. How could it be otherwise? There was really nothing left to discuss. It was hopeless. . . . It was finished. . . .

The rest of the evening in the tent was very silent. There was the quiet of a funeral, as if they were sitting by the body of some one dead. It felt like death. The death of a most vital part of themselves.

VI

All night it snowed. Next morning dawned bright and clear. But never had any one seen so much snow. The men wormed their way out of the half-buried tent, and found themselves in powder to their waists.

They looked up at the sweep of whiteness that rose to Rakiot Peak, and high against the blue, the Ridge. There it was, waiting, dazzling in the bright sunlight. Camp Five, Camp Six, Camp Seven, and beyond. . . . That the way they should now be planning to go—not toward the base camp. Might it not still be possible, by sheer will, to conquer the impossible? Herron faced toward the summit, and began to struggle up the plateau—he did not advance ten feet. On this upslope, he floundered breathless, in powder snow to his breast. He turned back. The other were laughing grimly at the ridiculous hopelessness of it all.

They had been keyed to a desperate fight. There could not even be any fighting. No final heroic effort toward the summit, to relieve the long pressure of desire. This was, simply, the end. . . .

Now they began to think, half-indifferent and half-uneasy, about the steep slopes and avalanche possibilities below them. They rather wondered whether they would ever get down alive.

3
CHAPTER

TRIALS AND TRAGEDY

March 1: Minus 148°

ART DAVIDSON

Alaska's Mt. McKinley, a stiff mountaineering challenge under the best of spring and summer conditions, is brutal in winter. Few had ever contemplated a winter ascent—and fewer still attempted it—when a determined group began up the West Buttress route in February 1967. Success came hard; a French team member, Jacques "Farine" Batkin, died after falling into a crevasse early in the ascent. Art Davidson, Ray "Pirate" Genet, and Dave Johnston reached the summit February 28, only hours ahead of a vicious storm that overwhelmed them on the descent. Pinned down by horrific winds, with minimal cover and cut off from the other expedition members in a lower camp, they faced one of the most horrid bivouacs in the history of mountaineering. From Minus 148°: The Winter Ascent of Mt. McKinley, *Art Davidson chronicles their struggle for survival. Other members of the team were Gregg Bloomberg, Shiro Nishimae, George Wichman, and John Edwards.*

NOTE: The expedition is split between Denali Pass [a high pass on McKinley, infamous for its dangerous exposure to high winds and vicious weather] and the 17,300 foot camp. With no means of communication, each group has no way of knowing what is happening to the other group. The narrative follows Dave, Pirate, and Art at Denali Pass, while diary entries written by Gregg, Shiro, George, and John during the isolation imposed by the wind record the course of events and the trend of their emotions.

17,300 FEET: GREGG, JOHN, SHIRO, GEORGE

Gregg's diary:

A frightening thing is developing, but let me start from this morning. Shiro got up early, and although there was some wind we decided to give it a go. We started off with Shiro and George and John and me roped in twos. From the time we started it was apparent we wouldn't go far. The winds aloft were howling. After a few hundred yards John pooped out, and I went ahead to tell the others. When I caught them George unroped to go back with John, and I rope in with Shiro. The idea was to go up and see that the others were all right. When we approached the pass it was evident why the others had not descended. The wind was howling like crazy. I tried to lead up to the pass but was turned back by the wind. We then traversed to a spot that we thought was directly under their bivouac site. Shiro went up and tried twice, but the wind was so fierce it was impossible. The wind was coming from our direction, and if we went one step too far it meant not getting back again.

Shiro tried another place . . . the same. . . . We retreated rapidly. Once, when Shiro had come back, I asked him what he saw. He said, "Three sleeping bags. They are in their sleeping bags." When we were just about back in camp he told me all he saw was one sleeping bag, lying up against the rock and flapping in the wind. Shiro surmises the three are on the leeward side of the rock, covered with the parachute [a piece of parachute had been taken for emergency cover], with possibly two in one bag. All I know is that they must have made it back to the bivouac site, and are in a bind. If we could have reached them—they were less than a hundred feet away—we could have told them that the wind wasn't as bad on this side of the pass. We could have told them to make a try.

It's a bad situation . . . winds up to a hundred miles per hour, possibly more. It's a whiteout up there. . . . I pray at this point that they make it through. . . . They must make it through.

* * *

Much later Shiro confided: "When I saw only one sleeping bag I was certain they were dead. I told Gregg I saw three. He is very emotional. I thought maybe dangerous to alarm him. He might lose his mind."

DENALI PASS: ART, DAVE, PIRATE

The wind woke us. The wildly whipping parachute billowed and snapped with reports like those of a bullwhip or rifle. The wind blasted against the rocks we were nestled among with a deafening eruption of noise; crosscurrents in the storm fluctuated its pitch to a groan or a prolonged whine. A dull, aching pressure along my backside was the cold, pressed into me by the wind.

I twisted in my sleeping bag to grope for the loose section of parachute thrashing me from behind. The moment I caught it my hands were pierced with cold; groggy with sleep, I'd forgotten that the nylon, like everything else outside our sleeping bags, was about −40°. The cold sank into my fingers while the parachute, jerking and cracking erratically, resisted my attempts to anchor it. As soon as I managed to gather the slack material under me, the weight of my body holding it down, I shot one hand under an armpit and the other into my crotch for warmth. I was out of breath from the effort.

Drawn tighter, the parachute made less noise, and I was able to relax for a few moments. My fingers, aching inside from being deeply chilled, began to gradually rewarm with strong tingling sensations. I pressed the length of my body against Dave to be warmer on that side, and I felt Dave shift inside his bag, trying to press against me. I snuggled close to him and lay quietly for a long time, hoping I'd fall asleep again, as if not thinking about the wind and cold would make them disappear.

I couldn't sleep, and the wind only grew more vicious. I tried to ignore the cold along my backside, away from Dave, but when the first shiver ran through my body I turned to check the sleeping bag where it touched my back. To my horror it was no thicker than its shell, two pieces of nylon. The wind had pushed the down away. I could hardly believe it possible that the parachute, designed to resist wind, was letting the wind eat through it and into my sleeping bag.

The parachute began cracking again. "Oh, hell," I mumbled. The cracking meant a portion of the parachute had broken loose again. Feeling I didn't have the strength for another attempt at anchoring it, I curled up in my bag, shivering occasionally, waiting for something to happen; I didn't know what. After what seemed like several minutes but was probably only a matter of seconds, I heard Pirate trying to tie down the parachute.

"Art." Pirate's voice sounded far off and unfamiliar. "Help me hold it."

Hearing his voice made me realize that the three of us had been awake for more than an hour before anyone had spoken. Burrowed into my sleeping bag, I didn't want to budge from its security, false as it was, for even a moment. While I was deciding whether to help Pirate or prolong my rest, I felt Dave get to his hands and knees and begin wrestling with the parachute, which was now pounding his head and back as it billowed and cracked back in rapid succession. Yanking and cursing, Dave managed to pull part of it around him again, only to have it whip off as soon as he settled into his bag.

"Look, we gotta get outa here!" Dave yelled.

"Where? We'd never make it down!" I said, grabbing onto the piece of parachute that Pirate was clinging. "Maybe it's a morning wind that'll die down."

"Morning wind?" Dave looked at me in disbelief. "It's a bloody hurricane, you fool! I'm checking the other side of the rocks."

"Awwghaaaaa. . . ." Pirate growled, staring up into the wind.

Instead of getting completely out of his bag, Dave tied the drawstring at the top tight around his middle. With his legs still in the sleeping bag and his arms free, he lurched toward the crest ten feet away. I was horribly apprehensive. If he lost his grip on the rocks he could easily be blown off the mountain. On the other side we'd never hear him again if he called for help. How far was he going? Maybe he'd be hidden behind a rock where we wouldn't be able to find him if we needed his strength. Besides the logic of my fear, I recoiled emotionally against Dave's leaving because it seemed to break our trust; it violated a fundamental law of survival—stay together.

"Dave," I cried. "Wait! I think it's safer here."

"Stay if you want!" he hollered back. "This wind's bad, and I'm gettin' out of it!"

"Where are you going?" Dave didn't hear me. "It's exposed over there!" He had disappeared over the crest.

Since my mittens were too bulky to grip the parachute, I pulled thick woolen socks onto my hands; my fingers were nearly numb already. I was astonished as I looked up to see Pirate holding the parachute with his bare hands. Just as I yelled at him to get something over them, one of my socks started to slip off. Pulling it back on, I shifted position, and the wind seized the wind parka I had been sitting on. Inside its main pocket was the tape recorder I had been using for the physiological testing, but at that moment I was much more concerned about the loss of the half dozen cookies I'd stashed in the pocket. One moment the parka had been next to me, then I saw it whirling through the air, fifty, a hundred feet up, sailing in the direction of McKinley's summit.

With Dave gone, his loose end of the parachute caught the wind, and this threatened to rip the entire piece of nylon from our grip. We gave up trying to wrap the parachute around us; the pull on our arms wrenched our whole bodies as we clung to it to keep it from escaping. The parachute was our only shelter.

"My hands are bad!" Pirate's voice was weak, almost a whimper. His face was drawn up into a hideous, painful grin. Ice caked his beard.

"Bring them in!" I yelled, though his head was only inches from mine. His fingers felt like chunks of ice against my stomach.

"They're stiff!"

"Move them!" I reached for a better grip on the parachute. It slipped. I lunged. Pirate caught it as it whipped past him. He winced in pain.

"Aw, the hell with it!" Pirate signed. As he let loose, the parachute twisted through the air. It snagged on a rock. I saw it starting to rip, then it was gone.

For the first time I noticed the sky. It was a blue wall, smashing into the mountain. Thin pieces of cloud shredding—everything grew blurred. My eyes were watering and stinging from squinting into the wind. Compared to anything I had ever experienced, this wind was like another element. It was as if gravity had shifted and, instead of holding us down, was pulling us across the landscape.

Pirate began digging his hands in under my parka. The top of my bag had fallen open to the wind. As I pulled it shut, I fell against Pirate. We grabbed each other.

"Hold onto me!"

"Art, let's get into one bag."

"How? There's no room. . . . Give me your hands." I felt his icy fingers grabbing the skin around my middle. My bag had opened again, and to keep the wind from getting to me Pirate pushed himself over the opening. I just leaned against him, trying to catch my breath. Shivering, teeth chattering, my whole body was shaking with cold.

"Pirate, it's no good!" Wind was coming into my bag. We were both losing our warmth. "Each in his own bag . . . it's better."

"I can't feel my fingers!"

"Put 'em between your legs!"

"I don't want to lose my hands!"

I remembered Dave. If it was less windy on the other side of the rocks, he would have come back to tell us. If it was just as windy, I thought he would have returned to be with us. Something must have happened to him. But maybe he had found a sheltered corner. How could he abandon us!

"Pirate, let's try the other side!"

"Naw . . . the wind's everywhere!"

We huddled together, hunched upright in our sleeping bags, wedged tightly between two rocks. Whenever we relaxed the wind caught us, started us sliding along the ice, which gradually sloped away, and forced us to push and fight our way back up into the rocks. Leaning against Pirate didn't make me any warmer, but it was comforting—I wasn't alone. We didn't talk. I could breath more easily with my head inside my bag. I wondered what the others were doing down in the cave. Shiro's cough, Gregg's foot, John's swollen ear—it was too frightening to think about.

Beneath me I felt the ice slipping. Slipping onto my side, I brought an arm out in time to grab Pirate's knee. I pulled myself back against the rocks. My arms trembled from exhaustion. Pirate stared blankly out of his bag. His head turned slowly toward me with a groggy nodding motion. Was he slipping into a stupor? I wondered whether I looked as awful.

"It's no use here," I sighed.

I could barely keep myself up against the rocks. There was nothing I could do for Pirate. Maybe Dave had found a safe spot. I had to check the other side of the rocks, but that would be deserting Pirate. Yet there was no way I could help. How could I just leave him? I had to do something for myself!

"I'm going over." He didn't move. "Pirate," I yelled, "I'm going after Dave!"

His head shook from side to side as he half mumbled, half shouted, something I couldn't understand. I grabbed at the rock above me and pulled myself up the slope. Another rock; its sharp cold cut through the wool socks. Another pull. I reached the crest. To my tremendous relief I saw Dave crouched on the ice only about fifteen away. His back was toward me.

"Dave!" He couldn't hear me. I worked a little closer to him. The wind threatened to throw me off the crest. Beyond lay bare glacier where I'd never catch anything to hold onto if I was blown from the rocks.

"Dave!" This time he turned and saw me. I was out of breath and must have been gasping as much as yelling. "Is it better where you are?"

I didn't want to go back, and waiting here on the crest was impossible because it was completely exposed to the wind. Before I'd decided which way to go, a crosscurrent gust caught me. I grabbed for rocks. One came loose. I caught another one nearer Dave. Somehow the sock on my left hand had blown off. I shoved the bare hand into my sleeping bag. The other hand held onto a rock. The wind flung and tossed my body as though it were weightless.

My right hand ached with cold from gripping the rock, and my forearm began cramping from the strain. I couldn't go back into the wind, but neither could my right hand cling to the rock much longer. The only other rock I could reach was three feet to my left, near Dave. My numb right hand had become so dead that I couldn't feel the rock it held onto. My shivering body seemed on the verge of going into convulsions.

I tried to think. If I lost my grip, I'd be blown across the ice. My mind was racing. I had to grab for the rock near Dave with my left hand: it was bare, no mitten or sock. It would be frozen. I had to. Suddenly, my bare hand shot out to grab the rock. Slicing cold.

I saw Dave's face, the end of his raw nose, frostbitten. His mouth, distorted into an agonized mixture of compassion and anger, swore at me to get a glove on. I looked at my hand. It was white, frozen absolutely white.

I pulled my body onto the rock. Dave was only five or six feet away on the ledge he had chopped in the slightly sloping ice.

"Christ, Art." His voice cracked. "You froze your hands!"

I pushed off from the rock, letting the wind throw me against Dave. He flung his arms around me. All I could do was lie across him, wheezing and shaking, trying to catch my breath.

"Man," he said, "we gotta dig in!"

17,200 FEET: GREGG, JOHN, SHIRO, GEORGE

John's journal:

The pass was roaring windy, and we had our first real concern for the summit . . . change of wind. Raven flew down buttress! Hypothesis concerning summit party: perhaps they had not gone to the summit the previous day, and had gone today. . . . Weather worsening rapidly all afternoon. Flying clouds, but mountain looked magnificent all afternoon. Blue shadows, yellow. . . . Shiro saw one sleeping bag against the bivouac rocks. At the time Gregg thought

Shiro had seen three, but had misheard under the roar of the wind, and was rather profoundly disturbed when back in camp Shiro said he had seen only one. . . . Very tired and anxious for the three. I am pretty sure they will break out despite the weather and come down tonight despite the whiteout. If not, we are in serious trouble indeed.

Sheldon flew in late this afternoon, low around the igloo, with landing lights on. Some discussion as to the significance of this flight, but probably a reconnaissance before the storm. Had Ray been in radio contact with Anchorage and given an emergency to Sheldon, or was this flight on his own or on someone else's account before the onset of the storm? George very apprehensive about storm. Solemn. There is not much we can do about it but wait for the others to move down. But if they don't. I have no great apprehension for the three above yet. I think they will fight their way down, that is, if they are all well. Art's altitude sickness? But then we may have seven days before Sheldon can take us out.

Gregg's diary, continued:

It's evening. We all stayed in case there is a need to help one of the others down. The wind has descended to this altitude, and we are huddled in the snow cave with a large mouth covered by a tent, weighed down with rocks which we hope will hold. If they come down tonight, we will be crowded, but we will be a happy crowd. If they make it back tonight, we will descend tomorrow as quickly as possible. The wind is from the southeast, right into the tent, but it will hold unless things get worse. Those guys only had a bunch of lunch, one stove full of gas, a pot, their sleeping bags, and the parachute with which to cover themselves up.

Please God, let us hear their voices. Let them descend unharmed. Give them a break in the wind and the wisdom and stamina to use it.

What can we do? I suppose the best is the prayer above. I am thankful that Shiro wanted to come down yesterday, or we would have probably been caught in the same trap. How proud and stupid we all are.

Edi [Gregg's wife—Gregg's journal was in the form of a continuous letter to his wife], you can't imagine how I long to be in your arms, to lay my head in your lap while you stroke my hair. this is nothing new. I have been longing to be with you since I started. I think you can tell by this journal. All my love, honey. Don't worry. I'll still call you about the fifth of *this month*. Good night. Pray for a happy morning.

With the provisions and personal reserves they have they could probably last two more days at the longest, but practically speaking they must make it down tonight or tomorrow morning at the latest. If they had only known today that the wind wasn't as bad on this side of the pass. Oh, pray to hear their voices urgently wanting to come inside.

On the bright side, they are the strongest of us. Dave and Art have plenty of experience. Ray has good sense. They're all tough as nails. With a tiny break in the wind, they can't help but make it! Oh Lord, what anguish we are all suffering for our friends' safety.

DENALI PASS: ART, PIRATE, DAVE

Dave cradled Pirate's feet against his belly and massaged them gently until they began to rewarm.

"Dave," I said, "you know you saved us out there." My words sort of hung in the air. They sounded hollow, and Dave bit at his lip self-consciously. I didn't say more, but my eyes followed Dave with admiration and a kind of love as he tucked Pirate into his bag and then reached for the stove.

For more than an hour I had clung to the ledge on the ice, feeling the frostbite blisters swell on my hands and watching helplessly while Dave dug a cave in the ice. Just before he had completed it, Dave had collapsed from exhaustion; by then Pirate had pulled himself together, and despite his hands and feet, which were beginning to swell with frostbite blisters, he had somehow made it over the crest to finish hollowing out the cave. Dave had recovered enough strength to help me through the small hole in the ice, which was the entrance to our new home.

Now inside the cave, Dave leaned on his elbows, and steadying the stove with one hand, he prepared some food with his free hand. In this cramped chamber under the ice cooking was more miserable than it had ever been in the last four weeks; Dave had quietly accepted the job because his were the only hands capable of working the stove. At least he had found some good food to fix—four pound-and-a-half cans of ham, bacon, and peas, which had been cached by a previous expedition among the rocks we had bivouaced against. Since our pot had blown away, he heated the ham in its own can, then used the can to melt water in.

Flattened against the wall while Dave cooked in the middle, I realized how small our cave was. At the wide end there was barely enough room for our shoulders, and at the narrow end our feet in our sleeping bags were heaped on top of each other. Because of the rocks behind us, Dave and Pirate had been unable to make the cave long enough for us to stretch out completely. Over our feet the ceiling was about a foot and a half above the floor; toward the larger end there was just enough height to turn or lie on our sides with one shoulder touching the ice on the floor and the other touching ice on the ceiling. We were quickly learning that our every movement bumped the next person. This cave certainly wasn't pleasant or comfortable by ordinary standards, but it kept us safe from the wind, and that was all that mattered, for the moment.

Dave looked for his journal and found it missing. We had lost too much to the wind—the use of four hands and two feet, an incalculable amount of body warmth, two packs with half our food in them, the parachute, my wind parka, and—perhaps our greatest loss—the foam pads that would have insulated us from the ice and helped to keep our bags dry. Yet we felt secure. We were supplied with enough gas to make water for another day, maybe two more days if we stretched it. With four lunches left, and three remaining cans of food, we needn't worry about starving.

That night ham and hot water were a feast, not filling, but delicious nonetheless; it was our first warm food since leaving the cave down at 17,200 feet more than thirty hours before. My hands had become so inflexible that Dave had to place each bit of ham—

there were five of them—in my mouth, then tip the can to my lips to let me drink. Eating made us giddy with pleasure and almost got us feeling warm.

We were actually exultant, not from any sense of conquering the wind, but rather from the simple companionship of huddling together in our little cave while outside in the darkness the storm raged through Denali Pass and on across the Alaska Range.

We agreed that the wind coming out of the northwest was funneling through the pass at least 130 miles per hour. We remembered that a wind of such velocity, combined with the $-30°$ to $-45°$ air temperature outside our cave, created an equivalent wind-chill temperature somewhere off the end of the chart; the last figure on the chart was minus 148°.

"One hundred and forty-eight degrees below zero."

It was frightening to say, but the worst was over, we thought. In the morning the wind would slack off; we would descend, greeting the others at 17,200 feet with the news we had made the summit; we would get off the mountain and go home. We wanted to believe the climb was over, that in a couple of days everything would be warm and easy again. Yet the wind, howling and pounding the slope overhead, reminded us that we couldn't move until it died down. We talked of the cave as our refuge, but the suspicion that we were being held captive in the ice must have entered each of our minds as we fell asleep listening to the wind.

Retreat Down K2

ROBERT BATES

Mountaineers often point to the 1953 American Expedition to K2 in the Himalaya as a paradigm of demonstrated courage, strength, and tenacity in the face of extraordinary odds. For seven days, a team led by Charles Houston huddled stormbound high on that unclimbed peak until one member, Art Gilkey, developed thrombophlebitis, a life-threatening affliction. With no choice, the team began his evacuation down treacherous slopes in a raging blizzard. The obstacles were overwhelming, the outcome was always in doubt. But as Robert Bates describes in K2: The Savage Mountain, *the climbers struggled together with a measure of will, self-sacrifice, and compassion seldom matched in the annals of mountaineering.*

We all knew now that some of us might never get down the mountain alive. Each had long recognized the near impossibility of evacuating an injured man from the upper ledges of K2. We had told one another that "if somebody broke a leg, you never could get him down the mountain," but now that we were faced with Gilkey's helplessness, we realized that we *had* to get him down. We didn't know how, but we knew that we had to do it.

Schoening in particular, and also Bob Craig and Dee Molenaar, had done a lot of mountain rescue work, and the rest of us placed great confidence in their faith that somehow we could get our casualty to Base Camp. Gilkey's high morale and his confidence in us was a great boost to our spirits and we faced the job ahead with strong determination. When on the morning of August 10 Charlie

Houston thrust his shoulders through the tunnel entrance of the tent where Schoening, Streather, and I, shoulder rubbing shoulder, had tossed during the long night hours, we spoke almost in unison: "How is he?"

"We've got to take him down," said the doctor. "His other leg has a clot now and he can't last long *here*."

The wind was hammering the tent fabric so hard that we had to yell at one another. Drifts of fine powder snow were sifting in through a strained seam in the tent vestibule, though we had done our best to keep the shelter airtight, and we could feel the whole tent vibrate as gusts stretched the fabric to the utmost.

"What? Move in this storm?" said someone.

"We've got to," said Houston. "He'll soon be dead if we don't get him down."

Nothing needed saying after that, for we knew what this decision meant. All of us had fought mountain storms before, but we had never seen anything like the duration and violence of this furious wind and snow that was still battering us. We all knew the story of the storm on Nanga Parbat in 1934, when nine members of a German expedition had died of exhaustion while battling the wind and snow. Willy Merkl, Uli Wieland, and Willi Welzenbach had been famous mountaineers, but a storm had exhausted them and killed them one by one. Here on K2 we had not only the storm to fight but the steepest part of the mountain, and we were trying to bring down these precipitous slopes a crippled companion as well!

We all realized that our adventure had now become grim, for the odds against getting Art down were obvious, and our own position was getting more critical all the time. While Houston and Schoening were easing Art out of his tent into the storm, the rest of us began packing light loads to take down. We would need one tent in case of emergency, and we took the Gerry tent, our lightest one. We also might need a stove and pot, and some meat bars, chocolate, or quick-energy food that needed no cooking. Often the effects of altitude so weaken one's determination that doing nothing becomes a positive pleasure, but this was no time for lethargy, and as we moved purposefully out of the tents into the stinging blasts of snow, we knew that we had to move fast, while fingers and toes still had feeling. Little was spoken. Each of us realized that he was beginning the most dangerous day's work of his lifetime.

Gilkey seemed in no pain as we wrapped him in the smashed tent, put his feet in a rucksack, and tied nylon ropes to him in such a way that they cradled him. Four ropes, tied to this cradle, could be held by one ahead, one man behind and one on either side. We had already put on all our warm clothing—sweaters, wool jackets, down jackets, and nylon parkas—and stripped our packs to the minimum. As we worked, the disabled man watched the preparations silently. He was an experienced mountaineer and realized what all of us were up against. But he knew that we would never leave him, and that we would bring him down safely if it were humanly possible. Art's cap was pulled down over his face, which looked drawn and bluish-gray, but he gave a wan smile whenever someone asked, "How is it going?"

"Just fine," he would say. "Just fine." And his mouth would smile. He never showed a moment's fear or the slightest lack of confidence, but he realized of course that he had been stricken by something that was likely to be fatal, that his condition was getting worse, and that he was 9,000 feet above Base Camp in a terrible monsoon storm. The nearest tent, at Camp VI, was 2,000 feet below. He knew that we could not carry him down the tricky route we had come up, and that we must go only where we could lower him. Even in perfect weather with all men in top physical condition, the task might prove impossible—yet Art Gilkey could smile, and his smile gave us strength.

While we were adjusting the tow ropes, Schoening and Molenaar strapped on their crampons and disappeared into the storm. They were to find the best route past the dangerous avalanche slope that had blocked us a few days before, and to go over to Camp VII cache to get a climbing rope that was strung on the ice slope just above. It would be useful in the descent. After their departure Houston called Base Camp on the walkie-talkie and told Ata-Ullah our plans. "It's pretty desperate, Ata," he said grimly, "but we can't wait. We're starting down now. We'll call you at three o'clock."

Each man took his place on a rope tied to Gilkey and for a couple of hundred yards we lunged hard at the tow ropes to pull Art through the knee-deep drifts of powder snow; then gravity took over and we had to hold back just as strongly to keep our helpless 185-pound load from plunging into the abyss. The steep slope we were on disappeared below us into nothingness. Was there a cliff there, a jumping-off place? We strained our eyes peering into the storm, but we could not wait for clearing weather. Instead we had to depend on Schoening and Molenaar, who had gone ahead to scout out the way. As we descended, Craig and Bell pulled the front ropes, one on each side, and Houston directed operations from a point immediately behind Gilkey, while Streather and I anchored the rope higher up. Gradually we worked our way to a rock ridge, climbed down alongside it, and then began to lower Gilkey down a steep snow slope leading to a snow chute and an ice gully below. This route was not the one we would have taken had Gilkey been able to walk, but now we had no choice: we could go only where we could lower our companion, and we had faith that the two men ahead would find a route down. Once we were well started, return to Camp VIII would be impossible for any of us.

The wind and cold seeped insidiously through our layers of warm clothing so that by the end of the third hour none of us had feeling in his toes any longer, and grotesque icicles hung from our eyebrows, beards, and moustaches. Goggles froze over and we continually raised them on our foreheads in order to see how to handle the rope. Moving the sick man was frightfully slow. We had to belay one another as well as Gilkey, and our numb fingers would not move quickly. Somehow, when we got to the steepest pitch, however, someone managed to tie two 120-foot nylon ropes together and we started to lower Gilkey down, down in the only direction the slope would permit. Houston and I, braced on the storm-swept ridge, backs to the wind, could feel the terrible gusts trying to hurl us off the rocks. We could not see where we were lowering Art, but we could hear faint shouts from Schoening and Molenaar, who were out of sight below. As we slowly payed out the coils of rope, thankful that they were of nylon and would not freeze in kinks, Bob Craig unroped from us and climbed down alongside the injured man to direct the descent. Soon he was completely obscured, too, but Streather climbed down to where he could see Craig's arm signals, yet still see us, and so we belayers had communication with Craig and Gilkey and knew whether to lower or to hold the rope. Alternately we anchored and payed out line until we were nearly frozen, and our arms were strained when Tony Streather, whom we could barely see, turned and shouted, "Hold tight! They're being carried down in an avalanche!"

We held. Our anchorage was good and the rope stretched taut. For a moment snow flurries blotted out everything, and then we could hear a muffled shout from Streather. "They're still there!" The rope had broken loose a wind-slab avalanche of powder snow that had roared down over both men, blotting them from sight. Craig clung to the rope to Gilkey, and held on to it for his life. The pull of the hissing particles must have been terrible, but the avalanche was of unconsolidated snow. The falling powder slithered out of sight and down off the side of the mountain, where it must have kept falling long after we could hear it. When it was gone, Craig still clung to the rope, gray and very chilled. Both men were safe. The grim descent continued.

Schoening and Molenaar, who were not far from Camp VII, soon were able to reach Gilkey, but it seemed like hours to the four of us on the icy rocks of the wind-swept ridge before they shouted up that they had him strongly belayed "on the edge of a cliff," and we could climb down. Stiffly we shifted from our frozen positions, and climbed clumsily down the steep, crumbly rocks to the snow chute above the ice gully. Houston and I were on one rope, Bell and Streather on the other. All were so cold, so near exhaustion, that moving down over dangerous, snowcovered ice stretched us to the limit. Through the murk of blowing snow we saw Schoening standing in front of a large, rounded rock that had become frozen onto a narrow ledge. His ice-ax was thrust deep into the snow above the rock, and the rope with which he held Art Gilkey was looped tightly around the shaft of the ax. The sick man was at the edge of a 20-foot cliff, beneath which we could glimpse the ice gully dropping

off steeply into the storm toward the Godwin-Austen Glacier nearly
two miles below.

Schoening looked like a man from another world. So much frost
had formed on our beards that faces were unrecognizable, and we
knew that we were fast reaching the breaking point. We could not
continue much longer without shelter from the driving storm and
food to renew our energy. Some 150 yards below us to the east was
the tiny shelf, nicked into the ice slope, where Schoening and Gilkey
had spent the night of July 30 during their reconnaissance above
Camp VI. We had called it Camp VII, or Camp VII cache. None
of us had expected anyone to spend another night there, but Bob
Craig, whose struggle against the avalanche had so completely exhausted him temporarily that he could hardly tie a crampon strap,
had been belayed over to this site to rest and clear some of the
avalanche snow that had seeped under his parka. We yelled to him
to try to enlarge the ledge. Meanwhile, with Schoening anchoring
the rope, we lowered Gilkey slowly over the short rock cliff until
he was resting against the 45-degree slope. Streather, who was roped
to Bell, climbed down to Gilkey. Schoening held Gilkey's rope
firmly while Houston belayed me across a delicate pitch of steep,
hard ice, and then Houston climbed down to a point opposite the
man suspended against the slope. The problem now was not to get
Gilkey down, but to swing him across the steep ice slope to the ice
shelf at Camp VII. Our plan was to get a firm anchorage and then
pendulum him across, but unfortunately the ice near him was too
hard for axes to be driven in and the slope was relentlessly steep.

Even during the best weather conditions the maneuver would
have been dangerous, and our position at that moment I shall never
forget. Schoening was belaying Gilkey, who hung 60 feet below
him, suspended against the sharply angled ice. On the same level
as Gilkey, and 40 feet across from him, five of us, facing into the
stinging, drifting snow, were searching for a place where we could
stand and anchor the rope to Gilkey as we pulled him across the
ice in the direction of Craig on the ice shelf. With our spiked
crampons biting the hard ice, Streather, Houston, Molenaar, and I
stood close together. Bell and Streather were roped together, Hous-

ton and I were on a rope together—and Molenaar had just "tied in" to a loose rope to Gilkey. He had done this when Craig had unroped and gone over to the ice shelf to rest, and it was Molenaar's precaution that saved us all. For George Bell, who was some 60 feet above us, began to descend a delicate stretch of hard ice in order to help with Gilkey's rope. At that moment, what we had all been dreading occurred. Something threw Bell off balance and he fell.

I never saw Bell fall, but to my horror I saw Streather being dragged off the slope and making desperate efforts to jam the pick of his ax into the ice and stop. Streather had been standing above the rope from Houston and me. In almost the same instant I saw Houston swept off, and though I turned and lunged at the hard ice with the point of my ax, a terrible jerk ripped me from my hold and threw me backward headfirst down the slope. *This is it!* I thought as I landed heavily on my pack. There was nothing I could do now. We had done our best, but our best wasn't good enough. This was the end. Since nobody was on the rope with Houston and me, there was no one else to hold us, and I knew that nothing could stop us now. On the slope below, no rock jutted on which the rope between us could catch. Only thousands of feet of empty space separated us from the glacier below. It was like falling off a slanting Empire State Building six times as high as the real one.

Thrown violently backward, with the hood of my down jacket jammed over my eyes, I had a feeling of unreality, of detachment. The future was beyond my control. All I knew was that I landed on my pack with great force, bouncing faster and faster, bumping over rocks in great thumps. The next bound I expected to take me over a cliff in a terrible drop that would finish it all, when, by a miracle, I stopped sliding.

I was on my back with my hood over my eyes and my head a yard below my feet. My arms, stretched over my head, were so completely tangled with the taut rope that I could not loosen them. I was helpless, and when I tried to move, I realized that I was balanced on the crest of some rocks and that a change in position might throw me off the edge. The rope had apparently snagged on a projection—though how and where I couldn't imagine—but it might not be securely caught. Whether it was firmly held, whether anyone else was alive, I did not know, but I didn't need to wait. Almost immediately I heard a groan coming from nearly on top of me. "Get me loose," I called, and immediately I felt the pressure of a leg braced against my shoulder and the rope was pulled off my arm.

Grabbing a rock, I swung my head around. Dee Molenaar and I were clinging to a rocky outcrop at the side of a steep ice slope, studded with rocks, about 150 to 200 feet below the place where we had been working on the ropes to Gilkey. Blood from Dee's nose trickled across his moustache and beard, and he looked badly shaken. My rope was tight to someone or something above, and I heard a distant yell, "Get your weight off the rope!" Fifty feet higher, through a mist of blowing snow, I could see Tony Streather staggering to his feet, a tangle of ropes still tight around his waist. Below I heard a cry, "My hands are freezing!" and, looking down, to my amazement I saw George Bell, who seconds before had been 60 feet above. Now about 60 feet *below*, he was climbing up over the edge of nothingness. He wore neither pack nor glasses and was staggering up over the steep rocks, obviously dazed, with his hands held out grotesquely in front of him. His mittens had been ripped off in the fall, and already the color of his hands had turned an ugly fish-belly white. If his hands were badly frozen, of course, we might never be able to get him down off the mountain.

Turning to Molenaar, I thrust my pack into his arms. Most of the lashing had ripped loose and the walkie-talkie radio, which had been on top, was gone; my sleeping bag was half off, held by a single twist of line. Without sleeping bags we were unlikely to survive the night, no matter how we tried! Since Molenaar wore no pack, I imagined that his sleeping bag also had been torn off in the fall. Whether or not the tent someone had been carrying had survived the fall, I didn't know. "For God's sake, hold this," I yelled above the wind, placing my load in Molenaar's arms. (For all I knew, mine was the only sleeping bag to survive the fall, and we must not lose it now.) The loose pack was awkward to hold securely while we were standing on such steep rock, but Molenaar grasped it and

I unroped and started to climb shakily down to meet Bell. As I climbed down, I wondered about the ropes that had saved us. They were snagged to something up above, but the driving snow kept us from seeing what was holding them. [Miraculously, and with incredible strength and will, Peter Schoening had held five men with his single ice-ax belay.] Luckily I had a spare pair of dry loosely woven Indian mitts in the pouch pocket of my parka, and when I reached Bell, whose face was gray and haggard, I helped him to put them on. Already his fingers were so stiff with cold that he couldn't move them, but balancing on projections of rock on the steep slope, we struggled to save his hands and finally forced the big white mittens past his stiff thumbs and down over his wrists.

Bell's fall had ended with him suspended over the edge of a ledge, below which the slope dropped away precipitously for thousands of feet. The weight of his pack pulled him head down, and he had lost it while trying to get right side up and back over the ledge. While Bell crouched down, working desperately to warm his hands under his parka, I left him, for Molenaar and I had seen a crumpled figure lying below a 30-foot cliff on a narrow shelf that seemed projecting over utter blankness below. It was Houston. Somehow a rope to him was snagged high above us, too. Climbing unsteadily but cautiously, for I was not roped and felt shaken by the fall, I worked my way down the steep rocks and across the ledge. Houston was unconscious, but his eyes opened as I touched his shoulder. When he staggered to his feet, I felt relief it is impossible to describe.

"Where are we?" he asked. "What are we doing here?"

He was obviously hurt. His eyes did not focus and he appeared to be suffering from a concussion. Again and again I tried to persuade him to climb up the cliff, while Molenaar anchored the rope still attached to him from above. He didn't understand. "Where are?" he kept saying, for my replies did not convey any meaning to him in his confused state.

The wind and blowing snow were searing our faces. We were all near exhaustion and in danger of crippling frostbite. If we were to survive, we had to get shelter at once, or we would be so numbed by exposure that we could not protect ourselves. What had happened in that Nanga Parbat storm which had taken so many men was a grim reminder. All of us working together did not now have strength enough to pull or carry Houston up the steep rock and snow to the ice ledge, 150 feet above, which we had called Camp VII.

"Charlie," I said with the greatest intensity, looking directly into his eyes, "if you ever want to see Dorcas and Penny again [his wife and daughter], climb up there *right now!*"

Somehow this demand penetrated to his brain, for, with a frightened look and without a word, he turned and, belayed by Molenaar, fairly swarmed up the snowy rocks of the cliff. Instinct and years of climbing helped him now in his confused state, for he climbed brilliantly up to Molenaar. I followed more slowly because, being fully conscious, I had great respect for this steep rock wall, and with great care I pulled myself up over the snow-covered slabs. When I reached Molenaar, he was looking puzzled and very unhappy as he tried to answer Houston's repeated question, "What are we doing here?"

Storm and Sorrow

ROBERT CRAIG

Perhaps more than any other hazard, climbers dread the fury of high mountain storms. During the 1974 American Pamir/USSR Expedition, nineteen American climbers and those from other nations were invited for the first time to climb in the Soviet Himalayas under the auspices of their Russian hosts. An International Base Camp was established in the Achik Task Valley beneath the huge peaks they would ascend. The early loss of American Gary Ullin in an avalanche overshadowed several climbing successes. Then a monstrous storm struck, trapping climbers on several mountains. The most vulnerable party, eight Russian women on the summit of Peak Lenin, attempted to descend while their tragic efforts were monitored from Base Camp by walkie-talkie. Robert Craig relates their grim struggle, and the anguish of the powerless climbers below, in this chapter from Storm and Sorrow In The High Pamirs.

In Base [Camp] on August 4 we were almost ankle deep in mud after another night of snow and rain. Climbers came down off Peak Lenin in a steady stream. [John]Roskelley and [Jeff] Lowe had returned from [Peak] Nineteen; Schoening, Higgins, Kpaczynski, and Sarnquist from Lenin, and the American sector of Base came back to life again. Austrians, Swiss, English, Russians, and Bavarians all came in as afternoon clouds again enveloped the range.

Jeff and John rapidly crossed the meadow into Base and while they were not jubilant at having completed the best route of the season, there was the quiet sense of satisfaction at having accomplished a worthwhile task. Peak Nineteen had been a challenge, a drama, a tragedy [The death of American climber Gary Ullin], and now what had begun with such high spirits and sunlight was completed quietly and in storm. There was no triumph, only a grave on the mountain and two friends safely returned.

With Pete Schoening back, we tried to take stock of the various Americans. Everyone seemed okay at Camp II and ought to be back in Base on August 5. We had not heard a thing from Jock Glidden, Al Steck, and Chris Wren since they left Base Camp. Then there was the report of the Siberians having sighted the Americans on Lipkin on the 2nd, but the latest long-range weather report had come in forecasting an extremely dangerous new storm. If they were not transmitting we wondered if they could be receiving. There was some reassurance for their safety in the many years of big mountain experience of Steck and Glidden, but the big Pamirs storm, with hard snowfall already hitting Base, was the beginning of real anxiety for all of us.

It snowed moderately the night of the 4th; still the storm did not materialize and we awoke with hopes that conditions would hold until everyone was in a safe position. The morning report of the Soviet coaches [These Soviet mountaineers directed and safeguarded the ascents of the international climbers.] at Camp III on the 5th indicated relatively calm conditions with little wind and partly cloudy skies. It had not snowed any appreciable amount the night before.

What was disturbing about their transmissions, especially to Abalakov and the other Soviet officials, was the report that climbers were still setting off for the summits in spite of the warnings from Base. Abalakov decided to send up several of the Soviet coaches to be in position to render assistance for those climbers on the Lipkin and Razdelny routes, should they need it on their way down the mountain. Boris and Valodya were already in Camp I and he would immediately dispatch Kostya and Oleg. They would go as high as they could, perhaps to the ice cave camp on the Lipkin.

Abalakov, Gippenreiter, and Monastyrski were in a corner of the mess tent in mid-afternoon when Pete, John Evans, and I approached them. We said we would like to help if support was needed. Aba-

Iakov noted it was too soon, that not enough was known about what was happening on the upper mountain. Monastyrski conveyed a sense of deep concern. By nature he was cheerful, and often humorous, even while functioning in a low-key, businesslike manner. He was obviously worried and tense, and appeared to be smoking one cigarette after the other. Gippenreiter, normally outgoing and urbane, looked thoroughly exhausted and was distinctly concerned. He had been high on the Lipkin with the Siberians and the Scots. He had had a meal with the Soviet women. Having climbed Lenin four times, he had decided to descend alone after reaching a point where the Lipkin joined the northeast ridge at about 22,000 feet. He said the conditions were as bad as he had ever seen on Peak Lenin. Abalakov was more impassive than ever.

Late in the afternoon of the 5th the storm, which we observed lashing the upper levels of Peak Lenin and the other peaks of the Pamirs within our view, moved down into the Achik Tash Valley. It began again to snow heavily, the wind rose, and we knew the major storm forecast by Osh had arrived. To make things even more ominous, the Soviet Meteorological Service was forecasting "winds of hurricane force." At about 5:00 P.M., Allen North came down off the Lipkin and reported the three Americans were camped solid at about 21,000 feet and planning to go for the summit with the first good weather.

At about 7:00 P.M. we were called to the communications tent, and informed by Abalakov and Monastyrski that the Soviets had indeed reported from the summit of Lenin that they were going to camp on top and that they were having trouble getting their tents up in the storm. It was never clear how many they were able to pitch, though it seemed they had started with three. Abalakov again had ordered them to descend immediately in the morning, returning down the Lipkin as that was the route they knew. It was almost a 4,000-foot descent to Camp III at Razdelny Pass with virtually no protection in between. By contrast, to the Lipkin ridge from the summit and some sort of lee shelter it was a 1,000 to 1,500-foot descent. In the back of his mind he hoped, too, that the women might encounter the Japanese or Americans holding out in the storm on the Lipkin. Abalakov suggested further that, as the storm was out of the southwest, they would gain some benefit from the lee of the northeasterly trending Lipkin ridge.

Equally ominous was Monastyrski's report that Viktor and Georg had called in a few minutes earlier with the news that it appeared the International Women were in trouble and that a rescue group was being formed at Razdelny to give assistance in the morning. They reported violent winds, heavy snow, and rapidly falling temperatures. Michael also noted that a large group of Siberian and Polish climbers was descending the Lipkin and northeast ridges but was too far below to be of possible assistance to the Soviet women.

The atmosphere in the mess tent that evening was extremely subdued. Over forty people were at 20,000 feet or above, eight of them at 23,400 feet in a great storm that had not even reached its peak. Still, there was no certain indication that anything had gone wrong. The movies went on as scheduled, but attendance was light, and as we returned to our tents it was snowing hard.

There were five inches of snow on the ground when we got up early the morning of August 6. The sun came out and took some of the chill from the air and we had the impression that things might be improving. But a look toward Peak Lenin was not reassuring: clouds enveloped the whole mountain down to the base, and where a rent occurred to reveal layer upon layer of clouds well above 30,000 feet, one could estimate that the winds aloft had to be enormous. This was soon confirmed.

At 8:00 A.M., Viktor and Georg reported from Camp III that the night had been desperate: two tents had been blown apart and the occupants forced to double up with others nearby. The three International Women, Heidi, Eva, and Anya, were still 1,500 feet or so above Camp III in God knows what shape. There had been over a foot of snow and the wind was blowing 70 to 80 miles per hour. A rescue team of Peter Lev, François Valla, Michel Vincent, Sepp Schwankener, Hans Bruntjes, and another Netherlander named Louie had left to render assistance in getting them back to the relative safety of Camp III. Three Japanese and a Swiss man were also unaccounted for, and the two Soviet coaches could only hope they managed to bivouac safely.

The Soviet women reported in rather matter-of-factly with a strong signal from their position on the summit of Lenin. They had had a bad night. The wind had destroyed two of their tents in the night. They were now four in each of the two remaining military tents. One of the women who had been in a collapsed tent was feeling poorly.

The tents had no zipper closures, but rather a double flap system of folds which were secured along the seams by wooden toggles passed through string eyelets attached to the flaps. This closure system hardly kept out the storm in the same kind of tents that were provided for us at Base, and a number of us were dumbfounded when we learned that this equipment was what the Soviet women were depending on. Even more depressing was the knowledge that the four poles providing the A-frame suspension at either end of the two-man tents were made of wood, and at least three or four of these poles had broken in various instances in Base Camp, most not involving heavy winds, but snow loads of a mere few inches. We made no mention of our feelings about the tent to the Soviet officials, but feverently hoped the women could somehow dig snow caves.

Shataeyeva did not specify how or to what degree her teammate was sick. She was apparently one of the two youngest. Michael Monastyrski and Eugene Gippenreiter translated for us alternately as Abalakov, speaking directly directly to Elvira, the leader, and to each of the women as teammates, ordered an immediate descent to the shelter of the Lipkin. As they verified their understanding, the roaring wind periodically obliterated their voices. Abalakov, speaking slowly, told the women they had to get down the mountain far enough to find snow suitable for snow caves. He repeated that snow caves and some lee shelter out of the wind were absolutely essential. Again, they must go down the Lipkin immediately. He did not say it directly, but it was implied that if the sick woman could not move and they could not achieve adequate shelter, they must leave her for the good of the group as a whole. He said this softly but he

was adamant that they descend. He exacted a promise from Shataeyeva that they would do so.

As we walked back to the American tents, Pete said, "We've got
to do something! We've got to persuade them to bring helicopters.
There must be some way. They're all going to die up there! Jock,
Allen, Chris—they're up there too. At least let's put a rescue or
support team together." We agreed to talk to the Russians, the
English, and the French and see what could be arranged.

At about 3:00 P.M. on August 6, Viktor called Base from Camp
III saying Eva Eissenschmidt had died while being evacuated to
Camp III. The other two women had been returned safely, but
frostbitten. He noted there was other frostbite amongst the climbers
in camp and that supplies of fuel and food in the camp were dangerously low. The three Japanese and the Swiss had survived their
bivouac and returned to Camp III as the rescue of Eva proceeded.
When Abalakov asked Viktor whether they could descend in the
storm, he said Peter Lev, the American avalanche specialist, had
stated emphatically that snow conditions were just too dangerous
for a descent at that time. He noted that he, Georg, and François
Valla, another avalanche expert, tended to agree, but he felt they
would be in equally grave danger if they remained too long at III.

At 5:00 P.M. the Soviet women called Base from just below the
summit of Lenin on the short, steep snow and ice slope leading
northeasterly down to the Lipkin. One of the women had died,
apparently while assisting the others down. It sounded as if she had
frozen to death while belaying the others down to a bivouac position.
The woman who had been reported sick was worse and another ill.
Under the circumstances of storm and extreme cold and 23,000
feet, being "ill" could only mean that two more were, in fact, dying.

Shataeyeva said they were trying to pitch tents on the steep ridge.
Abalakov tried to be stern as he questioned why they had not dug
snow caves, but he visibly sagged and seemed more desolate than
ever as Elvira replied they had tried but the snow was too hard and
that they were very cold and rapidly weakening.

Abalakov then said they must continue to climb down, there was
nothing they could do for the sick—they would all die if they tried

to remain in that spot. Shataeyeva replied with some detachment that she understood, that they would continue to try, and that they hoped to get further down the next morning. The Russian woman translating in English next to us said tearfully, "It is like a dream; she doesn't seem to realize what is happening to them."

As Elvira ended her transmission on a note of what seemed deep sadness and resignation, if not a dangerous kind of vagueness, the steady moan of the raging storm could be clearly head above her voice and, as it was snowing again at Base, one could only guess at the temperature at 23,000 feet, some 12,000 feet above us. At the adiabatic cooling rate of 5 or 6 degrees per 1,000 feet, it was probably somewhere between 60 and 70 degrees below freezing—30 to 40 degrees below 0°F. If one added the velocity of the wind, probably well over 70 miles per hour, the prospect of the women's surviving the night seemed very slim.

A crowd of climbers from every national group in Base Camp milled around the communications tent area in the falling snow and gloom. The final realization that a disaster of overwhelming proportions was in the making—a disaster that very conceivably might involve everyone on the upper slopes of Lenin—was painfully evident.

Pete and I talked with the British and French about mounting some kind of rescue or assistance effort. The response from Doug Scott and Benoit Renard had been immediate and affirmative. If the Soviets would agree, we would add four English, four French, and four Americans to their coaches at the bottom of the Lipkin and Razdelny routes. We would recommend bringing up helicopters at the earliest moment—tomorrow, the 7th (but requesting them immediately), if possible to attempt an airdrop to the women. An airdrop or any use of helicopters assumed a lessening of the storm, but experience had indicated that it took at least a day to move machines into position in the Achik Tash Valley.

We would also recommend that the Soviets strongly urge the evacuation of Camp III, despite the known avalanche hazard, in light of the strong possibility that its inhabitants, like the Soviet women, might soon experience the beginnings of hypothermia and reduced function.

We approached our three Russian friends after dinner. We outlined the situation as we say it and told them of the willingness, indeed the eagerness and necessity, of a group of top climbers' trying to assist the others. At first there was reluctance, even slight annoyance, and Michael said, "We feel this is our problem. We appreciate your spirit but we will do everything that can be done."

I replied, "Michael, we understand you are doing everything you can, but it is not enough. You have a rescue operation underway on the Saukdhara Glacier, your coaches are thinly scattered on Peak Lenin, and now there is a real question about the safety of over forty people distributed all over the mountain, a good many of them in places we're not ever sure of. We have twelve or so international class climbers, including a doctor, who are willing to go up to help. They may not succeed, but we must at least try. You must know we are your friends—we will do nothing to embarrass you."

Monastyrski looked at us, eyes slightly brimming, and said, "I know, we have already become better friends. I will discuss with Evgeny and Vitaly." The three were in session for over an hour. They called us back to the command post at about 7:30 P.M.

Abalakov was, as we had expected, uneasy about the thought of any further exposure of foreign climbers to the hazards of the full storm that was now enveloping the Pamirs, yet he recognized the soundness of our logic. There was no denying that Soviet personnel were stretched too thin. Too many things had happened, even the safety-conscious Soviets could not have predicted so many misfortunes.

Abalakov affirmed that he knew the British, French, and Americans would do nothing to embarrass or distort the situation. Still, what really could be done?—the "girls" were 12,000 feet above Base Camp.

Gippenreiter and Monastyrski, knowing as did Abalokov that the chances were very slim for the Russian women, felt there was a chance to render real assistance to those at Camp III and perhaps the Americans, Japanese, and Siberians on the Lipkin. They quietly urged the joint effort. Abalakov, for whom we had by now developed real affection in addition to respect, looked at us sternly and sympathetically and finally said in German, "Yes, we must, in the last analysis, try to do something."

Vitaly Abalakov staked his reputation and prestige on the enterprise of an all-woman's traverse of Peak Lenin. There had been considerable resistance to Abalakov's progressiveness in certain circles of the Soviet Federation of Mountaineering. Although the general lot of women in the Soviet Union is touted by the authorities as a kind of co-equal existence in all walks of like, and clearly Soviet women in athletics have been a formidable force in international competition, there had been a reluctance in the area of mountaineering to allow female teams to operate on their own in the highest mountains.

We outlined our thoughts regarding the form we thought the rescue group ought to take: the English would be Tut Braithwaite, Guy Lee, Paul Nunn, and Doug Scott; the French would send Bernard Germain, Yves Morin, Benoit Renard, and Michel Revard; and the Americans would include John Evans, Jeff Lowe, John Roskelley, and Frank Sarnquist.

The three Soviet leaders agreed they should go up in the morning and join forces with Kostya, Boris, Oleg, and Valodya. They had already requested helicopter assistance from Dushanbe and from Osh. There was no way to estimate when they could reach the Achik Tash. So far as the evacuation of Camp III was concerned, they agreed the Soviet coaches should be urged to descend, but that Peter Lev's concerns about avalanche hazard should be taken most seriously. In any event, the rescue group should divide to provide assistance to both the people on the Lipkin and those descending from Razdelny Pass.

The Soviets agreed to our assessments and recommendations, by now too overwhelmed by the staggering sequence of events to dispute, and apparently trusting our objectivity in a situation that involved a good many of our own teammates.

At 8:30 P.M. on the 6th, Shataeyeva came on the air again and the roar of the storm at various moments simply obliterated her transmission; the wind seemed to snatch her voice away from time to time, but the massage was all too clear. Two more of the women, the youngest two, had died in the last three hours. One more of their tents had been shattered by the wind and five of them were in the tent without poles on a ledge they had scooped out of the steep ridge.

They were taking turns going outside of the collapsed tent and trying to dig into the hard, wind-blown snow of the ridge. The snow under the surface was granular and very loose and did not submit to the forming of a cave. It was like digging into a tub of dry, loose sand.

Elvira was clearly beside herself with grief, yet she somehow maintained an almost eerie composure, talking calmly about problems with the tents, no stoves, no water, etc., faltering only when she referred to her dead companions. We remembered the lady interpreter's comment of just that morning—Elvira had seemed to have entered a dream.

It snowed another six inches at Base through the night of the 6th. By early morning of August 7 the temperature had dropped to around 22° F. The Achik Task appeared as if in winter. Elvira came on the radio at about 8:00 A.M. She sounded very weak, very tired, and distinctly disoriented. She repeated herself as she tried to describe the night just passed. They were all very cold, they had eaten nothing for a day and a half, and they had little strength left.

Abalakov pressed her to determine whether they were still trying to descend to the Lipkin ridge. She hesitated, did not answer the question directly, but said almost fiercely, "Three more are sick; now there are only two of us who are functioning and we are getting weaker. We cannot, we would not leave our comrades after all they have done for us. We are Soviet women. We must stick together, whatever happens!"

Abalakov knew well what was taking place and that whoever remained of his "girls" had little time left before their strength to go down would be totally exhausted. He again tried alternate haranguing and gently persuasion to get them to abandon their hopeless position on the ridge, but by that time the pattern of their agony seemed irreversible. In the spirit of group solidarity they were committed to stand by each "sick" teammate and, as they did so, one by one they began to die themselves.

As Abalakov kept the main transceiver open for instant communication with the women, we reached Jed Williamson and Peter Lev at Camp III with a Sony transmitter the Dutch team had brought. We apprised them of the overall situation involving the Soviet women and the lack of any communication from Jock Glidden's group. We stated that the weather forecast was for even worse weather for the next two days. We noted that Georg and Viktor had earlier reported that tents had been destroyed and that food and fuel supplies were crucially low. In the face of all this, we asked them how they felt about things. Through Jed, we gathered that Peter's position was that any party descending from Camp III under the current conditions was "in the most dire danger of becoming caught in an avalanche and if not buried, getting lost in the blizzard during the descent."

Jed seemed to lean toward descending and reported that several others felt the same way, and thus it was left that when they decided what they were going to do and if they decided to go down, they should call Base. In the meantime, on the chance that they might decide to descend immediately, a support party would leave Camp II that day to help guide them down. John Evans and the support group from Base should arrive at Camp I that evening. They would join Bruce Carson at I. Early in the morning, John and Bruce and anyone else who was available would leave for Camp II to back up Valodya. All the other rescuers would proceed toward the Lipkin ridge. In the meantime, Valodya would leave Camp II immediately and begin placing wand markers in the snow from Camp II upward toward Camp III. The Russians instructed Valodya to proceed with whomever he could persuade to go in the direction of Razdelny Pass. It was urged that he try to communicate by radio with Georg and Viktor every hour and, failing that, by voice signals.

Elvira came back on the air at 10:00. The roar of the wind was almost constant as she transmitted, but several standing nearest the receiver thought they could hear one of the women weeping.

"We are holding on. We cannot dig in; we are too weak. We have had almost nothing to eat or drink for two days. The three girls are going rapidly. It is very sad here where it was once so beautiful."

Her voice broke and she sobbed for the briefest moment, then regained her composure and said in a tremendously weary but steady voice, "We will carry on and talk again soon. Over."

We all asked: How could they have survived so long? Thirty to 40 degrees below zero, consuming wind, no tents, no food. What keeps them going? Why do these smiling, happy, cheerful women have to die?

It snowed intermittently but hard through the morning at Base. The mess tent was crammed to overflowing with people from the many nationalities who made up the International Camp. We continued to wonder what could be happening to Steck, Glidden, and Wren. The real (perhaps the only) hope of the day lay in Evans and Valodya giving assistance to the large group retreating from Camp III.

Shataeyeva came on again at noon. One more had died. Four were dead. Two were dying. The condition of the last two we could only guess. The transmission was brief. Elvira almost seemed delirious, but she said, "We will go down, there is nothing left for us here. They are all gone now. The last asked, 'When will we see the flowers again?' The others earlier asked about the children. Now it is no use. We will go down."

The mountain was totally closed in by clouds and the great wind roared across the ridges high and low. At Base we could just see across the valley, nothing above. The wind was gusting to 40 miles an hour across the meadow and the temperature remained around 28 degrees. In zero visibility, with the possibility of descending to the right and over the huge east face or to the left and onto the not so precipitous, but avalanching north face, the dying Soviet women had run out of alternatives. It was only a matter of hours and, though no word was spoken, virtually every person in camp hoped they would be mercifully few.

There was no transmission at 2:00 P.M. from Elvira and we wondered if they were moving down or if the end had come. The receiver had been on continuously since 6:00 A.M., so the batteries were changed to ensure that there was no failure either in transmission or receiving.

The rescue group called in from Camp I and reported that Jeff Lowe, the Englishmen, and the French were going to try to get up with Kostya and Boris to the ice cave camp on the Lipkin. We briefed them on the status of the women and reminded them we were still concerned for the Siberians, Japanese, and Americans.

Roskelley had contracted diarrhea and would remain at Camp I with Frank Sarnquist. Frank would treat the sick as they came down off the mountain.

Evans was on his way to Camp II with Bruce Carson, who had joined the rescue group at Camp I. One of the Swiss named Hans had joined up as well. They were to support Valodya and assist the large group descending from Camp III.

The Japanese on the Lipkin had been in touch with their people at Base, but not with anyone else. They must have been transmitting on a different frequency than any of the other groups since their voices were not heard on the communications tent receiver. Nor did the Japanese at Base make known until somewhat later that their four men on the Lipkin had heard the transmission from the Russian women and, although they spoke no Russian, sensed something was wrong. When this was confirmed by the Japanese at Base, two of the four set out to try to rescue the women. The storm was so violent and visibility so limited, the wind chill factor so great and loss of location of their own camp so likely, that they were forced to turn back after getting only a short distance. Several times in the attempt they were blown off their feet. They were probably less than 1,500 yards from the women when they started.

The barriers of language and cultural differences in judgments of value and importance within those barriers added the final sense of confusion to the International Camp. The Russians may never have known about these transmissions, but they never revealed it if they did; nor did they suggest at any point a tie-in with the rescue effort being mounted from Base. Most likely in the great confusion of large numbers of people in apparent trouble, they didn't know. In the face of the frightful conditions, it is significant that the Japanese on the Lipkin even tried to reach the Soviet women.

Elvira came on the air at 3:30 P.M. She spoke incoherently and then seemed to have lost track of time and referred to the illness of two of the women who had already died. The sound of the storm had momentarily eased and someone beside her (Valentina?) was audibly weeping. Then Elvira began to sob, "They are all dead; what will happen to us? What will happen to the children? [The two women who had youngsters had already died.] It is not fair, we did everything right."

Abalakov sat at the transmitter cutting in, trying to console Shataeyeva, "Viretska, my dear, beautiful girl, you have been very brave, all of you. Please hold on, we are trying to reach you."

Elvira came back on calmer, but distinctly weaker than she was three hours earlier. "We are sorry, we have failed you. We tried so hard. Now we are so cold."

"Elvira, don't give up. Stay awake; try to move your limbs. Kostya and Boris and others are trying to reach you. Keep calling us on the radio. We will not leave the receiver." The sad, thin-faced woman interpreter did a brave job of keeping us informed of the conversations as, frequently on the edge of tears, she helped us understand that Abalakov was not cynically trying to raise the hopes of his doomed friends, but simply trying to make their death seem less forlorn. He felt that anything he could do to ease the anguish of their slow and certain dying was a merciful thing.

The transmission at 5:00 P.M. was garbled, but we sense one more had died, leaving three still alive. The storm seemed to be continuing to build in intensity and for a brief moment we caught a glimpse of the clouds racing across Krylenko Pass. We estimated the wind velocity at 80 to 100 miles per hour.

Further below, Kostya and Oleg called in to report they could make no progress in the storm. They were worried about the large group of Siberians which were descending, but thought they were safely below the upper ridge line and thus somewhat protected from the most punishing winds. They said they would go up with the rescue team, whom they could now see below in breaks in the storm, in the morning.

At 6:00 P.M. we got the tremendously cheering report that the entire group from Camp III had made it down to Camp II and that some were continuing down to Camp I. It was thought that Heidi Ludi, Anya, and Sepp Schwankener had fairly serious frostbite and would need medical assistance if not helicopter evacuation from Camp I. Everyone else was apparently okay.

At 6:30 we heard several clicks of the transmitter key and then above the roar of the wind the very faint voice of Elvira, "Another has died. We cannot go through another night. I do not have the strength to hold down the transmitter button."

At this, the Russian woman interpreter burst into tears. People looked at one another in embarrassed silence. We saw Zina, the Russian camp dietician who had been so kind to all the Americans, across the meadow with tears streaming down her face.

At 8:30 the receiver registered a few of the clicks we heard earlier and then Elvira came on in a voice almost drained of passion. "Now we are two. And now we will all die. We are very sorry. We tried but we could not. . . . Please forgive us. We love you. Good-bye."

The radio clicked off and everyone in that storm-lashed meadow knew the cheerful Soviet "girls" were gone forever. Everyone in the meadow wept unashamedly as the fact of finality was driven home by the utter silence of the radio and the unforgiving wind. The Soviet men and women wept the hardest and caused the rest of us to weep even more as they, several Russian generations removed from the church, made the sign of the cross and with that almost forbidden gesture signified the end had come. And then there was only the wind.

The Accident

DAVE ROBERTS

Their climb a success, four alpinists began descending an Alaskan peak. It was July 29, 1965. Dave Roberts, Matt Hale, Don Jensen, and Ed Bernd, four Harvard students, had just audaciously captured a mountaineering prize: the first ascent of Mt. Huntington's steep and fierce West Face. Amid their celebrations, thoughts turned down and homeward. The single tent of their high camp was too crowded, so Roberts and Bernd elected to descent further to a lower camp. Midway to safety, the inexplicable occurred. From his book, Mountain of My Fear, *Dave Roberts tells the story of mountain joy turned to grief.*

The snow was in poorer condition than we liked; it hadn't refrozen yet, and might not that night since a warm wind was coming in. I knew the pitches below better than Ed, having been over then five times to his one, so I tried to shout instructions to him when the route was obscure. It got to be too dark to see a full rope length. I went down the twenty-ninth pitch, our ice-filled chimney, feeling rather than seeing the holds. But the fixed ropes [climbing ropes securely attached to the mountain and left behind to be used by the climbers on their descent] helped immensely, and since I came last on the two hard pitches (twenty-ninth and twenty-seventh), Ed didn't have to worry so much about not knowing the moves. Despite the conditions, we were moving efficiently.

At the top of the twenty-sixth pitch, the vertical corner Don had led so well in crampons, we stopped to rappel. We stood, side by side, attached to the bottom of the fixed rope we had just used on the pitch above. In the dark, we could discern only the outlines of each other's faces. Under our feet, we felt our crampons bite the ice. Just below the little ledge we stood on, the rock shrank vertically away, and empty space lurked over the chasm below. It was too dark to see very far down. Above us, the steepest part of the face, which we had just descended, loomed vaguely in the night. Up there, on another ledge, Don and Matt were probably sleeping. Beside us, in the mild darkness, icicles dripped trickles of water that splashed on the rocks. The fixed rope was wet; here and there ice, from the splashing, had begun to freeze on it.

We didn't have an extra rope, so we untied and attached ourselves to the fixed rope, setting up a rappel with the climbing rope. Ed attached a carabiner to the anchor, through which he clipped the climbing rope, so that we could pull it down from the bottom. He wrapped the rope around his body and got ready to rappel. We were tired, but were getting down with reasonable speed. It was ten minutes before midnight.

"Just this tough one," I said. "Then it's practically walking to camp."

"Yeah," Ed answered.

He leaned back. Standing about five feet from him, I heard a sharp scraping sound. Suddenly Ed was flying backward through the air. I could see him fall, wordless, fifty feet free, then strike the steep ice below.

"Grab something, Ed!" But even as I shouted, he was sliding and bouncing down the steep ice, tangled in the rappel rope. He passed out of sight, but I heard his body bouncing below. From the route photos I knew where he had fallen; there wasn't a chance of his stopping for 4,000 feet.

Perhaps five seconds had passed. No warning, no sign of death —but Ed was gone. I could not understand. I became aware of the acute silence. All I could hear was the sound of water dripping near me. "Ed! Ed! Ed!" I shouted, without any hope of an answer. I looked at the anchor—what could have happened? The piton was still intact, but the carabiner and rope were gone with Ed. It made no sense.

I tried to shout for help to Matt and Don. But they were nearly 1,000 feet above, hidden by cliffs that deflected and snow that absorbed my voice. I realized they couldn't hear me. Even the echo of my shouts in the dark seemed tiny. I couldn't just stand there; either I must go up or I must go down. It was about an equal distance either way, but the pitches above were more difficult. I had no rope. There was no point going up, because there was nothing we could do for Ed. His body lay now, as far as anyone could ever know, on the lower Tokositna, inaccessible. An attempt even by the three of us to descend the 4,000 feet to look for him would be suicidally dangerous, especially since we would have only one rope for all of us. If I went up, I should eventually have to get down again. All it could do was add to the danger. I realized these things at the time. Yet the instinct, in my isolation, to try to join Matt and Don was so compelling that for a while I didn't even consider the other possibility. But it became obvious I had to go down.

At least the fixed ropes were still in. I used two carabiners to attach myself to them, then began to climb down the steep pitch we had started to rappel. I moved jerkily, making violent efforts, telling myself to go more slowly. But I had to use the adrenalin that was racing through me now; it was the only thing that could keep the crippling fear and grief temporarily from me.

I managed to get down the hard pitch. The snow on the Upper Park [Significant features on the mountain had been given names by the climbers.] was in poor condition. I broke steps out beneath me, but held my balance with the fixed rope. I realized that I was going far too fast for safety, but slowing down was almost impossible. As I traversed to the Alley, I was sure the weak snow would break under my feet, but it held. At last I arrived at the tent. The seven pitches had taken eighteen minutes, dangerously fast. But I was there; now there was nothing to do but wait alone.

I crawled into the tent. It was full of water. Matt and I had left the back door open! In the dark I sponged it out, too tired to cry, in something like a state of shock. I took two sleeping pills and fell asleep.

In the morning I gradually awoke out of a gray stupor. It seemed to be snowing lightly. I felt no sudden pang about the accident; even in sleep I must have been aware of it. I forced myself to cook and eat a breakfast, for the sake of establishing a routine, of occupying myself. I kept thinking, *What could have happened?* The carabiner and rope were gone; nothing else had been disturbed. Perhaps the carabiner had flipped open and come loose; perhaps it had broken; perhaps Ed had clipped in, in such a way that he wasn't really clipped in at all. Nothing seemed likely. It didn't matter, really. All that mattered was that our perfect expedition, in one momentary mechanical whim, had turned into a trial of fear and sorrow for me, as it would for Matt and Don when they learned, and into sudden blankness for Ed. His death had come even before he could rest well enough to enjoy our triumph.

The time passed with terrible slowness. I knew Matt and Don would be taking their time now that it was snowing. I grew anxious for their arrival, afraid of being alone. I tried to relax, but I caught myself holding my breath, listening. Occasionally a ball of snow would roll up against the tent wall. I was sure each time that it was one of them kicking snow down from above. I would stick my head out the tent door, looking into the empty whiteness for a sign of them. My mind magnified even the sound of snowflakes hitting the tent into their distant footsteps.

I made myself eat, write in my diary, keep the tent dry, keep a supply of ice near the door. But I began to worry about Matt and Don, too. I knew there was no reason to expect them yet, but what if they had had an accident, too?

There were some firecrackers in the tent. We had tentatively arranged on the way up to shoot them off in an emergency. I might have done that now, but there was no emergency. It would be more dangerous to communicate with them than not to, because in their alarm they might abandon caution to get down fast.

I began to wonder what I would do if they didn't come. What if I heard them calling for help? I would have to go up, yet what could I do alone? I calculated that they had at most five days' food at the Nose Camp. I would wait five or six days, and if there was no sign of them, I would try to finish the descent alone. At the cave I could stamp a message for Sheldon; if he flew over, he would see it. If he didn't, I would eventually start the hike out, seventy miles down an unknown glacier, across rivers, through the tundra. . . .

But these were desperate thoughts, the logical extremes of possible action I might have to take; I forced myself to consider them so that no potential course of events could lurk unrealized among my fears.

Already I had begun to miss Ed in a way separate from the shock and loneliness. I longed for his cheeriness, that fund of warmth that Matt, Don, and I lacked. I had wanted so much to relax in the tent, talking and joking with him, reliving the long summit day. I hadn't climbed with him since July 11. Now it was the last day of the month, and he was gone.

I went outside the tent only to urinate. Each time, I tied a loop around my waist and clipped in to a piton outside, not only because I was afraid but because I couldn't be sure that the sleeping pills and the shock (if it was actually shock) were not impairing my judgment or balance. I felt always tense, aware that I was waiting, minute by minute. I could think of very little but the accident; I couldn't get the sight of Ed falling, sudden and soundless, out of my head.

The snow continued to fall lightly, but the tent got warmer as the hidden sun warmed the air. In the afternoon I began to hear a high, faint whining sound. It was like nothing human, but I couldn't place it. Could it be some kind of distress signal from Matt or Don? Impossible. . . . Could it be the wind blowing through a carabiner somewhere above? But there was almost no wind. Was it even real? I listened, holding my breath, straining with the effort to define the sound. I couldn't even tell if it was above the camp or below. I sang a note of the same pitch to convince myself the sound was real. It seemed to stop momentarily, but I couldn't be sure I hadn't merely begun to ignore it. Finally I noticed that when I went outside the tent, I couldn't hear it. Therefore the sound had to come from inside. At last I found it—vaporized gas, heated by the warmth of the day, was escaping from the stove's safety valve! I felt silly but measurably relieved.

I tried to relive every moment Ed and I had had together the last day, as if doing so could somehow salvage something from the tragedy. My recollections had stuck on a remark he had made in the Nose Camp as we rested after the summit. I had told him that it had been the best day I'd ever had climbing. Ed had said, "Mine too, but I don't know if I'd do the whole thing again."

I thought he was still upset about Matt's and my near-accident, and suggested so. Ed thought a moment, then said, "No. It's not only that."

We hadn't pursued it, but his attitude had seemed strange to me. For me, there was no question but that it would have been worth doing all over again. Nor for Don. And I thought Matt would have said so, too. But Ed had climbed less than we had; perhaps he wasn't so sure that climbing was the most important thing in his life, as we would have said it was in ours.

Now his remark haunted me. The accident, ultimately inexplicable beyond its mechanical cause, which itself we would never be sure of, seemed that much more unfair in view of what Ed had said. It would have been better, fairer, perhaps, had it happened to me. Yet not even in the depth of anguish could I wish that I had died instead. And that irreducible selfishness seemed to prove to me that beyond our feeling of "commitment" there lay the barriers of our disparate self-love. We were willing to place our lives in each other's hands, but I wouldn't have died for Ed. What a joke we played on ourselves—the whole affair of mountaineering seemed a farce then. But the numbness returned; I told myself to wait, to judge it all in better perspective, months, years from now.

By that night there had still been no sign of Matt or Don. I took another sleeping pill and finally dozed off. Sometime in the night, on the edge of sleeping and waking, I had a vision of Ed stumbling, bloody, broken, up to the tent, yelling out in the night, "Why didn't you come to look for me?" I woke with a jolt, then waited in the dark for the dream to dissolve. I hadn't considered, after the first moments, trying to look for Ed's body. For me alone, without a rope, to try to descend the 4,000 feet would certainly have been suicide. Yet because there was nothing to do, and because I hadn't seen Ed's dead body, a whisper of guilt had lodged in my subconscious, a whisper that grew to Ed's shout in my nightmare.

I took a sip of water and fell asleep again. In the morning I discovered my watch had stopped. An unimportant event, it hit me with stunning force. It was as if one more proof of reality were gone, one more contact with the others, Matt and Don first of all, everyone else alive in the world eventually. I set the watch arbitrarily and shook it to get it started.

That day, August 1, dragged by as the last one had. I was no more relaxed than I had been before. The weather was good for a few minutes in the morning, then clouded up again; but at least it had stopped snowing. I felt surer now that Matt and Don would get to me, but I began to dread their arrival, for it would open the wounds of shock in them, and I would have to be the strong one, at first.

I thought of how rarely an expedition is both successful and tragic, especially a small expedition. Something like 95 percent of the dangers in a climb such as ours lay in the ascent. But we had worked for thirty-one days, many of them dangerous, on the route without a serious injury before finally getting to the summit. Going down should have taken only two or three days, and it is usually routine to descend pitches on which fixed ropes have been left. I was reminded of the first ascent of the Matterhorn, when only hours after its conquest the climbing rope broke, sending four of Edward Whymper's seven-man party to their deaths. Then I realized that the Matterhorn had been climbed one hundred years, almost to the day, before our ascent. I thought also, of the ascent of Cerro Torre in Patagonia in 1959, still regarded by many as the hardest climb ever done. On its descent Toni Egger, one of the best mountaineers in the world, had fallen off a cold rappel to his death, leaving only Cesare Maestri to tell of their victory. But thinking of those climbs explained ours no better. I knew that Whymper, after the Matterhorn, had been persecuted by the public, some of whom even suggested he had cut the rope. I knew that, even in an age that understands mountaineering a little better than the Victorians did, vague suspicions still shrouded the Cerro Torre expedition. But even if we could explain Ed's death to mountaineers, how could we ever explain it to those who cared more about him than about any mountain?

Around 4:00 P.M. I heard the sound of a plane, probably Sheldon's flying near the mountain. I couldn't see anything through the mist, but perhaps his very presence meant that it was clear up above, possibly that he could see our steps leading to the summit.

Around 10:00 P.M. I thought I heard a shout. I looked out of the tent, but saw nothing, and was starting to attribute the sound to a random noise of the mountain, ice breaking loose somewhere or rock falling, when suddenly Matt came in sight at the top of the Alley. He let out a cheery yell when he saw me. I couldn't answer, but simply stared at him. Pretty soon, Don came in sight and yelled, "How are things down there?" I pretended I couldn't hear him. Matt said later that they had seen our tracks from high on the mountain and therefore known that Ed and I hadn't completed the descent to the cave. This had disturbed them a little, and their mood had acquired gloominess during the treacherous last descent, on steps covered by new snow, using ice-coated fixed ropes, once belaying in a waterfall that had frozen their parkas stiff. But as they approached, Matt had seen my head poking out of the tent and for an instant had thrown off his worries. Yet my silence made him uneasy again; then, before he got to the tent, he saw that there was only one pack beside. Then I said, "Matt, I'm alone."

He belayed Don all the way down before either of us said anything to him. When Matt told him, Don stood there frozen momentarily, looking only at the snow. Then, in a way I cannot forget, he seemed to draw a breath and swallow the impact of the shock. He said, "All right. Let's get inside the tent." His voice, calm as ever, was heavy with a sudden fatigue. But once they knew, once I saw that they were taking it without panic, being strong, I felt an overwhelming gratitude toward them: out of my fear, an impulse like love.

4
CHAPTER

SUMMITS

Measured Steps

JULIE TULLIS

*The summer of 1984, a Swiss expedition was attempting to climb
the Himalayan giant, K2. Accompanying the expedition to climb and
film an adventure series for English television were the famous Austrian
climber and filmmaker, Kurt Diemberger, and Britian's foremost
female mountaineer, Julie Tullis. Beset by a succession of high-altitude
storms, the expedition finally retreated from K2 and prepared to return
home. Refusing to accept defeat, Diemberger and Tullis set off alone,
across the Goodwin-Austin Glacier to make a fast, alpine-style attempt on another of the great mountains, Broad Peak. For Diemberger,
age fifty-three, it was a homecoming of sorts; he had made the first
ascent of Broad Peak years earlier in 1957. For Tullis, a former
housewife who had not even taken up mountaineering until she was
thirty-eight, it was an attempt to become the first British female to
climb an 8000 meter mountain. Tullis relates their attempt in this
excerpt from her autobiography,* Clouds From Both Sides.

On 15 July the expedition was due to go home. The closer the
date came, the more often Kurt and I discussed what we should do.
We could leave with everyone else. We were longing to see our
families again and return to the green and growing world after living
with stones, ice and snow for three months. Summer had passed us
by. But what about the film? The 23,000 feet of material we had
already shot were good, but the dramatic events on the mountain
had no conclusion. Our expensive cameras and film equipment were
also still scattered about various camps high on K2, unrescuable at

this time because of deep, dangerous new snow left by the last storm on the mountain.

The only satisfactory answer was to stay on by ourselves, with a couple of porters to look after our tents in Base Camp, and immediately try for the summit of Broad Peak. This was not such an isolated mountain as K2 and, therefore, although only four miles away, attracted a totally different weather pattern. This is what we eventually decided to do.

We talked to our expedition leader. Luckily, Stefan was a very practical Swiss, and Fakkar, our liaison officer [an official assigned each expedition by the host country], a likable, sensible, young officer from the Pakistani Air Force. It was Fakkar's first expedition, and he understandably wanted no complications if we got into difficulties by ourselves that might jeopardize his chances of going on future trips. The authorities in Islamabad have very strict rules governing the movements of expedition members, which they understandably do not like to bend. The wild area around the Himalayas is a dangerous place and they need to know where people are, and that they are safe. Fakkar tried hard to dissuade Kurt and me from staying on by ourselves, but finally, after we had written and signed several statements saying that it was our own decision and that we took full responsibility for our actions and safety, he agreed and wished us luck.

We felt very alone when our friends had gone. We were well aware that if either of us had an accident or became sick we would be in serious trouble. We had felt well protected with a group of thirty other mountaineers including a doctor around us, but now our isolation also made us feel closer to our surroundings, which was after all the reason why we were there.

The expedition's departure day was, ironically, beautiful: hardly a cloud in the sky. Could it mark the change in the weather at last? The monsoon is not supposed to affect this Karakoram area, but the weather we had been battling with over the past few weeks was typical of the monsoon syndrome, with fresh storms coming in almost daily. How frustrating for the others, who were already feeling very disappointed, having to walk away from the mountains, if the weather really was going to improve again.

Finally, at two o'clock, we were able to leave the now lonely-looking K2 Base Camp. Our three weather-beaten faded tents looked tiny and forlorn without the company of the other expedition tents as we looked back toward the soaring majesty of K2, its summit still hiding in the clouds.

The moraine in direction of Concordia had changed during the months of May, June, and July. The previously snow-covered humps of the central corridor of the Godwin-Austen Glacier had become stone-covered ice mini-hills; gaping crevasses cutting across the previously simple direct route made long detours necessary.

We finally turned off to the left, into the broad band of ice pinnacles that still separated us from the foot of Broad Peak. I began to feel apprehensive . . . would we have a chance to reach the top? I paused to look at our objective; its huge sprawling mass was beautiful in the late afternoon sunshine but it made me feel infinitesimally small.

"Come on, Julie," Kurt's voice broke into my musings. "We have to reach Camp 1 tonight to have any chance at all."

It was a complicated route through the ice pinnacles. We had to climb up and down over the maze of broken ice cliffs and skirt the icy lakes nestling in the hollows between the ice towers. The cold world was silent apart from the grating of our crampons against the ice, and it required concentration to find the safest and most direct way through to our objective on the other side. It had taken us three and a half hours, but finally we were plodding up the steep snow slope toward Camp 1. It was amazing to think that after twenty-seven years Kurt was once again climbing on Broad Peak. It was certainly in a better condition than K2, but this year many of its steep slopes were covered in ice instead of the normal snow, which would make the climbing more technical.

We had not gone far before we began to regret the sun-caused melting process. The lower snow slope was like sticky porridge which built up thick platforms on our crampons, and as the snow covering some small stones melted they began zipping down around us. We knew that it was more dangerous to be moving on such terrain in the late afternoon after a warm, sunny day, but we had no choice. It was only ten more days before our porters would arrive to help carry our gear back to civilization. It was already dark when I pulled up the last fixed rope into Camp 1, perched on a tiny rib like an eagle's eyrie. Several other expeditions were trying to climb Broad Peak this year. Over a hundred people had tried to reach the top, but so far only five had succeeded. Four tents were perched on the tiny platform, but luckily for us only three were occupied, and we thankfully retreated into the empty one and started to melt snow for a brew. [To speed their ascent, Tullis and Diemberger were using equipment and camps already established by previous climbers.]

We were starving. In our hurry to get away we had not eaten much and that little was eight hours before. For three hours we cooked—tea, soup, and powdered potato, which we mixed with sardines; and then more tea, biscuits and chocolate. It was after midnight when we finally snuggled into our warm down sleeping bags. We had been up since four in the morning helping our expedition get ready to leave, so it was not surprising that we soon dropped into a deep contented sleep.

At six we were awoken by the occupants of the other tents moving around. They were not too polite to us when we emerged rubbing the sleep from our eyes.

"What the hell were you doing last night?" demanded an angry Frenchman, who had obviously had his precious sleep disturbed by our nocturnal picnic.

Had we really been so noisy? The thin tent walls have no noise insulation properties, but we had really tried to be as quiet as possible. Perhaps he was suffering from the common problem of not sleeping well at altitude? We apologized profusely in our best French, but when, during breakfast, they discovered who Kurt was their mood changed and they became very friendly. They had only recently arrived and were still acclimatizing their bodies and minds to the arduous high mountain life with its thin, oxygen-depleted air. We followed in their tracks toward Camp 2, delighted that they were breaking the trail through the fresh snow as we would need all our energy that day.

We would have to "front point" up the icy sections, some of which had no fixed ropes, using only the two front prongs of our crampons, which stick out like a beetle's antennae, kicking these in to spear the ice and attach us to the mountain. As the whole base of the foot hangs over space, this technique places a lot of strain on the ankles and calves. We had planned not to stop at Camp 2 but carry straight on to Camp 3, 3,000 feet higher. Not only were we short of time, but the fine weather might not last for long. In fact, halfway to Camp 2, the clouds began to gather around the mountain. By the time we arrived there all the mountaineers from the German, French, and Italian expeditions were hurriedly packing their rucksacks and retreating to the safety of Base Camp. Our friends from Camp 1 also went down. It was not only the approaching bad weather that drove them down. Some of them had already been living on the mountain for several days and were too exhausted to continue. Sadly, two were suffering badly from frost-bitten feet.

However, Kurt and I were both committed to going on. We knew all too well how fickle the weather could be. It could just as easily change again for the better and already this year we had plenty of experience of living with fierce Himalayan storms. It is as much a mental endurance test as a physical one, even if you are simply lying in a tent. Many of our friends on K2 could not stand the constant noisy flapping of the tent fabric in the high winds for hour after hour, expecially at night. It is a strange form of torture for some people and certainly the imagination runs riot during the long hours of darkness as gale force winds batter the thin material shield protecting you from the elements. One sleepless night plays havoc with the energy level and your performance the following day; you feel totally drained.

We crossed the featureless snow plateau below the snow cliff leading to the next exposed ridge. Once past Camp 2 we found renewed energy. We had made a drink there, had something to eat and left a depot of everything we felt we could manage without. It wasn't a lot: my little Canon Sureshot camera, some of our spare batteries, an extra pair of gloves—we would use our spare socks as gloves if necessary—and other odd bits and bobs of food. It was more psychological than anything, but our rucksacks felt lighter and we felt better, the climbing was going well and we were gaining height.

At the top of a short snow slope Kurt stopped and looked down at a tiny stone platform. "This is where we put our Camp 3 in 1957," he explained. We sat down and idly looked at the debris left by other expeditions who had during the intervening years also used this place for a camp site. Suddenly Kurt's keen eyes spotted something, and he dug in the frozen stones. "Look," he exclaimed, "a piton which Herman Buhl used to anchor our tent, all those years ago." I looked at the heavy nine-inch metal spike with the two-inch ring through the top and began to understand where Kurt's incredible mountaineering strength, endurance, and tenacity had begun. To survive at these altitudes with the very basic and terribly heavy equipment they had to carry and use then was a training that would last a lifetime.

The next section was interminable. We were getting extremely tired with the effects of altitude, as well as over seven hours' extreme exertion. Our loads were heavy for climbing at over 23,000 feet as we were not sure about the tents of the other expeditions on the mountain, whether they would be already occupied or destroyed by storms. Consequently we were completely self-sufficient carrying our own tiny bivouac tent, sleeping bags, foam mattresses, stove and gas cylinders, pots, food, still camera and films, spare batteries, head torches, a few bits of spare clothing, rope, and ice-axes, etc. When you think that a modern rucksack weighs over four pounds when it is empty and that your high alititude clothing, boots, and crampons when they are snow free add a good few more pounds, we must have been carrying at least 40 pounds altogether. It would be quite an effort to carry this total weight around for eight hours at sea level, without going continuously steeply uphill.

Just after six o'clock we got a first glimpse of the tiny tent that was Camp 3. It was sitting high on a steep snow slope sheltered by a large ice cliff. I longed to lie in its protective depths and rest my weary limbs. Kurt took over the lead. Slowly we started to zig-zag up the last obstacle between us and a desparately needed rest. The last light began to fade and it started to snow lightly. My legs ached, and my arms, neck and back. . . . Would we never reach that damned tent? It is strange how suddenly the will to go on can leave you. If only Kurt would stop for a moment! But I knew that he could not. We had to keep going, it was getting so cold.

When it was completely dark, Kurt took out his head-torch. We decided to use only one, saving mine for an emergency. I stepped into each of his footsteps as his foot was leaving it, on, on, on. But we never seemed to reach the tent. We hit a particularly bad patch of snow and sank into it up to our waists. Hell! It was like being in a bog. After struggling out it took time-consuming careful probing with a ski stick to find a safer way in the now total dark.

Suddenly we were there! Nine hard hours after leaving Camp 1 we had made it. We were now at the same height as we had reached on K2.

After the first hot drink we felt revived—bad memories soon fade. But it was a somber thought that poor Dr. Peter Thexton had died suddenly of a heart attack at this very camp the previous year when he was climbing with Doug Scott's expedition. The next day we moved on and established our little bivouac tent at 24,200 feet on a shelf Kurt dug on the lip of a crevasse which had opened up on the steep side of the mountain.

The following morning we had to wait for the weather to improve before we could move. It was ten o'clock before the visibility cleared and we could get going

We struggled, so slowly, up the last four hundred feet leading to the col. Why did the snow have to be so soft and deep? I took a deep breath and swung my foot with a strong kicking motion into the steep snow slope, but as soon as I transferred my weight onto it, it sank down through the surface of the step I had just made as if it were made of expanded polystyrene granules.

Hell! One step up and two steps down! My top foot ended up just above my lower one, buried beneath the wet snow up to my thigh. I was already feeling tired and fed up, and we had only been going for two hours. But we had to reach the col.

I set myself a landmark, a tiny rock sticking out of the snow, and made a rough estimate of how many steps it would take to reach it. Two hundred and forty, I guessed. 'No cheating,' I warned myself, and set off. Kick, step up . . . "one," breath . . . kick, step up . . . "two" . . . Every ten steps I stopped to rest and recontrol my erratic breathing. It was a long exhausting way. Above me, the heavy grey stormclouds hung menacingly overhead.

'Concentrate,' I commanded myself. 'Don't start to feel sorry for yourself. Just think how lucky you are to be here!' I looked down at Kurt solidly plodding up the slope below me and tried to regain my rhythm.

It was just after twelve noon as we topped the col. The wind almost threw us off our feet back down the slope up which had just come, and it was bitterly cold. The wind-driven snow stung the tiny exposed areas of our faces not protected by climbing helmets and big snow goggles. We looked around desparately to find shelter to protect us from its stinging bite rather than retracing our steps back down the exit chimney on which we had just expended so much energy. 25,600 feet! Just 800 feet, but still well over a mile, from the top.

We found a snow alcove and huddled together, our backs to the fierce wind. We tried to light our little Gaz stove, but the lighter kept blowing out. We took it in turns to try again, as we could not leave off our gloves for long before our fingers became numb with cold. At last the stove worked and we set to melting snow to make a much-needed warming drink. We couldn't see much through the swirling snow flakes, but knew that on one side of us the mountain dropped steeply down nine thousand feet to the Godwin Austen Glacier far below; and on the other there was an even more severe drop—over ten thousand feet, into China.

As soon as we had finished one drink, we started to melt the snow for the next. It was a slow process, as each quarter pint took nearly twenty minutes to reach the reduced boiling point of around

80°C, due to the altitude. We both were very aware how important it is to drink as much as possible at such a height, when the body is required to work at maximum effort and the oxygen level is reduced by two-thirds.

Three brews later and we were still feeling cold and cramped.

"My feet are very cold," Kurt told me. "If they don't get better soon we'll have to go back down." I felt an overwhelming disappointment, but knew that with such weather our chances of reaching the summit were very slim anyway.

Kurt stood up and started to stamp his feet and exercise his legs. "Please, please let them warm again," I silently prayed to myself. It was not just the constant frustration of the past three months, continually driven down from K2 by fearsome storms. I wanted this summit for many reasons. I had looked up at Broad Peak, on the opposite side of the glacier from our K2 Base Camp, so often and had wondered what it would feel like to be up there, so high that you could look over all the surrounding giants of the Karakoram range, except of course K2.

I wanted it for my husband, who for the past three summers had so unselfishly encouraged my mountaineering adventures . . . for my children . . . for the film . . . for Kurt who had put in so much effort, and because this was his special mountain. But most of all, I wanted to reach the top . . . to stand with my own feet on the summit!

"Let's try moving round on the ridge to get out of this wind. I just can't get warm here," Kurt's voice broke into my thoughts. "We can wait for another half hour, but if it doesn't improve we'll have to go down," he added, and I knew in my heart that would be the logical course of action.

We picked up our rucksacks and moved slowly on, looking for a more protective spot. Neither of us noticed when the wind actually stopped, we were so involved in trying to reach the other side of a narrow steep-sided rocky ridge. Although it had some rather old fixed ropes to hold on to in places it still involved a delicate and airy rock traverse.

"I thought you said that the summit ridge was broad enough to walk along?" I said accusingly.

"Julie, in 1957 it was! It must have eroded over the years." Kurt was also taken by surprise.

We moved steadily on up. After another hour and a half I looked ahead and my heart leapt. The summit was there, at the end of the next curve of the ridge. I moved on with renewed energy, up a steep icy snow slope. Nearly there. Almost at the top . . . keep going. Step up . . . breathe . . . step up . . . breathe. I felt myself holding my breath as I took the last step. We had made it. . . .

What my eyes saw my brain failed to register for a moment. The summit was still far away, about half a mile or another long hour of concentrated effort. The summit ridge curved round still farther, but this had been hidden by the false summit we had just climbed. It was getting late in the day, already after five o'clock. On the Chinese side of the ridge the weather was almost cloudless, but on the Pakistani side clouds were closing in. I didn't tell Kurt that I thought we had reached the summit, keeping my disappointment to myself. Please don't stop because it's getting late, or because the weather looks bad, I silently begged him as despite my disappointment I felt well, and as if he had heard my plea Kurt moved on with measured steps along the ridge.

About half an hour from the summit, the effect of going for several hours in the so-called "death zone" at above 26,000 feet hit me; my legs would not carry me for more than twenty steps.

Kurt was very helpful and set targets to reach. "Try to get to those next rocks, then you can rest again," he encouraged, and so we went on in short bursts until, suddenly, almost unexpectedly for me, we arrived at the foot of the summit snow slope. It was only the previous year that the first women had stood on top of Broad Peak, and I wondered what her feelings had been.

Slowly we climbed the last twenty feet.

There were none of the immediate emotions I had expected to feel, overwhelming joy, relief, a feeling of conquest. Instead it all felt rather unreal. This feeling was heightened by shimmering snow crystals, which were floating in the air all around us, like tiny mother-of-pearl sequins. Because of their size and lightness they were carried on the wind, dancing freely in the air, almost transparent, their rainbow colors sparkling in the sun's dying rays. Their backcloth was gray storm clouds over the mountains of Pakistan, but when we turned to look out over the thousands of Chinese peaks topped by a clear blue sky they took on a new energy, a life of their own, and as if to check that they were really there, we both unconsciously reached out to touch them.

We stood pensively looking down the huge drop to the Gasherbrum Glacier more than 10,500 feet below us. Was it really only the previous summer that I had learned the thrill of exploring these wild places? It seemed a lifetime away since we had been down there, the first people in the world to enter this spectacular glacier, and see Broad Peak's secret side. The enormous scale of the mountains and landscape seemed to belong to a different timescale too.

It was half past six and the light was beginning to fade. "Come on Julie, we must hurry up and take our summit photographs." Kurt's voice jerked me back to the present.

I went as close to the summit edge as possible and in the pose of an intrepid mountaineer held my ice-axe aloft. Click went the camera shutter. We had made it! For Kurt a journey back in time—for me my first 8,000-meter summit. I was very happy.

Last Chance

DAVID NOTT

The third attempt to ascend the world's highest waterfall ranks as one of the most bizarre, but intriguing, expeditions ever. In January 1971, four climbers penetrated the deep and remote southeastern jungle of Venezuela and for ten days and nine nights—many of them in drenching rains and without sleep or proper rations—battled up a 3,000-foot face near the falls. The climb, a debilitating confusion of cold mist, dangerous passages, and false rock spires eventually brought them near the mysterious summit plateau, itself a labyrinth of deep gorges, which held success in doubt. From his book, Angels Four, *David Nott describes a unique but uncertain summit day.*

At first light I lifted the corner of the sop-blanket and peered up at a hundred-foot buttress of rock that rose to our left. It had the profile of a totem pole and its noses and beaks changed color from blurry gray to jet black as the rain and mist swept across them. My heart sank. It was the lousiest, soggiest weather of the whole climb, and on the very day, the final day, that should have been gold with sunlight.

This was our last chance to reach the summit. Once again we would leave everything behind except climbing equipment and make a dash for the plateau. We would not even carry food or water.

I

BEATEN

We crawled out from under the cover just as wet and a lot colder than we had been the night before. As I shuffled across the cave to the water container, I came to a halt, shocked. My legs were buckling. When I looked down at my feet, my head swam. I reached for the wall to steady myself and glanced quickly to see if the others had noticed. They hadn't, and I forced myself outside into the rain. I was talking aloud: "Move along the ledge a bit. That's it. Now turn to face the rock. Brace up, idiot. Now try to climb. Just two or three feet. Step up just *one* move, can't you? Just one . . ."

I couldn't do it. Facing outward I eased my back down the wall until I was crouching on my heels. I tilted my face up into the rain.

"Why are you sitting there? Get up. You ill or something? You might get to the top today. Do you hear? The *top*."

But I wasn't thinking of the top. I was thinking of the sop-blanket. If I rolled up in it maybe I could get warm. Maybe my brain would stop swimming. Maybe I could sleep.

I rose to my knees and slowly pulled myself up. I felt no outrage, not even disillusion. Just the realization that if I was to have any chance at all of getting down the face, which would be the hardest part of the climb, I could not try for the summit. I was beaten. I went back down into the cave and told the others.

"You *what*? What's wrong?" said Timo.

"I've had it. I'm shaky. If I go on another day I'll have nothing left for the descent. It would be dangerous for you as well as for me."

"Come on, Dave. You'll make it. We'll give you a hand. It's only hours from the top. After eight days you *have* to go on now."

"No, John. I can't even walk around this cave without my legs folding. I'll stay behind and pack up so we can move off right away when you get back."

They looked at me and at each other. Then Straub gave himself a sort of rousing shake, "David. You come on now. We'll *shove* you up. There's three of us."

I studied that bedraggled trio. They looked stooped and wan. They were busted too. I felt I was about to get either exasperated or wet around the eyes, so I ended the palaver abruptly, turning away and pulling out my tatty notebook and a stub of pencil.

"You'll need a message to leave on top if you get there. I'll write it in English and Spanish."

I scribbled hastily and read it out: "This paper was placed here by the first team to scale the East Wall of the Auyan-Tepui, slightly right of the Angel Falls. The route took ten days climbing. The members of the team are: John Timo, Jr., George Bogel, Dr. Paul Straub, David Nott."

We signed beside our names and added a note that the first two were members of the Pittsburgh Explorer's Club.

East Wall of the Auyan-Tepui? We didn't even know where we were, for God's sake. Even Timo, who had lived and dreamed of the route for four years and had been on two previous expeditions, was so bone-weary, so totally absorbed in getting to the summit, that he failed to notice the mistake. The East Wall was miles away. We were on the West Wall of the Churun Gorge, which cuts into the Auyan-Tepui from the north. Moreover, we had been on the wall eight days so far, not ten. This was the morning of the ninth day. Later we were to realize these were not my only errors.

II

A CALL FROM SOMEWHERE

I handed the note to Timo and watched somberly as the three left the cave and traversed back in the direction of the chockstone, but at a high level. Once alone I stood for some time, thinking things over and getting nowhere. My notion of creeping back under the wet sleeping sack faded in disgust. I couldn't face the soggy, muddy feel of it, nor the squelch of the ground beneath it. So I packed everything and sat beside the fire's ashes to wait.

Seeping rain fell from the different levels of the roof, plumping and pattering on the floor, tinkling in the pools of water, splattering on the rocks. I had just about worked out the various rhythms of this demented drumming when I thought I heard a call from somewhere above. Shuffling stiffly out of the cave, I shouted, "Say again!"

There was no answer in the sound-deadening mist.

"Where are you?"

Again no answer.

I stood outside maybe a quarter-of-an-hour, staring dully at the rain, when suddenly I heard Timo calling out: "Dave. Are you coming?"

His voice was startlingly clear through the clouds and drizzle. I felt a pulse of excitement and jumped down into the cave, grabbed my slings and karabiners, got back out and stumbled along the slope at the foot of the ramparts, in the direction of Timo's voice, yelling "Yes!" and "Hold on!" and "Bloody Good!" I found him grinning at the top of an easy chimney. I nipped up quickly, grinning myself.

"Dammit! That's better! I'd never forgive myself for staying down there!"

I felt very grateful. But it was difficult to know whom to be grateful to. Providence, I guess. Because we still don't know who called first. Timo says he heard me shout and, thinking I was on my way to join them, came back to the top of the chimney to guide me up.

Probably the first voice I heard had been a call between themselves. It might have been Bogel sounding off at someone or something. But whatever it was, I was on my way, astonished at my lifting spirits and more so at my legs, which were trundling me along a higher ledge toward the final wall of rock. My knees were bent and creaking a bit, but I was moving, by God, and about to enter some of the weirdest terrain on earth: the Labyrinth.

III

THE LABYRINTH

The last couple of hundred feet to the top of the face of Angel Falls are more a cluster of towers than a continuous wall. Over the ages, streams from millions of tons of tropical rain have cut deep channels into the edge of the plateau. The falls itself shoots out from one such gorge 200 feet below the summit. These gorges are almost as immense and far more complex than the skyscraper canyons of Manhattan. This was the maze we were about to penetrate.

Before us the wall was split by a narrow cleft two feet wide and sixty feet high. We followed this forbidding passageway for several yards until it opened dramatically into a sort of moon crater scooped out of the plateau and cradling a crumbling ruin of stone. It was like bursting into the internal intricacies of a medieval castle through an underground tunnel. We had got in at the base of its front wall. We wanted to get out at the top of its rear wall, for up there was the flat plateau of the tableland mountain.

We could not believe our eyes. Everywhere we looked there were pinnacles, corners, angles, cracks, walls, and overhangs, all rising perhaps sixty feet from our level and, as we soon discovered, all dropping to unknown depths below. It was like traversing within the crevasses of an Ice Age glacier or through some fearfully deep and complicated cave from which the roof had been lifted. Moreover, in the Labyrinth, wherever there was a nook or cranny, we found earth or mud in which grew plants fit for a madman's window box, a vegetable world undisturbed in all history by any man or animal: plants two feet high and two feet wide clinging to a half-inch of dripping dirt; plants whose roots twined up their own stems; mosses we sank into up to the knee; and here and there, incredibly out of place, a pale palm tree, straight and slim.

Our own course was unplottable: twenty feet up, three across, thirty down, ten to the right, double back through a tunnel, around a ledge. Every step had to be taken with extreme care, for these giant, jumbled boulders, slabs and blocks had never felt the weight of anything but insect life, and we feared that any moment the balance of geological ages would be disturbed by our intrusion and the whole structure would collapse, grinding us to nothing in its thunderous fall. We kept glancing up, trying to memorize the main features of the rim of rock above so we could find our way back. Through all the passages of the maze blew a thick drizzling mist. If this was the Lost World, it was far older than that of Conan Doyle's fiction; here, the dinosaurs were millions of years in the future, and we, the first men, were aeons out of our time.

This fanciful notion gave way to a concrete problem. There was a forty-foot-high wall blocking our passage through the maze. On climbing it, however, we found it was not a wall but the tip of a colossal chockstone jammed across a great rift, the Number Two gully, which had repulsed us below. Up to now the chockstones in the maze had been so thickly clustered we had thought we were in a corridor with a floor. Now we saw we were once again on a huge boulder with nothing beneath it but air.

The other side of this boulder sloped down to a gap ten feet wide. Across the gap was another chockstone that sloped up thirty feet.

"My God," said Straub. "That gap drops through into the rift. That's more than a thousand feet deep!"

So far only Bogel had fallen into a hellhole. Now it was my turn. Timo took a few coils of rope in his hand, skidded down the slippery rock, leaped across the gap and scrambled up the slope of the second chockstone as if the devil were after him. An extraordinary performance.

I was next. I had a rope from Timo and one from Bogel. I slid cautiously down the latter to the edge and peered into the rift. It was an appalling drop and sapped the nerve I needed to make the leap across. Instead I moved a few yards to the right, where the gap narrowed. Here I could jump across to a small ledge and then climb up.

I was giving the knots at my waist a final check when I slipped on the wet rock. Cartwheeling over the edge I plunged headfirst into the rift, glimpsing a whirling patch of sky above my boots. My head hit the rock with a bang as I went through the gap, then the ropes stopped me with a jerk. But I was below the chockstones, unable to reach the rock on either side. I swung back and forth over that drop like a skydiver beneath his parachute. As I pendulumed I heard the ropes rasping on the edge of the chockstones.

My head cleared and I shouted frantically to Bogel to slack off. He did so and I swung across to the other side, where Timo hauled me until I could pull up onto the ledge and climb to him.

"You okay, Dave?" he asked.

I nodded, trembling.

We brought the others across. There was no time for sympathy, nor even a sly crack from Bogel. Beyond the second chockstone we could see that the maze continued as difficult and complex as ever.

IV

"YOU FIRST, JOHN"

Again I felt a twinge of panic and disbelief. The summit might be no more than fifty feet above. But had we chosen the wrong line up to it? Would we ever find the right line in this confusion?

Timo seemed to sense what was on our minds. "We can't backtrack now," he said. "It's this route or nothing. But let's get out of this rift."

He pointed to a slippery finger-crack cutting up an overhanging wall. There was not a hold on it for twelve feet. "Quick, Paul," he said. "Brace yourself at the bottom there."

Timo climbed from the doctor's knee to his shoulder, then to his head and, amazingly, up onto his hand, held straight up. Straub was shaking from the strain and clearly couldn't hold him a second longer. Timo fought his way up, slipped, recovered and flung himself up onto a ledge.

"Beautiful! Beautiful!" Bogel yelled. We whooped and applauded.

Straub shoved me up as far as he could, Timo heaved me the rest of the way and we hauled the others up on the rope. We traversed along the ledge, stooping under an overhang, turned a corner and found ourselves at the bottom of a crevasse. But this time its walls were only twenty-five feet high and above them we could see the open sky. To our left the crevasse was jammed with huge greasy boulders rising in steps toward the rim.

"That's got to be the plateau!" Straub cried.

"Don't count on it," warned Timo. "There may be another series of walls above this."

We moved carefully up the boulders, glancing down at the deep drop between them. With every move upward the light grew brighter. There was a new freshness in the air. Above the last boulder, in the last eight feet of the crevasse, a rickety tree sprouted from a crack.

I turned to Timo with suppressed excitement. "You first, John. You never know . . ."

He climbed up and over the ledge, looked around briefly, leaned down to us and said,

"Gentleman, this is the top."

V

THE LOST WORLD

The Auyan-Tepui plateau at this point was flat, black, slippery rock dotted with rainpools and boulders, split by deep crevasses. We could see only thirty yards in the churning clouds and here and there weird towers and blocks loomed and shifted as the mist moved across them. It was utter desolation. If astronauts were to land on the moon in a heavy drizzle, this is what they would see.

We crossed two crevasses with immense care, for it was like walking on ice, and suddenly we were on grass—thick mountain turf, flat and soft. Timo gave a whoop and ran around in a little circle. Then we were all skittering about. We had been nine days and eight nights on a vertical wall where not a single step could be taken without thought. Now we dodged this way and that, played tag, jumped sideways and backward.

Our jig of freedom became a dance of triumph. We waltzed around in a four-man bear-hug, slapping and punching each other.

"We did it!"

"We're up!"

"We got it!"

"Wha-ha!"

More quietly we shook Timo's hand and said, "Congratulations, John."

We had two tasks to complete before we began the descent. The first was to cross to the 200-foot-deep gorge through which the Angel River runs before dropping over the face to form the falls. It would be dangerous to lose our way here; in the mist we might never find our route down again. So we moved thirty yards leftward, stopping at a point from which the entrance to the Labyrinth was still in sight. Here I stayed while the others went on, leaving one man at each limit of visibility until Timo went on alone toward the edge of the gorge. He was looking for the aluminum tube in which the 1968 expedition [This nonclimbing expedition, sponsored by the Explorer's Club and the Zoological Society, both of Pittsburgh, and by the Venezuelan Air Force, was the first to reach the brink of Angel's Falls by a nontechnical route in August, 1968] had left a record of its visit; he wanted to add our ascent to it. But in the thick clouds he never found it.

In fifteen minutes we were all back at the entrance to the Labyrinth and the next job was to build a cairn of stones to mark the spot. I found a black and green rock fourteen inches long. One crack with a piton hammer split it cleanly across the middle. Inside, it was a lovely pale pink. This was the base of an eighteen-inch pile we erected on a boulder and under which we put an aluminum 35 mm. film container holding the message I had written that morning.

Before we put it in, we noticed I had dated it January 13, 1970, instead of 1971. We stared at it in bewilderment. In a small way this was a matter of history and the pencil stub was down in the bivouac. Finally Bogel exploded, "What the hell! Everybody writes down the wrong year for a couple of weeks after January 1. And anyway, we've spent the whole of what's gone of the year on the trail. We've never had to write 1971 before."

We screwed the cap on and fitted the container into the cairn.

It was the moment for pictures. Straub and Timo balanced their cameras on a boulder with delay-action springs set and scuttled across the rock to get all four of us in the shot. Out came the flag of the Pittsburgh Explorer's Club, and, in miniature, the Stars and Stripes, and the yellow, blue, and red banner of Venezuela.

"I have a surprise for you, David," Timo said, and he pulled out a Union Jack, five-and-a-half inches by four. I'd never been so taken with a gesture in all my life. I really was most absurdly pleased.

So there we stood, four dripping, mud-soaked tramps, close to exhaustion, holding up our little wet flags and beaming selfconsciously at the cameras as they clicked off pictures like robots. No one in the whole world knew where we were, and all we could see was mist.

. . . And Miles to Go . . .

THOMAS HORNBEIN

What is it like to set foot atop the highest point on earth, the summit of Mt. Everest? For Thomas Hornbein and Willi Unsoeld, those minutes, historic ones in mountaineering, were charged with memories of the struggles they had endured to reach that point: team resistance to their attempt up the unknown West Ridge; devastating windstorms; the earlier death of teammate Jake Breitenbach; the nagging uncertainty of climbing beyond possible retreat. Hornbein's chapter from Everest: The West Ridge *relates those compressed moments on top of the world, and the beginnings of the long way down.*

> *I believe that no man can be completely able to summon all his strength, all his will, all his energy, for the last desperate move, till he is convinced the last bridge is down behind him and that there is nowhere to go but on.* Henrich Harrer

Just rock, a dome of snow, the deep blue sky, and a hunk of orange-painted metal from which a shredded American flag cracked in the wind. Nothing more. Except two tiny figures walking together those last few feet to the top of the earth.

For twenty minutes we stayed there. The last brilliance of the day cast the shadow of our summit on the cloud plain a hundred miles to the east. Valleys were filled with the indistinct purple haze of evening, concealing the dwellings of man we knew were there. The chill roar of wind made speaking difficult, heightening our feeling of remoteness. The flag left there seemed a feeble gesture of man that had no purpose but to accentuate the isolation. The two of us who had dreamed months before of sharing this moment were linked by a thin line of rope, joined in the intensity of companionship to those inaccessibly far below, Al and Barry and Dick—and Jake.

From a pitch of intense emotional and physical drive it was only partly possible to become suddenly, completely the philosopher of a balmy afternoon. The head of steam was too great, and the demands on it still remained. We have a long way to go to get down, I thought. But the prospect of descent of an unknown side of the mountain in the dark [Unable to return down their steep West Ridge, Hornbein and Unsoeld planned to descend via the South Col, a route neither of them had ever seen.] caused me less anxiety than many other occasions had. I had a blind, fatalistic faith that, having succeeded in coming this far, we could not fail to get down. The moment became an end in itself.

There were many things savored in this brief time. Even with our oxygen turned off [Bottled oxygen is sometimes used by climbers on Himalayan peaks to offset the thin atmosphere and increase safety.] we had no problem performing those summit obeisances, photographing the fading day (it's a wonderful place to be for sunset photographs), smiling behind our masks for the inevitable "I was there" picture. Willi wrapped the kata given him by Ang Dorje about the flag pole and planted Andy Badewell's crucifix alongside it in the snow; Lhotse and Makalu, below us, were a contrast of sun-blazed snow etched against the darkness of evening shadow. We felt the lonely beauty of the evening, the immense roaring silence of the wind, the tenuousness of our tie to all below. There was a hint of fear, not for our lives, but of a vast unknown that pressed in upon us. A fleeting feeling of disappointment—that after all those dreams and questions this was only a mountaintop—gave way to the suspicion that maybe there was something more, something beyond the three-dimensional form of the moment. If only it could be perceived.

But it was late. The memories had to be stored, the meanings taken down. The question of why we had come was not now to be answered, yet something up here must yield an answer, something only dimly felt, comprehended by senses reaching farther yet than the point on which we stood; reaching for understanding, which hovered but a few steps higher. The answers lay not on the summit of Everest, nor in the sky above it, but in the world to which we belonged and must now return.

Footprints in the snow told that Lute and Barrel had been here. [Lute Jerstad and Barry "Barrel" Bishop had reached the summit earlier that day via the South Col route which Hornbein and Unsoeld were to descend.] We'd have a path to follow as long as light remained.

"Want to go first?" Willi asked. He began to coil the rope.

Looking down the corniced edge, I thought of the added protection of a rope from above. "Doesn't matter, Willi. Either way."

"Okay, why don't I go first then?" he said, handing me the coil. Paying out the rope as he disappeared below me I wondered. Unsoeld tired? It was hard to believe. Still he'd worked hard; he had a right to be weary. Starting sluggishly, I'd felt stronger as we climbed. So now we would reverse roles. Going up had been pretty much Willi's show; going down would be mine. I dropped the last coil and started after him.

Fifty feet from the top we stopped at a patch of exposed rock. Only the summit of Everest, shining peak, remained above the shadow sea. Willi radioed to Maynard Miller at Advance Base that we were headed for the South Col. It was 6:35 P.M.

We almost ran along the crest, trusting Lute and Barrel's track to keep us a safe distance from the cornice edge. Have to reach the South Summit before dark, I thought, or we'll never find the way. The sun dropped below the jagged horizon. We didn't need goggles any more. There was a loud hiss as I banged my oxygen bottle against the ice wall. Damn! Something's broken. I reached back and turned off the valve. Without oxygen, I tried to keep pace with the rope disappearing over the edge ahead. Vision dimmed, the ground began to move. I stopped till things cleared, waved my arms and shouted into the wind for Willi to hold up. The taut rope finally stopped him. I tightened the regulator, then turned the oxygen on. No hiss! To my relief it had only been jarred loose. On oxygen again, I could move rapidly. Up twenty feet, and we were on the South Summit. It was 7:15.

Thank God for the footprints. Without them, we'd have had a tough time deciding which way to go. We hurried on, facing outward, driving our heels into the steep snow. By 7:30 it was dark. We took out the flashlight and resumed the descent. The batteries, dregs of the expedition, had not been helped by our session with Emerson's diary the night before: they quickly faded. There was pitiful humor as Willi probed, holding the light a few inches off the snow to catch some sign of tracks. You could order your eyes to see, but nothing in the blackness complied.

We move slowly now. Willi was only a voice and an occasional faint flicker of light to point the way. No fear, no worry, no strangeness, just complete absorption. The drive, which had carried us to a nebulous goal, was replaced by simple desire for survival. There was not time to dwell on the uniqueness of our situation. We climbed carefully, from years of habit. At a rock outcrop we paused. Which way? Willi groped to the right along a corniced edge. In my imagination, I filled in the void.

"No tracks over here," Willi called.

"Maybe we should dig in here for the night."

"I don't know. Dave and Girmi should be at 6." [Camp 6 was the highest climbers' camp on the South Col Route.]

We shouted into the night, and the wind engulfed our call. A lull. Again we shouted. "Helloooo," the wind answered. Or was it the wind?

"Helloooo," we called once more.

"Helloooo," came back faintly. That wasn't the wind!

"To the left, Willi."

"Okay, go ahead."

In the blackness I couldn't see my feet. Each foot groped cautiously, feeling its way down, trusting to the pattern set by its predecessor. Slowly left, right, left, crampons biting into the snow, right, left . . .

"Willee!" I yelled as I somersaulted into space. The rope came taut, and with a soft thud I landed.

"Seems to be a cornice there," I called from beneath the wall. "I'll belay you from here."

Willi sleepwalked down to the edge. The dim outline of his foot wavered until it met my guiding hand. His arrival lacked the flair of my descent. It was well that the one of lighter weight had gone first.

Gusts buffeted from all directions, threatening to dislodge us from the slope. Above a cliff we paused, untied, cut the rope in half, and tied in again. It didn't help; even five feet behind I couldn't see Willi. Sometimes the snow was good, sometimes it was soft, sometimes it lay shallow over rocks so we could only drive our axes in an inch or two. With those psychological belays, we wandered slowly down, closer to the answering shouts. The wind was dying, and so was the flashlight, now no more than an orange glow illuminating nothing. The stars, brilliant above, cast no light on the snow. Willi's oxygen ran out. He slowed, suddenly feeling much wearier.

The voices were close now. Were they coming from those two black shapes on the snow? Or were those rocks?

"Shine your light down here," a voice called.

"Where? Shine yours up here," I answered.

"Don't have one," came the reply.

Then we were with them—not Dave and Girmi, but Lute and Barrel. They were near exhaustion, shivering lumps curled on the snow. Barrel in particular was far gone. Anxious hungering for air through the previous night, and the near catastrophe when their tent caught fire in the morning, had left him tired before they even started. Determination got him to the top, but now he no longer cared. He only wanted to be left alone. Lute was also tired. Because of Barrel's condition he'd had to bear the brunt of the climbing labor. His eyes were painfully burned, perhaps by the fire, perhaps by the sun and wind. From sheer fatigue they had stopped thinking. Their oxygen was gone, except for a bit Lute had saved for Barrel; but they were too weak to make the change.

At 9:30 we were still a thousand feet above Camp 6. Willi sat down on the snow, and I walked over to get Lute's oxygen for Barrel. As I unscrewed Lute's regulator from the bottle, he explained why they were still there. Because of the stove fire that had sent them diving from the tent, they were an hour late in starting. It was 3:30 P.M. when they reached the summit. Seeing no sign of movement down the west side, they figured no one would be any later than they were. At 4:15 they started down. Fatigue slowed their descent. Just after dark they had stopped to rest and were preparing to move when they heard shouts. Dave and Girmi, they thought. No—the sounds seemed to be coming from above. Willi and Tom! So they waited, shivering.

I removed Barrel's regulator from his empty bottle and screwed it into Lute's. We were together now, sharing the support so vigorously debated a week before. Lute would know the way back to their camp, even in the dark. All we had to do was help them down. Fumbling with unfeeling fingers I tried to attach Barrel's oxygen hose to the regulator. Damn! Can't make the connection. My fingers scraped uncoordinately against the cold metal. Try again. There it goes. Then, quickly, numb fingers clumsy, back into mittens. Feeling slowly returned, and pain. Then, the pain went and the fingers were warm again.

Willi remembered the Dexedrine I had dropped into my shirt pocket the evening before. I fished out two pills—one for Barrel and one for Lute. Barrel was better with oxygen, but why I had balked at his communal use of Lute's regulator, I cannot say. Lack of oxygen? Fatigue? It was fifteen fours since we'd started our climb. Or was it that my thoughts were too busy with another problem? We had to keep moving or freeze.

I led off. Lute followed in my footsteps to point out the route. Lost in the darkness sixty feet back on our ropes, Willi and Barrel followed. The track was more sensed than seen, but it was easier now, not so steep. My eyes watered from searching for the black holes punched in the snow by Lute's and Barrel's axes during their ascent. We walked to the crest, three feet down, ramming our axes into the narrow edge. Thirty feet, and the rope came taut as Barrel collapsed in the snow, bringing the entire caravan to a halt. Lute sat down behind me. Got to keep moving. We'll never get there.

We had almost no contact with the back of the line. When the rope came taut, we stopped, when it loosened we move on. Somewhere my oxygen ran out, but we were going too slow for me to notice the difference. Ought to dump the empty bottle, I thought, but it was too much trouble to take off my pack.

Heat lightning flashed along the plains to the east, too distant to light our way. Rocks that showed in the snow below seemed to get no closer as the hours passed. Follow the ax holes. Where'd they go? Not sure. There's another.

"Now where, Lute?"

"Can't see, Tom," Lute said. "Can't see a damn thing. We've got to turn down a gully between some rocks."

"Which gully. There's two or three."

"Don't know, Tom."

"Think, Lute. Try to remember. We've got to get to 6."

"I don't know. I just can't see."

Again and again I questioned, badgered, trying to extract some hint. But half blind and weary, Lute had no answer. We plodded on. The rocks came slowly closer.

Once the rope jerked tight, nearly pulling me off balance. Damn! What's going on! I turned and looked at Lute's dim form lying on the snow a few feet further down the Kangshung Face. His fall had been effectively if uncomfortable arrested when his neck snagged the rope between Willi and me.

We turned the crest, toward the rocks. Tongues of snow pierced the cliffs below. But which one? It was too dangerous to plunge on. After midnight we reached the rocks. It had taken nearly three hours to descend four hundred feet, maybe fifteen minutes' worth by daylight.

Tired. No hope of finding camp in the darkness. No choice but to wait for day. Packs off. Willi and I slipped into our down parkas. In the dark, numb fingers couldn't start the zippers. We settled to the ground, curled as small as possible atop our pack frames. Lute and Barry were somewhere behind, apart, each alone. Willi and I tried hugging each other to salvage warmth, but my uncontrollable shivering made it impossible.

The oxygen was gone, but the mask helped a little for warmth. Feet, cooling, began to hurt. I withdrew my hands from the warmth of my crotch and loosened crampon bindings and boot laces, but my feet stayed cold. Willi offered to rub them. We removed boots and socks and planted both my feet against his stomach. No sensation returned.

Tired by the awkward position, and frustrated by the result, we gave it up. I slid my feet back into socks and boots, but couldn't tie them. I offered to warm Willi's feet. Thinking that his freedom from pain was due to a high tolerance of cold, he declined. We were too weary to realize the reason for his comfort.

The night was overpoweringly empty. Stars shed cold unshimmering light. The heat lightening dancing along the plains spoke of a world of warmth and flatness. The black silhouette of Lhotse lurked half sensed, half seen, still below. Only the ridge on which we were rose higher, disappearing into the night, a last lonely outpost of the world.

Mostly there was nothing. We hung suspended in a timeless void. The wind died, and there was silence. Even without wind it was cold. I could reach back and touch Lute or Barrel lying head to toe above me. They seemed miles away.

Unsignaled, unembellished, the hours passed. Intense cold penetrated, carrying with it the realization that each of us was completely alone. Nothing Willi could do for me or I for him. No team now, just each of us, imprisoned with his own discomfort, his own thoughts, his own will to survive.

Yet for me, survival was hardly a conscious thought. Nothing to plan, nothing to push for, nothing to do but shiver and wait for the sun to rise. I floated in a dreamlike eternity, devoid of plans, fears, regrets. The heat lightning, Lhotse, my companions, discomfort, all were there—yet not there. Death had no meaning, nor, for that matter, did life. Survival was no concern, no issue. Only a dulled impatience for the sun to rise tied my formless thoughts to the future.

About 4:00 the sky began to lighten along the eastern rim, baring the bulk of Kangchenjunga. The sun was slow in following, interminably slow. Not till after 5:00 did it finally come, its light streaming through the South Col, blazing yellow across the Nuptse Wall, then onto the white wave crest of peaks far below. We watched as if our own life was being born again. Then as the cold yellow light touched us, we rose. There were still miles to go.

The Highest Man in the World

RICK RIDGEWAY

When Jim Wickwire stepped wearily to the top of 28,253 foot K2 with Lou Reichardt in 1978—the first Americans to ever do so—"Wick" lingered longer than Reichardt on the summit, aware of the price he might pay for those precious moments. When he finally began his descent, it was too late. Darkness fell and Wickwire was stranded and forced to endure an unplanned bivouac, alone, near the top of the world's second tallest peak. This extraordinary tale of endurance is told from the vantage point of Wickwire and others on the mountain, and is from Rick Ridgeway's book, The Last Step.

SEPTEMBER 6. SUMMIT PYRAMID, ABRUZZI FINISH. 26,500 FEET. 7:30 A.M.

The direct morning sun lit the rock to his left, and feeling evermore in a dream world, Wick slowly, step by slow step, worked toward a small flat spot on that ridge. Lou was already there, sitting, resting. Making the last steps, Wick unloaded his pack and looked around. To his surprise, he found more than just rock, ice, and snow. On the lonely shelf at 26,500 feet, in the heart of Central Asia, he also discovered a high-altitude garbage dump: an empty fuel canister and a fragment of aluminum wrapper from a drink mix, or possibly a soup package. He wasn't certain which since the label was in Japanese. They had stopped at the site of the Camp VI of the 1977 Japanese K2 Expedition.

Wick decided to start using oxygen [Bottled oxygen is many

times used by climbers to offset the dangers of ascending at extreme, atmospherically-thin, altitudes.]; Lou was going to wait until a bit higher, until the narrow couloir they could see above them. Opening the top flap of his pack, Wick exposed the yellow fiber-glass-wrapped aluminum bottle, and with his fingers unscrewed the brass cap protecting the valve opening. He had made certain, before leaving camp, the cap was only finger-tight; we had all been wary of carrying our oxygen bottle a total of 9,500 vertical feet (the altitude distance to Base Camp) only to find a cap that couldn't be removed without a wrench. He next screwed the regulator into the fitting and tightened it with a wing nut designed to operate with mittened hands. He cracked the valve and looked at the gauge, then looked again. At first he couldn't believe it, then he tried to imagine how it had happened, how he could have hauled the bottle that far without knowing it was only partially full. The gauge read 2700 psi, well below the 3900 to 4100 psi of a full-pressure bottle. Somehow, precious gas had leaked. Despite the extreme altitude, Wick was still thinking clearly enough to realize that to make the summit before the bottle emptied he would have to climb with a slow rate of one liter a minute. That would be far less than the two- to four-liter rate climbers normally use at comparable altitudes on Everest.

With the mask fitted and the rubber bladder-reservoir ballooned in front of his face, he signaled to Lou he was ready. Lou led out, but just before the bottleneck, where it became the steepest, Wick took the lead and worked up, carefully placing his crampons on the ice-covered rock and making sure the pick of his axe was securely in the ice before making each move. He realized his thoughts were slowing, and he knew he had to think through each move carefully, but he was feeling more strength—the benefit of the oxygen.

At the top of the couloir Wick stopped and pulled the rope up, and Lou followed. Despite not yet using oxygen, Lou was keeping up with Wick. In the narrowest and steepest part, one of Lou's crampons suddenly popped off as the icehold under his boot gave way, and he just caught himself. He had to breathe rapidly before he felt his oxygen-starved body regain strength sufficient to try again. He wondered if he could make the move with the weight on his back. But he did—he had to—and together he and Wick studied the next obstacle.

Straight above them loomed the enormous ice cliffs of the summit pyramid. To overcome the obstacle they would be forced to traverse left over rock covered with loose snow and ice. It looked spooky. Above the narrow catwalk was vertical ice; below, a ten-thousand-foot drop down the south face to Base Camp.

"You should probably use your oxygen," Wick said.

"Okay."

Lou removed his pack to screw on the regulator, then fitted the mask. Shouldering the pack, he slowly led across the traverse. He gingerly made each crampon-step, trying to keep the metal point off the rock where they would more easily pop off. Wick belayed the rope around his ice-axe, but they both knew the anchor would not hold a fall.

Making the moves across the traverse was hard enough, but it was even more difficult because Lou was having trouble with his oxygen apparatus. It didn't seem to be delivering any gas; his bladder was limp and only partially inflated. Balancing with one hand on his axe and his feet carefully placed in the ice-covered rock, he removed the mask with the other hand, took several breaths of ambient air, replaced the mask, and made several more steps, only to be forced to do the same thing. He fiddled with the flow rate, opening it to a maximum eight liters a minute. Even then the bladder remained deflated. Something wasn't working; it had been easier climbing without the mask.

He finished his pitch and belayed the rope as Wick crossed. He enviously noted Wick's bladder puffed like a tight balloon, and knew without doubt he either had an obstruction or a leak. Wick climbed past and Lou followed, continuing to fiddle with the apparatus. He mentally rummaged through his pack for something to jury-rig a leak.

Adhesive tape, he thought, but I don't have any.

Then he realized it was hopeless. He looked up and saw a rock above, the next "goal," and knew he couldn't possibly reach that, much less the summit, carrying a seventeen-pound security blanket that wasn't even working. He stopped, removed the mask, and examined the rubber tube leading to the bladder. There were several holes, possibly caused by a crampon puncture while being transported in the pack lower on the mountain. He removed his pack and set everything—mask, cylinder, even the pack—in the snow and continued to catch up with Wick.

Wick had been slowly punching steps up a long snow slope beyond the end of the ice cliff, realizing the most technically difficult sections were now behind him. From there it would be a long, slow trudge to the top. It was already past noon and they had some twelve hundred vertical feet to go. Much time had been lost while Lou worked with his faulty regulator. It would be all-important to keep a steady pace, and there would be no time for rests.

The snow had once again softened in bright noon sun, and Wick struggled to maintain his pace. He looked behind to check on Lou and was amazed to see him take off his oxygen mask, set his pack in the snow, unrope, and continue, leaving everything behind. Without the weight of his pack, Lou was much faster, and Wick waited for him to catch up.

Wick thought, Is Lou going back down? What's up?

Before Lou arrived, Wick made up his mind to continue, even if Lou was planning to descend, alone to the summit.

"What are you doing?" Wick asked when Lou arrived.

"I'm going without oxygen. My oxygen set wouldn't work. There was a leak or something. It's a gamble, but there's no choice."

Lou was concerned; he didn't know what his body's reaction would be at twenty-eight thousand feet without oxygen, and he feared it might dangerously impair his judgment. Recalling stories of previous climbs to the earth's highest summits where climbers had gotten in trouble when their oxygen ran out, Lou's subconscious notified him it was time to be careful and not to expect his judgment to be sound.

"Watch me, and tell me if I exhibit any bizarre behavior," he said to Wick.

"Okay, I'll talk to you every so often, and that way tell if you start to act weird," Wick said, then added, "You realize, though, I'm going to the top regardless?"

"Yes," Lou replied.

Wick continued slowly. His hopes for better snow conditions dissolved as his feet, calves, and then thighs disappeared in the mushy snow. Another hour passed. He traded leads with Lou, then switched back. One foot, then another, then breathe several times. Wick looked behind to see that Lou had started an angled traverse toward the ridge to their left, and Wick realized he was searching for better snow. Both men forged separate paths for another hour until finally Lou reached the ridge and appeared to have better footing. Wick began to traverse to merge with Lou's tracks. By the time he was in them, Lou was some distance above.

Wick tried to catch up, but it was all he could do to match Lou's pace.

Maybe something's wrong with my oxygen, he thought. He checked the flow rate, looked at the bladder. It was puffed full, still pressurized, still delivering gas. But he couldn't understand why Lou was maintaining distance. Wasn't he, the one with oxygen, supposed to be faster than Lou—the one without?

As they climbed to even more extreme altitudes, Wick slowly closed the distance, then passed Lou. It was like a crossing of the performance curves, if you could have graphed the trade-off of going with or without oxygen. Lower on the slope, Lou had been able to maintain his lead on Wick who, while breathing oxygen, was nevertheless handicapped by the seventeen-pound bottle and other equipment in his pack. As they approached 28,000 feet, though, the benefit of the oxygen exceeded the difficulty of the added weight, and Wick slowly worked ahead.

Other than a few sips from Lou's bottle, they had climbed all day without water. The small matter of the water bottle lost from Wick's parka was having its effect. Lou, in leaving his pack behind, had also left his parka, and he was starting to shiver in the increasing cold. The sun dropped behind the summit ridge, and the cold intensified. It was 4:30 P.M. Above, they could see the silhouetted, nearly horizontal ridge. Would the summit be there, or some distance beyond? They would make it, there was no going back, but it would be late.

It seemed deceptively close, yet it receded with each footstep. Wick continued in the slow, steady pace. Neither of them had rested for more than a minute or two since Lou had set down his pack. With each step Wick thought of his family, his wife, his children, his mother and father—all who had given such support to his quest for this summit. He thought of several of the earlier climbers who, except for the vagaries of bad weather and bad luck, might have been the first Americans to walk those last steps. He thought of Dusan and Al and Leif.

There were only a few more steps to the ridge crest. Excited, Wick picked up and made the final moves up the steepening snow face. Suddenly he stepped onto the ridge crest tinted gold in late afternoon alpenglow. He was gasping for air; he thought he had somehow pinched off the supply of oxygen, then realized it was because he had made several rapid steps. He fell on one knee, exhausted.

His head down, he slowly looked to his right, hoping he would see the summit only a few feet away. Instead, the ridge continued level, then seemed to drop away into China. He could see the burned Sinkiang hills before the setting sun. He looked in the other direction. To his surprise, Lou was only inches away, making the final steps up the ridge crest. For Lou, increasingly cold without parka, the psychological warmth of the direct sun rays—then so low on the horizon—seemed to raise the temperature thirty degrees.

Wick looked past Lou, and now the ridge gently arched up, wider than he expected. The snow was gold. Seventy-five feet away he could see the ridge round off, then descend toward the west. It was a little larger than he expected, but still no bigger than a large dining table. He was in no way disappointed. He stood up and said to Lou:

"We've come this far. Let's make the last step together."

Arm in arm, they walked to the summit of K2.

* * *

The second highest point on the surface of the planet. The summit of his dreams. Wick stared across the mountains stretching endlessly below him, summit after summit painted gold. They were all below him. The world curved away, in all directions, falling away, below his feet.

For Lou it was an even more remarkable victory. He was the first man to climb K2 without oxygen. The magnitude of his feat was measured in his blue lips, in the ice frozen thick in his beard. Although the moment seemed dreamlike, he was still thinking coherently, and unlike Wick, one thought predominated: Get Down. It was 5:15 P.M. Ninety minutes until total darkness. There would be no moon. Lou had no parka. He was fiercely cold. He knew he could not survive a bivouac.

When the pair had crested the summit ridge a few minutes before, Lou had said, "I'm going to walk to the top, then turn around and come right down."

"You've got to at least stay there long enough for me to take a picture of you," Wick had replied.

There was a tacit agreement that Wick intended to stay longer and Lou would descend. But first there were several things to do, and Lou waited impatiently while Wick rummaged in his pack for the American and Pakistani flags, for an eagle feather we had promised the United Tribes of All Indians Foundation, who had helped the expedition raise funds, we would carry to the summit. There was also the microfilmed list of all who had contributed $20 or more. Wick handed Lou the flags and the feather and took several photos. Wick then handed Lou his camera, since Lou had forgotten his own when he abandoned his pack, and Lou took a duty shot of Wick.

"Let's go."

"I want to get a panorama first," Wick said. "But I've got to change film. Go ahead. I'll be along in a minute."

Lou was cold. It was nearly 5:30, and the sun was dropping below the horizon. The first stars emerged in the blackening sky. Without hesitation, he turned and began to descend rapidly. Wick fumbled to change film. He had to remove his mittens, then work quickly to open the camera and thread the film. It was too cold to work for more than a few seconds before replacing his mittens. He waited for his fingers to warm. The wind was blowing harder, and he had to be careful not to let spindrift in the camera. He concentrated on the task; he hadn't been using oxygen since reaching the summit, and everything seemed so weird, so hard to do. He took his hands from the mittens, worked, put them back in. Finally the camera was loaded, but then he noticed the lens had iced, and he gave up.

He studied the terrain around him. He could see down the west side, to where he had tried to climb in 1975. He noted the Savoia peaks to the west. All the peaks of the Karakoram and especially the Baltoro dotted the horizon. He followed the horizon 360 degrees, trying to identify each peak. He was impressed by the brownness of China. All the peaks basked in gold light; the sky was nearly cloudless. Finally he thought to look at his watch. It was 6:10. He had stayed too long; he had to move fast. Shouldering his pack he descended the summit ridge, then glanced down the route. A thousand feet below he could see Lou nearing his pack. It was then Wick first knew he could not make it down; he knew he would have to bivouac alone, without sleeping bag, without tent, just below the summit. The wind began to pick up, and already it was fiercely cold.

SEPTEMBER 6. CAMP I, 18,400 FEET. 5:25 P.M.

It had been an exciting day. After Rob [Schaller] shouted, "They're on their way to the summit," that morning, everyone awoke immediately, looking bleary-eyed out their tents toward the summit, and without exception, jubilant. It was a very cold morning—the thermometer in Camp I read ten below zero Fahrenheit, but it was windless. They could see there was no wind on top, either, and it looked like a perfect summit day. Clear and crisp.

It was easy to watch the progress through the telescope. They could distinguish Lou from Wick. They studied their slow progress, watching them make four or five steps, then lean on their axes exhausted. They knew the snow was deep; they could even see the trail as they postholed up the soft snow in the gully leading to the summit slopes. It was painfully slow, but they followed the two each step.

Spirits were very high. There was a relief that all the work and toil was paying off. Each person had played a crucial role in the drama they were witnessing; every person on the team was in no small way a player integrally part of that final scene. Whatever rancor had existed, whatever disappointments and disillusionments had divided the team, dissolved with each step that placed Lou and Wick that much closer to the summit.

Concern mounted as shadows fell across the face at 3:30, and the two were still some distance below the top. Finally, about 5:15, they watched Lou and Wick crest the summit ridge. The mountain was backlit as the wind picked up, and a plume of snow blew off the ridge. The dots moved antlike the last few yards to the summit. Then, at twenty feet from the top, they disappeared behind the crest. Everyone realized the true summit was out of their view, but there was no doubt. Jim Wickwire and Lou Reichardt had reached the top.

People cheered, bear hugged, slapped backs. The moment of victory was theirs. There was still concern, however, about the late hour. Rob continued glued to the telescope. Five minutes after they had disappeared, he saw a figure bound off the summit ridge. He could tell it was Lou; he had studied each of them so carefully all day, he could distinguish their idiosyncrasies. He waited. Where was Wick? Lou continued with much haste down the slope, as if panicked. Had something happened to Wick? Why was Lou almost at a run? The cheering stopped, and quiet came over them. They waited. One minute, two minutes, three minutes. Each had the same thought: He should have appeared by now. Something has gone wrong.

They quietly discussed the possibilities. Five minutes, six, seven. It was getting dark. Wick would not stay on top this late because he wouldn't be able to get back to high camp before total darkness. They watched Lou continue his rapid descent. He was several hundred feet down the snow slope below the summit. Ten minutes, eleven, twelve . . .

Fifteen minutes, sixteen, seventeen. Lou was over five hundred feet below the summit.

"It could have been a summit cornice," Bill [Sumner] speculated.

"Is there a cornice on this summit?"

"I don't know. I don't remember reading about one."

"It's not uncommon. Remember Bruce Carson on Trisul. He was on the summit, peeking over the edge, and didn't realize he was on a cornice. It broke off."

"There could even be a crevasse. Like the Japanese who just died on the summit over on Gasherbrum."

It was unusual to have a crevasse on a summit, but it was not unusual to have a cornice. Bill's speculation and fear was based on several case histories . . .

Twenty minutes, twenty-five. There seemed little doubt something had happened to Wick.

Thirty-five minutes. Lou was now a thousand feet down, nearing the place where that morning they had watched him inexplicably leave his pack. Forty minutes . . .

"There he is!"

Everyone bolted up, staring hard at the darkened face and the still backlighted ridge crest.

"I can see him," Rob said, fixed to the telescope. "He seems to be okay."

Suddenly everyone went crazy, hugging, cheering, dancing. Wick was alive. For some reason he had stayed longer on the summit, but he was on his way down . . .

"But it's late," someone said. "He can't make it back to Camp 6 before dark."

"And there's no moon. He probably can't downclimb without moon light."

The cheering quieted as everyone realized the implications. Above, the last light disappeared, the plume off the summit crest grew with the mountain wind. Already, in Camp I, it was much below zero. Ten thousand feet higher it had to be incomparably worse. They had made the summit, and Wick was alive—there was much relief in that—but everyone knew the real fight was just beginning. Rob Schaller walked slowly back to his tent. As the team's chief physician, his most important and demanding duty still lay ahead.

SEPTEMBER 6. CAMP VI ABRUZZI, 25,750 FEET. 6:30 P.M.

"I apologize for being so hard to get along with these last couple of days. Must be the altitude."

"Don't worry about it," John {Roskelley} said. "I haven't been so easy to live with myself. This is our third day at eight thousand meters, and our second night without sleep. What do you expect?"

I lay my head back down on my boot—I used it each night as a pillow—and smiled.

"Yeah, I guess you're right. I'm pretty bushed. But I'll try and be a little more even-tempered."

Actually, I was completely exhausted, more than at any time on the expedition. After leaving Camp VI Direct {The high camp of Roskelley and Ridgeway, established for their failed attempt to climb a difficult, direct route to the summit.} that morning we had descended only two hundred feet when we took off our packs, tied a line on them, and started dragging them, thinking it was easier to sled the heavy loads than to shoulder them. We passed Terry {Bech} on his way down and learned that Lou and Wick had gotten an early start. {Terry Bech had assisted Lou and Wick in establishing Camp VI Abruzzi, from which they gained the summit.} We reached Camp VI Abruzzi about three o'clock; the last hundred feet with those heavy loads had brought me close to my limit.

As soon as we arrived John complained that his feet were frozen again, so we crawled into Wick's and Lou's tent and for the third day in a row he put his feet on my chest. I decided I might as well do the same, so we lay there for nearly an hour, feet up each other's parkas, and I blew warm air down my jacket as much to warm my chest as John's feet. I wanted so much to lie back and fall asleep, but I couldn't. There was still so much to do. About four I put my boots back on and went out to dig a platform for our tent.

"My toes are still numb," John said. "I'd better stay in and warm them."

"Yeah, you'd better stay inside," I said with deliberate irony. "Relax. I'll dig the platform."

The last two days I had been very irritable, downright crabby. Every little thing seemed to rub me wrong. Normally little inconveniences don't bother me much, but of late I had been short with John, and he noticed it. Each time he wanted me to defrost his feet seemed like a major sacrifice of my time. It was as thought the altitude was changing my personality; as though I couldn't remember all the times he had gone out to shovel snow off the tent while I lay in the sack, or all the mornings he was up first to start breakfast, or all the times he took over and did most of the postholing to break trail.

Now he couldn't help me with the tent just because his feet were frozen. Cursing under my breath I madly hacked away at the snow with my ice-axe, working with what little reserve of energy I had left to level a spot and pitch the tent before dark. After an hour I could see I might not make the sundown deadline. I was getting very cold and starting to shiver.

"I'll come out in a minute," John said. "Let me get my boots on."

"Thanks."

By dark we had the tent pitched. I crawled in my bag but continued to shiver for some time. As soon as I got a hot brew down me, I warmed up and was able to laugh at myself and apologize to John. We put a hot water bottle down John's bag to warm his toes, and soon he felt better too. We still had a couple hours of melting snow and cooking, but we looked forward to a few hours' sleep before again getting up about one o'clock to prepare for our own summit bid.

We received a garbled radio call from Camp I and managed to decipher that Wick and Lou had reached the summit. The expedition was a success. Now we only hoped they made it back without bivouacking. The wind had been picking up all evening, and the sides of the tent were flapping with increasing pitch.

By eight we were worried. It was very dark. We had a policeman's whistle along for just such an emergency, and leaning out the tent door, we blew it while flashing a headlamp beam, hoping to beacon them in. Another hour passed.

"Did you hear something?"

"Blow the whistle again."

We listened carefully. Above the wind we distinctly heard Lou's voice. We looked at each other, smiled, and grabbed the light to signal them in.

Lou had overshot our camp in the dark and was a hundred yards below the tents when he spotted our light. He had nearly given up finding camp and was hoping instead for a crevasse suitable for bivouac. When he saw the light all the strain of the last several hours gave way and the tension flowed out, as he realized he was safe. Consequently, he had an extremely difficult time climbing back to the tent. When he finally arrived he was shaking with cold, drained, on the edge of collapse. Few men would have been equal to the physical endurance of Lou that day.

We heard him arrive outside our tent, but before we could get out to help him he jammed his head through the vestibule door. I knew the hour was late, that Lou had been climbing at extreme altitude all day without stop, that he had been through a superhuman ordeal, and that all this would no doubt read in his face, but I was not prepared for the apparition that met me eye to eye.

"Good god," John said.

"Jesus," I confirmed.

His face was frozen, looking like a specter raised from a frozen underworld. Large clumps of ice were frozen in his beard—not just snow, or spindrift, but heavy pieces of blue ice. There was a large icicle hanging from his nose. His lips were puffed, red, and split from the ordeal. But his eyes still glowed with life; there was no hiding there the joy he felt to be in our tent.

We pulled him in, careful not to upset the stove, and helped him off with his crampons and boots. While John did that I mixed a brew of hot Gatorade. Lou was shaking and had difficulty speaking.

"Just a minute. You can tell us all about it in a second. First get this down."

I held the cup to his lips, but was aghast to discover so much ice in his beard I couldn't get the rim of the cup to his lips. I set down the cup and tried to remove the ice. I pulled and yanked, and finally a big hunk broke loose and with it a clump of hair. Lou said nothing, oblivious to what I was doing, still shaking. With the larger ice hunks gone, he was able to drink the hot liquid. Wearily he leaned against John, and appeared almost to fall asleep.

"We made the summit," he said, a quiver in his voice.

"Yes, we know," we said, excitement in our voices.

"I made the summit without oxygen."

John and I looked at each other, realizing the magnitude of Lou's words. He said it simply, but with pride.

"Where's Wick?" we asked. "Is he behind you?"

"I don't know."

"What do you mean, you don't know?"

"I'm not sure where he is."

"Where did you last see him?"

"On the summit. I think he's bivouacking."

John and I looked at each other again, but this time with grave expressions. The wind was worse than ever, and it was already extremely cold. For a moment, none of us said anything.

"Maybe he's still coming down."

"I don't think so. It's very dark, and I think he had it in his mind to bivouac; it was something he almost anticipated."

"No headlamp?"

"It was in my pack."

"If he has his half-bag and parka, it might not be too bad."

"He doesn't. The half-bag got soaked this morning when he spilled water. He left it behind. He's got a pair of down pants he borrowed from Cherie [Bech]. Just that and his sixty/forty parka."

"Are there any crevasses up there to bivvy in?"

"I don't think so."

We continued to melt water and feed Lou steaming drinks. He stopped shivering, and with the ice out of his beard he looked not nearly as frightful as when he poked his head through the tent. He still leaned against John. He was weary and extremely tired, nearly asleep.

"You feel rehydrated?"

"Yeah. A lot better."

"Let's get you in your bag."

"Thanks. I can't tell you what it felt like to find you guys here, with hot drinks ready."

We all smiled, and John and I patted Lou's shoulder as he crawled out to move to his own tent. There was an unspoken feeling—more than just camaraderie (that word doesn't quite describe it), more perhaps a feeling of fraternity—of men sharing a common stress and hardship, a common danger, and together achieving a common victory. If only we could be with Wick to see him through his ordeal.

On his way out Lou uprooted one of our tent's guy lines, and John went out to fix it. He quickly came back in, already shaking.

"It's cold out here. As cold as it's been."

"Let's make sure we're ready. Go over everything: mask, regulator, tank packed, water bottles ready for the morning brew, lunch packed, goggles, sunscreen, face mask."

"Should we take a bivvy sack?"

"No—we've got to stay as light as possible."

"Leave the stove, then?"

"Yeah, Keep it light."

"And no rope 'cause we aint' got one."

We turned off the stove and snuggled in our bags. In the warmth I felt safe, secure, and aware that at that moment Wick was struggling for his survival. I listened to the wind, gusting perhaps to forty knots, and felt the cold air on my face. That survival, I thought, would be marginal.

"What time is it?"

"A little after midnight."

"We'd better get ready again about one-thirty."

"I'll let you know when it's time."

"What do you think Wick's chances are?"

"Pretty grim."

"So do I. I think in the morning we're as likely to be on a rescue mission or a body detail, as on a summit attempt."

John did not answer. We both lay quiet, listening to the wind, waiting for the hour to pass until we would make preparations. I did not look forward to climbing into the cold blackness.

SEPTEMBER 6 OR 7. SUMMIT PYRAMID, ABRUZZI FINISH. A LITTLE LESS THAN 28,000 FEET. AROUND MIDNIGHT.

I am slipping, slowly, closer to the dropoff. Inch by inch, my bivouac sack slides down the icy slope. I dig in my boot heels, trying to jam them through the thin nylon sack that I am huddled in. I still slide. The wind is blowing hard, it is so cold. I cannot stop the slipping. It must be the empty oxygen bottle in the sack, and the empty stove. They are both empty. I wonder why they are still there? Why haven't I thrown them away?

I only wish the stove was still working. I had it going for a while, but the fuel ran out. I thought to bring an extra cartridge, but something happened. I think the rubber O-ring, the gasket, fell off. Something like that. Anyway, the gas all hissed out of the new cartridge when I screwed it down. I threw the thing in the corner of my bag, in disgust. I went easy on my oxygen. Wanted it to last. Took only a few sucks now and then. But there was not much left after using it all the way to the summit. It ran out awhile ago. About 11:00, I think. I'm not sure when, really.

I still have the cylinder in my sack. I wonder why?

I am still slipping. I chopped a platform up higher. I was going to bivouac there. Then the sack started slipping. It still is.

It is so cold. So windy. I am shivering. I cannot control the shivering. I move my hands and feet, my arms and legs, constantly. I must maintain circulation; I must avoid as much frostbite as possible. I must survive.

Okay. You got this far. You made the summit so you must get down. You can't come this far and not get down. You will survive.

I am still slipping. Wait. Isn't there a ten-thousand-foot dropoff here?

Ten thousand feet. The thought makes me laugh. That is a long way, ten thousand feet.

It is too dark to see. And so cold. When will it end? When will this be over? Every second creeps by.

You had better do something, Wickwire. You might be close to the edge. The edge, Wickwire. You are at the edge.

I must do something. I do not want to get out of this sack. I have to. I pull down the opening, and crawl out. I seem so stiff. The wind is so strong. I am out, and I start pushing the sack back up the hill. It is a long way, Ten, then twenty, then thirty. There, I find the platform I chopped earlier. I put the sack back on it.

Now what is to keep me from sliding again? I have an idea. No, under these conditions, it is an inspiration. In one corner of the bivvy sack I take my ice axe and jam it through the fabric, pinning it to the snow. I do the same to the other corner, using my ice hammer. Then back inside the sack to escape the wind. But not the cold. Good thinking, Wickwire. Not bad under these conditions. Now you won't slide anymore. You do not have to worry about that ten thousand feet.

Now you can concentrate on staying alive until dawn. It will not be easy. You are shaking with no control. The first stage of hypothermia. Your toes no longer have feeling. Keep wiggling though; keep moving them inside your boots. Maybe it will not be as bad that way. Keep tensing, keep moving, keep circulation going. Survive, Wickwire. You know you can make it until dawn. You have done this kind of thing before. Cold nights in crevasses bivouacking on Mount Rainier.

But you will survive. You have made the summit. You have gone this far. It is all downhill from here. It is that simple. Keep moving your toes, your fingers. Shift your arms, your legs. Keep the circulation going. The night will end. The sunlight will return. You will survive.

SEPTEMBER 7. SUMMIT PYRAMID, ABRUZZI FINISH. ABOUT 26,200 FEET. 4:30 A.M.

Hard snow, wind tortured to small crescents like the surface of the sea frozen, and a sense of time in slow motion. The sound of crampons biting hard snow, squeaking, and the sound of quick, conscious breathing. Dark. Wind. Cold. Extreme cold. The feel of fingers frozen, hard and lifeless, and a momentary fear from the imagery of missing digits. Other imagery, other fears: a companion lost, or worse, near death, and us helpless to save him.

John was ten feet away, and together we climbed, at a slow, even pace, the steepening snowfield above Camp VI, the base of the summit pyramid. It was black and moonless, but in the rarefied atmosphere starlight was sufficient to see above us the major features of the upper mountain: the enormous ice cliffs like ramparts guarding the summit fortress, and below the cliffs, the constricting couloir through the rock band. A ground blizzard blew spindrift over our boots, and studied care was necessary to place each step on the crescent sastrugi that patterned the hard snow surface. I was conscious, in the dark, of the absolute necessity for precise footwork because we had no rope.

Despite the heavy oxygen [bottles], the extreme cold, and the altitude—eight thousand meters—I felt strong. We planned to go on oxygen above the couloir, and without it I was surprised at the fast pace we kept. I felt much stronger than I had at the same altitude on Everest two years before, and it confirmed my hope that my difficulties at that altitude had been a result of pulmonary congestion and not a physiological limit of the altitude to which my body could adapt. It was our fourth day at eight thousand meters, and our third night with little or no sleep, but nevertheless I felt I had sufficient strength to reach the summit. I also thought there was only a chance we would reach it; it seemed more like our duty would be to rescue Wick.

Silent speculation on Wick's chance of survival had overshadowed our preparations. We had started the stove as 1:30, first warming water, then our boots and mittens. We tried to drink as much hot liquid as we could, but it was not possible to hold the warm mug of cocoa—the heat so comforting to cold fingers—without thinking how desperately Wick was in need of that cocoa. Was he still alive? Was he, somehow, to survive the forty-below-zero temperature and the fierce wind that was buffeting our tent? With no sleeping bag or parka we expected to find him that morning, if alive, at least seriously damaged by the ordeal.

At 3:30 we crawled out of the tent, packed the last items in our rucksacks, and left Camp VI.

"Good luck, you guys," Lou called from the next tent. "I have a feeling Wick will be okay."

Lou had felt more confidence than either John or me. He thought that Wick had been mentally prepared for a bivouac, and that even without bag or parka he would be able to see it through without serious injury. Lou thought that perhaps Wick had found a site to dig a snow cave. The night had been so fierce, however, it was hard to share Lou's optimism.

We immediately set a fast pace as much to warm our bodies as to make quick progress, so that by 4:30 we were several hundred feet above camp. I climbed just a few steps behind John in a zig-zagging route up the slope. I was thankful for each switchback because I moved my ice-axe (always held uphill) from one hand to the other, that way thawing my fingers frozen from gripping the metal tool. The fingers were still numb, but I felt with enough care—enough moving them inside the mitten, enough flicking my wrists to force blood to the fingertips, enough alternating of the axe between hands—I could prevent frostbite.

Our first rest came at the site of Japanese Camp VI. We sat on our parkas and picked through the refuse preserved in amber ice, and watched dawn over the Karakoram. We were at the same altitude as the summit of Broad Peak, across the valley of the Godwin-Austin Glacier and the closest mountain to the Abruzzi Ridge.

"There's enough light to see," I said. "Wick might be moving by now."

"I hope so."

"God knows what kind of condition he's in. We're going to have trouble getting him down if he's in bad shape. Especially with no rope."

"If he's that bad, I don't think we could get him down."

We sat still, silent, staring. The dawn filled the shadows in the lee of the great peaks. New mountains rose on the horizon, not visible from the lesser altitudes. The glaciers so far below flowed inexorably in their timeless path to the sea. We hoped Wick was also witness to such grandeur.

SEPTEMBER 7. SUMMIT PYRAMID, A LITTLE LESS THAN 28,000 FEET. FIRST DAWN.

You have to remember, Wickwire, to keep moving your toes. You forgot to do that too often. There's no feeling left in them. Your fingers are gone, too. Maybe it won't make any difference whether you move them or not. No, you've got to try. You know it will help in the end.

This night has to end sometime. This would be so much easier if somebody else were here with you. Somebody to talk to. Remember how Ed Boulton helped when just the two of us bivvied on Rainier's Willis Wall. We sort of bouyed each other—when one was down, the other was up. Then you survived that night alone on the south face of McKinley. This is certainly higher, maybe colder, but you know you can survive this night. You must.

Wiggle your toes and fingers.

It will get light outside. No sense looking, though. Keep covered inside this sack. You'll know when it's light. You can see it through the nylon.

Wiggle your toes.

Shaking uncontrollably.

The night will end.

It must.

You are the highest man in the world right now. Somewhere around twenty-eight thousand feet—there is certainly no one else on earth right now standing anywhere higher than you are. Alone. Surviving this awful night.

Wiggle your toes.

Shaking so bad. So cold.

Wish the shaking would stop. No, that would mean you are freezing. How much time has passed? Who knows? It will be over sometime.

Remember, there is no way you can come this far and then not make it. You have been to the summit. You are on your way home. This whole thing will soon be over. You must survive the night.

Getting rummy. Not thinking right. So cold.

It's finally going to end, isn't it?

The walls of the sack are getting lighter. It must be light outside. It must be dawn.

No sense going anywhere. Wait for the sun. The night is over.

It is so cold. It is dawn. Maybe you should look out. There. Still clear—another good day. Only those small clouds so far away. Everything looks surreal. Sunshine on Broad Peak. Almost like you could touch it. And the glacier moving down to Concordia. So far below. Remember when you camped there on the way in. It was Fourth of July, and we slept under the stars and played Handel's Royal Fireworks on Rick's little cassette machine. So long ago, like another life.

You have to go down.

What a place this would be to spend an eternity. Frozen up here forever on the summit of K2. The highest man in the world. That's kind of funny. . . . But you should go down. Even if it's harder to do that. It would be so easy just to stay. There is plenty of time. Stay inside the bivvy sack. Plenty of time.

There is still no warmth. So cold. Remember how warm it was on the approach march. One day it was 126 in the shade.

Maybe you should think about moving. That means you will have to crawl out of this magnificent bivvy sack. What a way to spend the night, huh. Covered with a piece of half-ounce rip-stop in a full gale at twenty-eight thousand feet. This is going to be one to tell stories about.

Probably be ice this morning. There was some yesterday; guess that means there will be some today. You should put your crampons on. Let's see, they are outside the bivvy sack here somewhere. Yeah, here they are. Now get out of the sack and put your crampons on. Okay, ol' crampon, there you go on the boot. Now lace the strap through the eye here, then it goes over the boot and crosses to this loop, then back again. Now buckle it down and make sure it is fastened. Okay. One crampon on. Sun feels good, but it is still so cold. My fingers are awfully hard. I wonder how the toes are doing inside that boot. Wait a minute, Wickwire. Look at your boot. The crampon is loose. Two steps with that rig and it would pop off and so would you. A long fall. All the way to Base Camp.

Ha, ha. That's funny.

Who needs crampons anyway. Just lie back and relax. You can go down later. Put the crampons on later. You probably don't need them anyway.

Feel the sun. Things seem so strange.

Relax.

What a magnificent view, huh. There are the four Gasherbrums, then Broad Peak, and farther to the right Chogolisa and Masherbrum. And the summit, just up above, an easy walk.

Look how ridiculously close I bivouacked to the cornice. Might have fallen through. So far down the south face.

Go down later.

Mary Lou?

Mary Lou and our five wonderful children. I can see all of you so clearly. Going to the airport and the rest of the team is getting off the plane, but where is Wick? Where is Dad? Mom, isn't Dad going to come home?

Sit up, Wickwire. Focus. You're in bad shape, now straighten up. Snap out of it. Concentrate, Wickwire, concentrate. Strap the crampon tight. Put the other one on. Tighten it. Keep warming your fingers. Keep moving them. Double-check crampons. They look better, now. That will work.

I'm coming home. I love you.

Stand up. Careful. Awfully stiff. Get your axe. Put the bivvy sack in your pack—keep it around as a souvenir. Okay. Ready? Maybe you should go down facing in. No. You're not that bad, and it is not that steep. Not right here, but be careful at the traverse. Now start moving. Keep thinking. Concentrate. You'll loosen up in a minute. Remember, most accidents happen on descent. Be careful.

You'll be down soon.

I'm coming home, Mary Lou.

I love you.

5
CHAPTER

BACK INTO THE WORLD

The Descent

GENE MASON

Gene Mason was one of the first climbers to ascend the tallest peaks of North and South America, and Africa. He and five others attempted 20,300 foot Mckinley by its seldom climbed Karstan's Ridge. After seventeen punishing days on the mountain, they descended back into the world of color and smells, of life and reflections. The following chapter from Mason's book, Minus Three, *describes their return.*

We were awakened by Jon wafting a bowl of hot stew laced with caribou pemican under our noses. It tasted unbelievably good. In my sleepy hunger I felt that I owed him a debt so large that I might never be able to adequately repay him. The snow had become deep and soft here, so we packed our crampons away; from now on we would descend on snowshoes.

After our nap and nourishment we were moving down the mountain at a decent pace, but I worried a little about Jon. He had cooked while the rest of us slept. Would this catch up with him later? I filed it in my mind.

Most of the glacier traveling was rather routine now. Keep ropes taut, probe suspicious areas, travel until you're sure you can't take another step, then rest a minute or two, and walk again. Step over most crevasses, jump others, down into some huge ones, and up the other side—on and on.

The crevasses had increased in width since our last passage over them. Several marked with wands where we had jumped, now gaped widely out of jumping range. New routes were explored and found, but always with the reassuring knowledge that we didn't have to return to lug equipment over them, as we had done during the ascent.

Many times I looked back on Karsten's Ridge, building a permanent mental image of the snow billowing along its windswept edge, silhouetted against the bluest of blue skies, and its foreboding slopes rising to the Harper's Glacier like a stairway. I felt an inner thrill that I had been there and returned.

Jon was leading now, stepping, probing with our eight-foot probing pole, withdrawing the pole, another careful step, maybe a sideways step, looking, listening, like some giant insect moving a feeler through this forest of gnarled ice. [A procedure they used to detect crevasses hidden beneath the surface snow.]

As time passed, fatigue was becoming a more constant companion, and a more difficult one to shake for more than short periods. It was after midnight and we were enshrouded in dense clouds when our exhausted rope teams were passing under the immense hanging ice cliffs on the east wall. We were forced to pass under them, as we did on our ascent, because our attempts to find an alternate route had failed. I felt an enormous uneasiness, but it couldn't be helped. I knew that we were traveling slower and slower, but we were doing the best we could.

Jon finally sat exhausted in the snow. I was stunned when he began making an earnest plea for camping right there, ignoring the mountainous icy cornices hanging over us. It took many minutes to dissuade him. I recalled his lack of rest. Kenn picked up the lead.

By two in the morning we had traveled toward the center of the glacier, clear of the avalanche danger, and virtually free of crevasses. We had to be getting close to our airdrop camp. [To avoid long and costly equipment hauls along Mt. McKinley's remote approaches, supplies are often airdropped to designated sites.] Ron and I voted to continue until we reached the old site. The rest voted against us, and we wearily set up our tents.

* * *

The fog had cleared during the early morning hours, and we were greeted by a bright crispness in the air. We packed our gear and headed for the food cache at our airdrop site. Our trip down so far had been hurried, and with little attention to nutrition. Much food had been abandoned to ease the carrying load. We keenly looked forward to a meal of variety and volume.

We crested the small knoll at seventy-two hundred feet that had been our campsite, and broke out our shovels. Snow had covered our mound of supplies during our seventeen-day absence. We dug quietly at first, and finally vigorously with a shocked realization that our supplies had been attacked by something. We dug through the snow only to find our food packages ripped and scattered. Piling the unbroken canned goods in the snow, we sat in mournful silence. There were no tracks or droppings to indicate our tormentor, the destruction probably having been done weeks ago. We assumed that a wolverine or perhaps a flock of huge ravens had done the damage. We knew that a wolverine had been following us toward the mountain, but we had thought he had stopped when we moved onto the glacier at five thousand feet.

We prepared a stew from what remained and tried to enjoy our last meal, knowing that we wouldn't reach civilization for at least two days.

Leaving the glacier, we were now traversing the steep side of the ridge paralleling the glacial valley. Avalanche hazard was also extreme in this location. Moving along as rapidly as we could, we stole furtive glances upward at the huge, overhanging ice cliffs, listening for any sound that might warn us of its downfall. An avalanching fragment alone would be sufficient to sweep us into the gaping crevasses below us.

As I carefully slammed each boot into the slope to gain footing, I wondered if the mountain would allow us to pass these ramparts, or would it hurl a final bombardment of snow and ice to forever hide this conquest of its summit?

The tension grew as our two rope teams were strung out along the slope. Jon, Helen, and Ralph were perhaps a hundred yards ahead of us, out of sight most of the time due to the irregularity of the slope.

"Hold up," shouted Kenn, "I've got to fix a boot."

I dreaded the pause under the menacing ice wall hanging above us, but I knew Kenn hated it equally. Several hour-long minutes passed while he solved his problem. As he stood up to signal his okay, a thunderous roar filled the air. Part of the hanging cliff had broken loose, starting a tumbling, crushing avalanche. We prepared to jettison our packs, but then it became evident that the avalanche course would pass several yards ahead of us. We froze in our tracks, awaiting the end of the fury, realizing Kenn's pause had probably saved our lives.

But what of the other rope team? They were almost directly in its path. Their footprints had disappeared into the icy rubble.

"Yaooo," shouted Kenn in almost a yodel.

We listened for a reply. Nothing but the tinkle of ice particles tumbling over the now quiet avalanche debris.

"Yaooo," Kenn shouted again.

Only quiet. Had our expedition ended in a final tragedy?

And then, "Yahoo," in the distance.

Quickly we moved out to join them. When we caught up, we were no longer under the hanging ice walls. Jon explained how the avalanche had broken loose directly above them, roared down, and was diverted to either side of them by a large rocky prominence. Our best and most apt comment was a slow shake of the head and a smile.

As we continued on we came upon the solitary tracks of a wolverine. We wished him no good.

The going was fairly easy now, and we were almost to the point where we would return to the glacier. Suddenly I stopped. My attention had been drawn to a small glistening puddle about the size of a grapefruit. I knelt to examine it. I placed a bare finger in the water and gave it a quick stir. It was the first naturally occurring water in three weeks. It seemed like years. I knew the image would find its way into the indelible portions of my memory. The rope was tightening. Quickly I stood up and moved on. We had only a few miles of glacier now; crevasses were few and of minimal significance. The danger had melted into little more than a long slog.

The foot-weary hours passed slowly. At five thousand feet we finally left the Muldrow Glacier. The surrounding hills were no longer snow-covered. It had been three weeks since we first looked hopefully up the glacier toward the mountain. Tiny alpine flowers had bloomed in all their varicolored enthusiasm. I felt as if I had returned to the earth I knew and loved.

We unroped and removed our snowshoes. I felt an incredible feeling of freedom in being able to walk without the annoyance of rope handling, and with neither the weight of snowshoes nor crampons to burden me. We walked as far as we could, and finally crawled exhausted into our sleeping bags beside a gurgling stream to remind us that we were off the mountain.

Seven hours of refreshing, danger-free sleep had charged us with enthusiasm for the twenty-five miles of green wet grasslands, hills, and rivers between us and our destination at Wonder Lake. We stuffed our sleeping bags into our packs and were quickly on the move, but not before donning our mosquito head nets. Although we had exchanged our frigid, odorless, colorless world of snow boredom for one of warmth, fresh smells, and spectral color, we had accepted mosquitoes in the trade—thousands of hungry mosquitoes. Swarms followed us continuously, necessitating a slightly louder conversational tone to be heard over the unrelenting buzzing. The occasional mosquito getting inside the head net was vulnerable to the snapping of a food-short mountaineer.

Since we were covered all the time, we wouldn't bother to strike at them unless a kill of at least four was in the offing. We began to make a game of it when I announced a kill of seven in one slap. Ground rules were quickly established. Dead mosquitoes were counted on the struck surface and on the striking hand, while a slight blowing through pursed lips prevented new live ones from fouling up the official count. Jon stole my thunder with a record of seventeen. The record passed around several times before falling to Ron with a tally of twenty-one mosquitoes with one slap.

As the hours and miles passed by, I wondered if I would have to readjust to civilization. The thought occurred to me that I might be tempted to carry a wad of toilet paper in my pocket, and go when and where the urge struck me, as I had for the last month—a month without plumbing, beds, baths, music, coffee, or news of civilization. I wondered if I would ever lose the keen appreciation of the beauty and tranquility of the world I had returned to.

Many of the streams we were crossing now had flecks of gold rolling haphazardly along the edges.

In the distance I heard a faint roar. The mighty McKinley River was announcing itself. I knew we would reach it after a mile or two of thrashing through the willow swamps. We had passed across the snout of the Muldrow Glacier during our ascent of the mountain, and with the late spring had only had to cross several small tributaries of the river.

By midnight we stood on the banks of this gigantic river—a mile-wide torrent of rushing, gurgling, frigid water generated from melting ice, filled with rocky, glacial silt and occasional pieces of bobbing ice. Its expanse was laced with sandbars every couple hundred feet. I smiled as I thought of the many parties which had been frustrated by this huge moat and had never even completed their approach to the mountain. However, to us its formidable barrier was dampened somewhat by what we had already experienced. I knew that generally it was no more than mid-thigh or waist deep, unless one of us were unlucky enough to drop into a hole.

We would have to cross it with our packs loose. If we stumbled we would probably experience no more than a freezing ducking, and quite likely the loss of a pack, but it didn't seem to constitute a threat to life.

We searched the banks until each of us possessed a sturdy pole to use as an upstream brace to assist our crossing. I sat in the sand and removed my heavy boots, coarse socks, and wool pants. I slipped into my nylon windpants and replaced the rubber boots. My wool pants and socks were crammed into the top of my pack. Heaving my pack onto my back, leaving the waist strap dangling, I trudged to the edge of the current with my rough pole grasped firmly. I was ready.

The first almost painful sensation as the icy water poured into my boots was followed by a series of thoughts and instructions to myself: lean heavily against the staff, keep moving, can't stay in one spot long, water washed footing out, slipping! Move another foot, quick! Annoying goose flesh sensations when I almost fell. Getting deeper, better try another direction. End of staff stuck in rocks. Careful. There, its dislodged. Move it over. So far so good. More than halfway now. Feet getting numb, cold. Getting shallower now. Foot sinking in mud. Ease it out. That's it, don't let your pack slip and throw you off balance. Don't fall now. Steady. Almost over. At last—God, my feet are cold.

We walked up and down the sandbar, looking for a likely crossing to the next sandbar. Then, carefully into the chilling, gritty water, and another crossing, and another sandbar, and so until a mile of rushing, frequently white water interspersed with rocky bars had been forded.

Sitting heavily upon the bank, I quickly dumped the icy water from my boots. My wool pants, socks, and then my boots were pulled back on over shivering wet legs. I tied my windpants to the back of my pack to dry, and took some moments to gaze back at the mountain. My eyelids began to droop heavily as fatigue overtook me. I jerked my head suddenly. Can't let up quite yet, I thought.

We were about to enter a forest of black spruce; about six miles would see us plod wearily into the ranger station at Wonder Lake to announce our survival. This might be my last opportunity for a final look at the mountain.

As I watched, a huge bank of clouds suddenly shielded the mountain from my view, as if to draw the curtain on our adventure. My mind was wandering over the many moods of Mount McKinley: Denali, the great one, the intense burning heat, the bitter cold, the ripping wind, the quiet, the gentleness, the awesome magnitude will continue though no eyes, no senses now perceive its might.

In the Woods of Lete

MAURICE HERZOG

Modern-day mountaineers sometimes utilize air transport to approach and depart from distant peaks with dazzling speed, but for most the treks still occur slowly on foot. They may be arduous, but are necessary if one is to climb the remote mountains of the world. Annapurna, in the Himalayas, was both remote and unknown when a French expedition led by Maurice Herzog climbed it in 1950, man's first ascent of an 8000 meter mountain. Their descent was difficult and followed by a lengthy and trying evacuation across torrential streams, through dangerous gorges and over endless ridges. They were racing to escape the monsoon rains and reach the Indian frontier from which their adventure had begun. Herzog and his climbing companion, Louise Lachenal, both disabled by frostbite, were confined to stretchers and forced to endure painful injections of drugs that were administered by the team doctor to counteract their injuries. For Herzog especially, as described in this chapter from his book, Annapurna, *his "triumphal return" became as much a battle of will and endurance as had been the fight for the summit.*

These wild-looking creatures, most of whom we recognized, arrived in small groups [Local men, called coolies by Westerners, were hired to transport material and food.] By miracle they had kept the rendezvous we had fixed with them a fortnight before, and Ichac was overjoyed. Soon he got the radio going; it was just about time for the weather report. A bulletin, specially broadcast for us, warned us of the approach of the monsoon proper:

This is All India Radio, calling on 60.48m. You will now hear a special weather bulletin for the French Expedition to Nepal: Monsoon extending over all eastern Himalaya will be reaching your area by June 10. Barometer pressure at Gorakhpur 980 millibars. I repeat: you have just heard a special bulletin . . .

So the storms of the last few days, which had added such hazards to our enterprise, were nothing but forerunners of this enormous disturbance which spreads over Asia at this season every year. The rains, which are torrential over the rest of India, become a solid deluge within a few hours of reaching the mountains. Tomorrow the skies would open and the floods would be upon us; but we heard the news calmly enough now that we were clear of the mountain.

A coolie handed a scrap of paper through the door of the tent: it was a note from Schatz, who had gone ahead to discover an easier crossing of the Miristi Khola gorges than we had made on the way up, and who now wrote that the volume of water had doubled in a single afternoon. So it became urgent to get away from this valley, which might easily become a vast trap, and though we said nothing we were all thinking of what had happened on Nanda Devi [an expedition that had had its retreat across a stream blocked by rising waters].

As forecast, the weather was bad next morning and rain fell ceaselessly. The Sherpas broke camp with feverish haste. We had given them orders to distribute to the coolies, before leaving, all the food we were unable to take down with us. The porters pounced gleefully on the tins and tubs which Sarki and Ang-Tharkey threw into the air by handfuls. Here was unlooked-for *bakshees*! Oudot, on the contrary, was beginning to run short of essential medical supplies. Bad luck lent a hand, too, for the needles had been dropped, and the syringes broke as he struggled with my arteries which were practically impossible to find.

The situation was serious; there were only two ampuls of acetylcholine left. Lachenal had had his two injections and my arms and right leg were done, and there we had to stop; but I was unmoved by this news which so distressed the others. I lay there like a dying man, in a state of extreme nervous excitement, knowing that these sessions were a terrible strain on my general condition.

While the last loads were leaving the camp under Ang-Tharkey's supervision, Lachenal started down. After a few yards the coolies abandoned the stretcher and the sledge was tried, but with no success. Oudot sent for the *cacolet*.

"We *must* get away at all costs," he said.

Before fixing him in it he gave Lachenal an injection of morphine. For me they found a wicker basket. The Sherpas hoisted me up and tucked my legs into a sleeping-bag covered by a *pied d'elephant*. Everything was soaked. From the walls all around us came echoes of rumbling avalanches mingled with the continual noise of falling stones loosened by the rain. The porter's naked feet sank into the soggy ground of the moraine on which they were walking, and we sent boulders flying down as we went. We were like the ragged remnant retreating in a disorderly rout from the scene of some catastrophe.

The column, composed of the two invalids, and of Oudot, Terray, Couzy, Ichac, Sarki and eight coolies moved with painful slowness. Should we be able to reach the prearranged stopping-place before night? Judging by the time we had taken on the way up, it *should* have been possible, even easy, but seeing the porters struggling beneath the weight of their burdens, and constantly sliding on the moraine where every step was a problem, we began to have our doubts. Time was passing but the clouds lifted and the rains stopped for a while. We lacked flashlights and food. Ang-Tharkey, unaware of our difficulties, had not made any provision for the party in the rear, so Sarki was sent on ahead with a message.

We were soon completely lost in a featureless country with neither color nor horizon. The scree of the moraine had given place to enormous boulders surrounded with a prickly vegetation which hindered our movements still further. The porters showed great fortitude, and made no complaint. Night fell and three flashlights discovered among our baggage were brought into action. The sahibs guided the coolies in the mist and the rain which had started up again harder than ever. It was past eight o'clock when the porters and their burdens, exhausted and disheartened, halted after an acrobatic descent of a slippery chimney down which somehow we had managed to come.

Lachenal and myself were placed under shelter; the others judged that we were in no fit state to go any farther that night. Terray decided to stay with us, while Couzy, Ichac, and Oudot went off rapidly toward the camp. They had only just left us when they met Sarki and Foutharkey coming up—with nothing but a flask of coffee by way of supplies! They sent Sarki on up to us and took Foutharkey back with them to the tents, which they reached after an hour. They told Schatz and Noyelle that it was not possible to carry the two casualties over such dangerous ground at night, and described our wretched bivouac. Immediately Schatz offered to take us up food and equipment, and Dawatondu went with him. In our shelter the situation wasn't ideal, in spite of Terray's efforts to cheer things up. Lachenal was still under the influence of morphine, but I was furious that we had failed to reach the camp, which I knew to be so near.

When we were no longer expecting anyone, Schatz arrived; water streamed down his face as he raised his startled eyes to mine, and with a little smile announced triumphantly that he had brought up sleeping bags, warm clothing and food. What more did we need? Soon a primus stove was roaring away. None of us had eaten since the morning and the smell of the open cans of food made Terray's mouth water. Meanwhile Dawatondu had inflated the mattresses and, though the food didn't tempt me, I enjoyed the comfort of a mattress. All night long it rained and I couldn't sleep. Deathly cold, my teeth chattering, I was haunted by anxiety and a shameful fear.

In the morning the weather improved. The formation of the clouds had changed, and they now tended to creep along the walls, and move upward. When this happens in Chamonix it means fine weather. Getting back into my wicker basket was unpleasant, and Lachenal, too, found little pleasure in returning to his *cacolet*. We were in a hurry to reach the camp and every few minutes I kept asking:

"Are we there?"

I always got the same answer, as though I were a child:

"Five minutes more!"

At last we saw the yellow roofs of the tents at the far end of a small flat space. The sky was clear when we reached the camp where Ichac, Noyelle, and Oudot welcomed us. We were not yet at the end of our troubles; the bridge which Schatz had built would not hold out until the evening: already it was only a foot above the water, and would in any case have to be reinforced before the loads and the casualties could be taken across. None of the coolies would volunteer to carry us over; and even the Sherpas thought it dangerous. Finally Adjiba made up his mind, and the others stood by to help him at the start and at the finish. From my tent I heard Lachenal being taken across, then Adjiba returned, I was hoisted on his back and with a firm step he went toward the bridge. This consisted simply of four or five tree trunks lashed together with liana and fixed somehow or other to either bank; the river went swirling by beneath, only just clearing the bridge, and spray wet the porters' feet, making them liable to slip. The feeling of helplessness was so awful, I wanted to shut my eyes. But I had to look, and though he carried me with great care I whispered in Adjiba's ear:

"Slowly, Abjiba!"

Would he be able to keep his balance on this rickety, slippery footbridge? Oudot, who was watching the operation, tried not to show his anxiety; his expressionless smile was intended to be encouraging. The moment we set foot on the bridge I could feel the precariousness of our situation. Adjiba calculated his moves and put each foot forward gingerly.

"Slowly, Adjiba!"

A few inches more—and then helping hands brought us safely to the bank. I heaved a deep sigh of relief, but at the same time felt a strong desire to cry: the inevitable nervous reaction after an ordeal. Adjiba took me at once into a tent and settled me there while the rest of the party hastily crossed the river, which was rising visibly. The coolies lined up to cross, and two hours later everything had been taken over. The expedition would not be trapped in the Annapurna massif, though by the following morning the bridge would have gone—swept away by the rushing torrent.

Oudot began to examine us at once, for he feared that the cold and damp of the previous night would have caused a deterioration in our condition. Lachenal's feet were very swollen and the improvement of the last few days was arrested. As for me, it was mainly my right hand that had suffered from our unfortunate bivouac. Oudot had assured me that the damage would not go beyond the end joints of my fingers. Now he said that at least two joints would have to go. [The frostbite had been severe enough to require the eventual amputation of several toes and fingers.] All these emotions tried me sorely.

We all gathered together in one tent for lunch. Schatz, who the day before had gone off to reconnoiter the Miristi gorges, told us that there was not the slightest chance of our being able to follow these gorges direct to Baglung and the Gandaki valley. This route would have avoided a long detour, but it was quite impractical: gigantic walls fell sheer to the river's edge over a distance of several miles, so that almost immediately we should have been forced to climb up out of the gorge to the ridges above—in other words to take the same route by which we had come on April 27.

We decided to dispatch Pansy as a special messenger to New Delhi to send off the telegrams we had written a few days ago. [These were to inform home countries of the successful ascent of Annapurna.]

I took little part in the conversation. When my attention was not needed I preferred to doze and not think about the present. My strength was ebbing and I dreaded the next stages of the march. After examining me once again Oudot did not hide the fact that it was difficult, in view of the extensiveness of my injuries, to foretell the course things would take. With half-closed eyes I heard him explaining to Ichac how dry gangrene can turn into gas gangrene, which necessitates immediate and extensive amputation. Ichac shuddered when Oudot told him that the toxins spreading from the affected parts to the living tissue become diffused over the whole body and produce general septicemia. Or sometimes it concentrated in one organ, the liver for example, particularly after antibiotic injections such as penicillin.

Meanwhile Terray was very adroitly constructing a chair in the shape of a hook, like those used for carrying in the Alps. He made it out of sticks fastened together with wire—it would enable the legs to be supported at the same level as the rest of the body, thus avoiding the wounded man's principal cause of suffering. The Sherpas copied Terray's model for me. The rain drummed ceaselessly on the tents, almost making us wonder whether the canvas would give way beneath the enormous bulletlike drops.

After a bad night I woke slowly and was told that the weather had improved. If only it would keep fine till evening! Today, they told me, we should have to go up from 12,000 to 15,000 feet over extremely steep slopes without any hope of a bivouac site before the pass of April 27. At all events the chairs were satisfactory. Thanks to Terray's ingenuity both Lachenal and I were slightly less apprehensive about the next stages of our journey.

The coolies climbed up steadily, although there was no track and sometimes steps had to be cut in the earth, so steep was the slope. Noiselessly as ghosts, they labored heroically through the mist to complete the allotted stage before nightfall. Shadows appeared and disappeared, outlines faded into the mist. This retreat would have seemed like a dream, and the men mere phantoms, had it not been for the jolting of my chair, which caused pain in every part of my body. I tried my best to keep drowsy and semiconscious, and envied Lachenal who managed to go to sleep on the back of his porter.

A little before noon the main contingent had ascended the grassy gullies and reached the C.A.F. shoulder—the point at which Schatz had left a Club Alpin Français pennant on the way up. The coolies wanted to camp here, saying that higher up there would be no better site, but Ichac and Oudot turned deaf ears to this suggestion. They sent the casualties ahead and themselves walked with the Sherpas; the coolies were obliged to follow. The long, long traverse across the pass of April 27 had begun.

Visibility was down to ten yards, and the porters walked in single file. They kept warm while they were moving with their loads, but as soon as they stopped their teeth began to chatter, for their only clothing was a small blanket. I tried to adjust myself to the swaying rhythm of my bearer, but he continually upset my calculations by hesitating, taking a longer or a shorter step, or, in certain awkward places, striding sideways. I could not stop trying to stretch out my arms in an endeavor to hold back or help on, or with the idea of protecting myself. Far away in the depths of its infernal gorges I heard the roar of the Miristi.

At the end of the afternoon we came upon the site of a shepherd's camp, the only one before the pass, which there was obviously no question of our reaching that evening. Prudence demanded that we should remain where we were for the night, and all that I asked was to be put down in a tent where I could lie still.

Dawn was sullen and we left in pouring rain, with visibility less than twenty yards. We had to continue the flanking movement and cross a whole series of streams which would be no easy matter. It was a sad day for me. I felt quite definitely that my condition was getting worse: I was aware that I had no reserves and I was profoundly disheartened.

For some time Schatz had been trying to encourage me with the assurance that the ridge was no longer very far off. There came a shout of triumph, but although Ichac was only a few yards away I could barely hear him:

"Maurice, you're on the Krishna side now!"

I was not particularly elated, although it was an important moment. As I passed in front of Ichac I saw him shooting with his movie camera. It struck me as a crazy proceeding—surely it wouldn't come out—there was no light, and this, as he had often enough told me, was essential for color film.

We began to descend gradually to the pass. At each step the porters let themselves slide down the slope, feet foremost, and the violent jerking caused me unbearable pain. To go on was madness, and, moreover, I just didn't feel capable of standing another couple of hours of this torture. I implored Ichac to stop everyone and go up again to the site we had passed. Very unwillingly those in front retraced their steps, while the Sherpas pitched the tents on the soaking ground.

We had now come to the last really hard day: we should have to descend for some 6,000 feet to the Chadziou Khola and the shepherd's camping ground. How would all the porters manage, especially those who would have to carry the two casualties across the terribly steep slopes on this part of the route?

Right at the beginning, on leaving the gap marked with a *chorten*, one of the coolies slipped and rolled down for fifty yards or so. We feared he would disappear into the river 6,000 feet below but he clung on and brought himself to a stop; for a moment he lay stretched out on the ground. The sack he had been carrying went bowling down the slope as well as a container, which burst open. The sack bounced, described a fine curve and disappeared into space. The man was only dazed; he picked himself up and came back toward us. He was a Tibetan from Tukucha, and one of the few who had consented to wear expedition boots!

I heard a frightful yell. I couldn't see what was happening, but I could guess from the shouts: a huge stone had fallen above Lachenal in the *couloir*. Terray succeeded in diverting it from its course, but the rock had hit Lachenal's bearer. The man fell without being able to protect himself; his arms were caught in his *cagoule*, and the block hit him on the nose. His face was covered with blood and he had an enormous bruise. It was not exactly an encouraging portent.

Ichac, Rebuffat, and Schatz went down the great pass *couloir*, the haunt of the marmots discovered by Rebuffat on the way up. They stopped at the first trees while the rest of the party came carefully down in their turn. To find out the owner of the sack that had fallen into the Chadziou Khola, they decided to check the loads as they were carried past on the porters' backs.

"I think it was mine," said Schatz, "and for once both my fountain pen and wallet were in it!"

Schatz was staring at a porter—he lifted up a sack that was concealing another and saw the name written plainly for all to see on the main pocket: "M. Schatz."

"There's no doubt," said Ichac, proceeding by elimination, "it must be Gaston's."

Rebuffat wasn't pleased. This retreat had been an ordeal for him too: and his frostbitten feet were still giving him some trouble. I saw him sitting down disconsolately, thinking of what he had lost. Suddenly Ichac had an inspiration.

"Gaston, look what you're sitting on!"

He shot up like a jack-in-the-box and read on the sack: "G. Rebuffat." The lost sack turned out to be the only one that belonged to no one: it contained spare clothes.

We were now in the forest, which was extraordinarily thick and tangled; we felt as if we were walking through submarine scenery in a damp, unhealthy jungle, expecting at any moment to meet hideous monsters. It was here that, on the way up, we had seen those giant rhododendrons of such magnificent shades of red. We entered the "triumphal way," a natural archway of flowers, which we had noticed on the outward journey. The coolies in front had stopped here—and why not? There was a general halt and soon fires were crackling. Oudot was of the opinion that the hardest part of this stage still lay ahead, and he wanted to go on at all costs. He gave me fresh injections of morphine and spartocamphor—these were the more painful because I had grown so thin, and I lost consciousness for a few moments. I felt the eyes of the Sherpas and coolies upon me. What a sight I must have been! There was a new expression in their eyes, which I had not seen before. Was it pity, or grief, or a kindly indifference? Before we left, they arranged on my knees a garland of the most beautiful flowers they could find. This gesture touched me deeply, and from now on during the whole course of our long retreat, whenever it was possible, the Sherpas never once forgot to put flowers beside me.

Now began the descent through the dead trees of the dense jungle. The Sherpas went ahead, and with great sweeps of their *kukris* cut away the branches and bamboos that barred the way. The ground was soaking and everyone kept slipping—there was scarcely a man who did not fall that day. Couzy, Ichac, Oudot, Schatz, and Terray went on to reconnoiter the route: Noyelle, according to plan, was always one march ahead, and Rebuffat stayed with Lachenal and myself. The injections Oudot had given me were very effective: I was completely worn out, but I felt less pain, and most of the time I dozed with my eyes half shut. Lachenal followed immediately behind me. The last bit before the river was particularly steep, and I would never have given myself one chance in a thousand of coming through alive. The slope was practically vertical and the minute track crossed it at an angle; the coolies had to cling to the trees growing alongside.

My bearer was in trouble; he could move neither backward nor forward. Finally he pressed himself up against the wall and went along sideways step by step. The hook-shaped chair in which I was stowed hung right over the precipice. Now and again the Sherpas dug their ice-axes into the wet ground and clung to them desperately the better to help my bearer. I was painfully aware of the slightest jolt. With bulging eyes I looked under my feet at the swirling Chadziou Khola into which I was in danger of falling at every step. If the porter slipped there would be no chance—perhaps he would be able to stop himself, but who could stop me? I no longer had the strength to fight my fears, and I knew now what fear really was. Lachenal also was petrified by fright. Fortunately for him, his arms were free and occasionally he was able to help himself. Every step was a reprieve, for it brought us nearer our goal. Before we arrived there was one last ordeal. For about five yards the track, which was always sketchy, disappeared entirely. A little ledge ran across a slab or rock and the feet had to be shuffled along it. My bearer carried on with great courage—my admiration for these men who unhesitatingly tackled such dangerous work was unbounded. He moved along sideways, clinging to the smallest holds, and letting the other porters guide his feet into the next steps.

At long last we reached the Chadziou Khola, swollen by the monsoon rains, which we had nonetheless to ford. Lachenal was following me over this dangerous crossing, and for all his fear, seemed completely master of himself, while I was a mere human wreck. Standing shoulder to shoulder and holding each other up, the porters succeeded in bracing themselves against the force of the current. We climbed up a hundred yards through strongly scented jungle and then, in the distance, I saw the shepherd's camp.

The porters halted before making this final effort, but after a few minutes I asked my bearer to get to the camp as quickly as he could. At the foot of a cliff it seemed to me that he took the wrong direction—on the way out we had traversed across, but the Sherpas who accompanied us seemed to be quite sure of the route. On we went, and the way ran up such a steep grass slope that we had to adopt the technique we would have used for traversing on ice. The Sherpas persisted and here we were embarked on a regular climb. I called nervously to Ichac to intervene, saying that we were about to have a frightful fall, but the porters were obstinate. We were beneath a sort of cornice overhanging a practically vertical wall and the rock was rotten. Perched up on my bearer and sticking out a yard from the rock, I was able to gaze into the very depths of the gorge below me. The Sherpas were worried and told me that my bearer could not turn around; he must go on. I could not stand any more and called for help—but still, I reflected, my luck had held during many a long day. After a few steps the going became easier and we got back onto grass and picked up the track which we ought to have followed from the beginning, and which Lachenal now took profiting from our experience. We reached the camp just as the rain stopped.

As I went into my tent I longed for nothing but peace and quiet. I scarcely had the strength to speak, but I murmured to Oudot that the hard part was over now—there was a good path as far as Lete. I remembered a larchwood near the village and beautiful meadows dotted with granite boulders which reminded me of the Chamonix Valley. During the long retreat I had thought of this idyllic little wood as a welcoming haven. I hoped we should make a long halt there, and my friends agreed. It was unnecessary for everyone to go up to Tukucha and back again to Lete. We would reorganize the whole expedition in this wood before beginning the long trek homeward through the valleys of Nepal to the Indian frontier.

"Where's my ice-axe?" I asked Schatz.

I set great store by it; as Lachenal had lost his, it was the only one to have been to the top of Annapurna. No one had seen it since we had left Base Camp. Schatz inspected all the Sherpas' axes, but it was not to be found. I felt this loss deeply. Though in itself it was of no importance, I had intended to present the axe to the French Alpine Club on my return. It turned up two days later.

The next day we had only a short march. As Oudot reckoned that we should reach the woods of Lete before midday, there was no need to hurry, and we might just as well enjoy the few rays of sun that had appeared as if by magic. The coolies started off and then we, too, left the shepherd's camp.

We arrived together at Choya and we were enthusiastically received. The inhabitants rushed toward us and looked at the casualties with curiosity. Dawantondu's throat must have been dry as he remembered the pleasure of the outward journey, and Ang-Tharkey volubly explained to Ichac and Oudot that this would be an excellent place to pitch camp—there was water, wood, and food.

"*Good place!*" insisted our Sidar. There was also good *chang* at Choya. But somehow the Sahibs didn't seem to understand. *En route!* Unwillingly the party moved on and soon we came to the banks of the Krishna Gandaki. Its clear, pure waters had become a dirty black flood, foaming and swirling and making an infernal noise. We crossed over by a bridge without any incident, and after a short hour's walk at last reached the resting place of which I had dreamed so long.

We chose a good-sized grassy site, bounded by three enormous granite boulders, and surrounded by the soft green of the larches— a cool and restful place. The wind played among the tall trees, and, closing my eyes, I fancied myself back in Chamonix. The tents were pitched where the Sherpas pleased. The sun was warm, and Oudot decided to make his examinations out of doors. One of my feet had begun to suppurate, and my hands were in an awful state. There was a most unpleasant nauseating smell; all the bandages were soaked with pus. Oudot broke into his last reserves of dressings—he knew that fresh equipment would be coming from Tukucha. For the first time he took his scissors and began "trimming," or cutting away the dead and affected parts. My feet did not hurt too badly, but my hands were so sensitive that the slightest touch made me cry out in pain, and I broke down—I could fight no longer. Oudot decided to stop. He painted the wounds with mercurochrome.

"Stay outside while I do Lachenal," he said.

Lachenal's condition had improved. He had come through the ordeals of the retreat very well indeed, and his morale was high, now that we were down in the valley; his excellent appetite had not deserted him.

In the afternoon Ichac, Oudot and Schatz left for Tukucha, where they were welcomed by Noyelle and G. B. Rana. That evening, in the few tents still standing, they talked at length, but not very cheerfully, for their main topic was Lachenal's and my condition. Oudot was of the opinion that I would undoubtedly have to undergo an operation before we reached the Indian frontier, which would not be until the first fortnight of July.

The next day the dismantling of camp was completed before a circle of coolies and children who squatted there hour after hour, keeping a lookout for tins or old tubes of milk. Noyelle saw to paying off the porters, and there was a grand distribution of rupees. In the afternoon Oudot finished his preparations and left to return to Lete and his patients.

Twenty-four hours later everything was ready for the others to leave the village, which had given us such a kindly welcome and had been our headquarters for nearly two months. The coolies and the inhabitants paid their farewell respects to the sahibs with a series of shouts. At four o'clock everyone was back at Lete.

The condition of the casualties, of myself in particular, was now distinctly alarming; when Oudot returned the day before he pronounced the situation critical. He had been hard at it since morning, resuming the agonizing injections. I presented an increasingly distressing picture. I had lost over forty pounds and become extremely thin. The fever steadily mounted—that evening my temperature was 105°!

"102°," announced Ichac without batting an eyelid.

I was oblivious of everything now, unconscious most of the time, in a coma.

"Heavy dose of penicillin," ordered Oudot.

Shadows appeared close by out of the mist. They leaned over, then disappeared noiselessly. The silence awed me. I no longer suffered. My friends attended to me in silence. The job was finished, and my conscience was clear. Gathering together the last shreds of energy, in one long last prayer, I implored death to come and deliver me. I had lost the will to live, and I was giving up—the ultimate humiliation for a man, who, up till then, had always taken a pride in himself.

This was no time for questions nor for regrets. I looked death straight in the face, besought it with all my strength. Then abruptly I had a vision of the life of men. Those who are leaving it forever are never alone. Resting against the mountain, which was watching over me, I discovered horizons I had never seen. There at my feet, on those vast plains, millions of beings were following a destiny they had not chosen.

There is a supernatural power in those close to death. Strange intuitions identify one with the whole world. The mountain spoke with the wind as it whistled over the ridge or ruffled the foliage. All would end well. I should remain there, forever, beneath a few stones and a cross.

They had given me my ice-axe. The breeze was gently and sweetly scented. My friends departed, knowing, that I was now safe. I watched them go their way with slow, sad steps. The procession withdrew along the narrow path. They would regain the plains and the wide horizons. For me, silence.

"Tenzing Zindabad!"

TENZING NORGAY

Mountaineers normally conduct their lonely sport far from the public eye and the media—that is unless the prize is great. Then, nationalism and politics often intrudes, as when Adolf Hilter awarded several German climbers Olympic Gold Medals for their first ascent of the highly contested Eiger North Face. No conquest was more nationally celebrated, however, than that of Mt. Everest by Colonel Hunt's British expedition in 1953. When the Sherpa Tenzing Norgay first stepped to the summit with Edmund Hillary and then descended victoriously, he thought only joy and personal satisfaction would follow. He was wrong. Describing the aftermath of their climb in his autobiography, Tiger of the Snows, *Tenzing relates the pleasures and pratfalls of becoming an international climbing hero in a typically obscure sport.*

Yes, the happiness came. And later other things too.

But first the happiness.

The next day the weather was again fine. The sun was shining. And though we were, of course, still tired, and a little weak from our three days at such great heights, it was with a joy and peace of spirit that we made the long descent from the South Col. The sahibs left most of their things at Camp Eight, but I carried three or four bags of equipment, a flask, and also one of Lowe's two cameras, which he had forgotten in the excitement. On the way we kept meeting our friends who had been waiting for us below. At Camp Seven were Major Wylie and several Sherpas. Below Camp Six Tom

Stobart came up to meet us with his moving picture camera. And at Camp Five were several more Sherpas, including Dawa Thondup and my young nephew Gombu. At each meeting there was much talk and excitement, and at Five the Sherpas gave us tea and insisted on carrying my load for the rest of the way down.

Then at Camp Four, the advance base, we met the main part of the expedition. As we descended the long snow slope of the cwm they came out to meet us, and at first we gave no sign of what had happened. But when we were about fifty yards away Lowe could keep the secret no longer. With one hand he made the "thumbs up" sign and with the other he waved his ax toward the summit, and from that minute on I think there has never been such excitement in the history of the Himalayas. Even with their boots and in the thick snow, they came almost running toward us. Hunt embraced Hillary and me. I embraced Evans. Everybody embraced everybody. "Is it really true? Is it really true?" Hunt kept saying over and over. And then he hugged me again in joy. Anyone who had seen us then could never have thought about distinctions between sahibs and Sherpas. We were all mountaineers together, who had climbed our mountain.

For hours then we drank and ate and rested—and talked and talked. It was a wonderful evening; the happiest, I think of my whole life. But, although I did not know it then, certain things had already begun to happen which were later to cause much difficulty and misunderstanding. A short while before, a false report had gone out over the Indian Wireless News that we had failed in our attempt. Now the true report was sent: first down to Namche Bazar and then by radio from there to Katmandu. But it was sent in code, and only to the British Ambassador, Mr. Summerhayes, who forwarded it to London but did not inform anyone else for more than a day. The idea, I believe, was for the Queen of England to have the news first, and for it to be made known the next day as a special feature of her coronation. For the British the timing was perfect, and there was a wonderful celebration. But for many Easterners it was quite the opposite, for they did not receive the news until a day later—and then from the other side of the world. This was true even for King Tribhuvana of Nepal, in whose country Everest stands.

At the time, as I say, I knew nothing about all this. I myself could have sent the news right away by Sherpa runner to Namche Bazar, and perhaps things would have worked out differently. But I asked myself, "Why should I?" I was working for the British. As we Sherpas say, I was "eating their salt." They had run the expedition; why should they not handle this in their own way? So I sent no message, and I told the other Sherpas not to break the news until it was official. Later there was loose talk that I had been paid by the British to do this—and even that I had been bribed to say that Everest had been climbed when it really had not been. To the first of these accusations I can say only that it was completely untrue. The second is so ridiculous that it is not worth answering.

When I say I sent no message I mean no public one, to be announced at once. But now for the first time in weeks and months I was able to think of something besides climbing—besides getting to the top—and my mind turned to my loved ones who were waiting for me back home. That night at Camp Four one of my friends wrote a note for me to Ang Lahmu. *This letter is from Tenzing*, it said. *Myself along with one sahib reached summit Everest 29th May. Hope you will feel happy. Cannot write more. May I be excused.* And at the bottom I myself signed my name.

I spent only one night at Camp Four. Half of it was celebration, half rest. The next morning my only thought was to get down off the mountain, and in one day I descended the cwn and the icefall, all the way to base camp, with the Sherpa Ang Tshering and my nephew Gombu. "Now I am free," I kept thinking. "I have been freed by Everest." And luckily I could not know yet how wrong I was. At base camp, too, I stayed only one night, and then, in another single day, I went thirty-five miles down the glacier and valleys to Thamey, to see my mother. I told her we had had success, and she was very happy. Staring up into my face, she said to me, "Many times I have told you not to go to this mountain. Now you don't have to go again." All her life she had believed that there was a golden sparrow on the top of Everest, and also a turquoise lion with a golden mane; and when she asked me about them I was sorry to have to disappoint her. But when she asked if I had seen the Rongbuk Monastery from the top I was able to say yes—and this pleased her.

I had come to Thamey alone. Now I spent two days there with my mother and my younger sister, who lived with her, and it was the first time since I had been a child that I had been so long in my native village. All the people came around, the *chang* flowed, and I am willing to admit that, as the English say, I "broke training." Then, remembering my duties to the expedition, I collected a hundred men to serve as porters on the return trip to Katmandu and left with them for Thyangboche. Before going, I asked my mother if she would like to come with me and live in Darjeeling; and she said, "Yes, I would like it. But I am too old. I would be too much trouble to you." Though I tried to persuade her, she would not come, and once again I had to tell my *ama la* good-bye. But on the way from Thamey to Thyangboche I met my older sister, Lahmu Kipa, with her husband and two daughters, and being younger, they decided to come along.

At Thyangboche the expedition was coming back in sections from the mountain, and everything was excitement and confusion. One of the worst problems was to get enough porters for the return trip, for the monsoon rains would soon be beginning, and few people wanted to go. Also, there was almost as much complaining as rejoicing that Everest had been climbed, for now they were afraid there would be no more expeditions and no more jobs. And the lamas (who had never encouraged its climbing) were afraid that our success would bring bad luck from the gods. After a little while, though, we got at least some sort of organization and made ready to leave. Colonel Hunt said that he was going ahead of the main party, to make various arrangements, and that one of them would be back to take me along to England. This idea had not occurred to me before. If I had thought anything about the future it was only that I would go back to Darjeeling and rest, and later, if I had enough money, build a small new house. I still hadn't any notion at all of what was going to happen to me.

It was not long, though, before I began to see that things were going to be very different from before. Already at Thyangboche there was a wireless for me from Sir Winston Churchill, and from then on the messages were like a flood. Also, there was one message I wanted to send myself—to Ang Lahmu, asking her and the girls to meet me in Katmandu—and I spoke to Major Wylie about this, saying I would pay for a special runner. As always, he was kind and helpful; the message was sent at expedition expense. And in the days that followed, as we took the long trail at Katmandu, he was good to me in many ways—giving me sound advice, helping me with strangers and even acting as a sort of secretary for me with all the messages that were coming in. "Now you see what sort of life you have to face," he told me. But this was just the beginning and I was still to learn my lessons the hard way.

Up and down we went across the hills and valleys of Nepal. And each day there were bigger crowds and more excitement. After about ten days, when we were some fifty miles from Katmandu, I received word that Ang Lahmu and the girls had arrived there—and that was fine news. But most of the people who came out were not bringing news, but looking for it, and soon I was walking along in the middle of a whole parade of journalists. Some were Nepali, some Indian, some British, and some American, and besides the story of the climb, many of them wanted me to make all sorts of statements about nationality and politics. Major Wylie had warned me this might happen and told me to be careful; and I tried to be. But it was not easy, with so many people crowding around and asking questions all at once, and half the time, it seemed to me, they were not only asking the questions but giving the answers, too. At a place called Hukse I had a good interview with James Burke of *Life* magazine, which had bought the American rights to the expedition story from the London *Times*. And a little farther on I met a representative of the United Press Association, with which I later signed a contract for a series of articles. The English climbers could not do anything like this. Before starting out they had signed an agreement that all stories and photographs would belong to the expedition as a whole, which in turn had its contract with the *Times*. But, though ranked as an expedition member, I had not been asked to do this, so that now I was free to deal with whom I chose. When we reached Katmandu, and later New Delhi, there was some discussion and argument about this, for the *Times* thought it had the rights to the story of *everyone* on the expedition; and Colonel Hunt offered me 500 rupees a month if I would sign the agreement like the others. But I declined to do this. For the first time in my life I was in a position to make a considerable sum of money, and I could not see why it was not right and proper for me to do so.

This, however, was only a small trouble. The big one started at a place called Dhaulagat, a little before Katmandu, when a crowd of Nepali came out to meet me and almost tore me away from the rest of the expedition. I have been often asked since if they were Communists, and this I do not honestly know. But I do know that they were nationalists, with very strong ideas, and what they were interested in was not Everest at all, or how Everest was really climbed—but only politics. They wanted me to say that I was a Nepali, not an Indian. And, also that I got to the top ahead of Hillary. I told them I was not concerned with politics or arguments with the British. I begged them to leave me alone. "Up till now," I told them, "nobody cared about my nationality. Why do you care now? Indian—Nepali. What difference does it make?" I tried to say again what I had said in the interview with James Burke: "We should all be the same—Hillary, myself, Indian, Nepali, everybody."

But they would not stop. They drove me almost crazy. They put answers in my mouth and made me sign papers that I could not read. And all the time the crowd grew bigger and bigger. I was separated from my companions, pushed and pulled around like some sort of child's toy. "What are they going to do with me?" I wondered. "If I had known it was going to be like this I would have stayed up in Solo Khumbu." When, on June 20, we walked down the last hills into the Valley of Nepal they were still pushing and pulling. At Bonepa, where the road begins, the put me into a Jeep and made me change into Nepali clothes, and by this time I was so exhausted and confused that I let them do as they like. In every town and village through which we passed there was a big celebration. People crowded around, waving flags and banners. *"Tenzing zindabad!"* they shouted. "Long live Tenzing!" And in a way it was wonderful to be so warmly greeted. But I confess I would rather have returned simply and quietly, as from every other expedition on which I had ever been.

Three miles outside Katmandu my wife and daughters were waiting for me, and we had warm embraces of happiness and victory. Ang Lahmu put a *khada*, or sacred scarf, around my neck. Pem Pem and Nima covered my shoulders with garlands, and I told Nima with a smile that I had put her pencil where she had asked me to. Later I learned that, during those past few weeks, things had been almost as confused for them as for me. They had first heard the great news on the morning of June 2, a rainy, gloomy day in Darjeeling, from friends who had been listening to the radio; and from that minute on their lives had changed completely. Important officials had come to call on them. There had been all sorts of messages, many plans and counterplans. Pictures of me, they said, were all over the town, and my friend Mitra had had a poet compose a song with music about me that was soon being sung up and down the streets. It had all been wonderful and exciting for them, but what they had wanted most of all was to hear from me, and the message I had sent telling them to come to Katmandu had never arrived. Ang Lahmu, on her own, had wanted very much to come, but had been afraid I might be angry if she did so unexpectedly. "Why is there no wire from my husband?" she had kept asking. "I will pay ten rupees to the boy who brings it from the telegraph office." But still my wire did not arrive (what went wrong I had never found out), and after waiting eleven days she decided to come anyhow. She had neither money nor proper clothes, but Mita gave her a hundred rupees he had made from the sale of my photographs, and later, with the help of Mrs. Henderson, of the Himalayan Club, and other friends, he raised another four hundred rupees toward the expenses. She and the girls had left Darjeeling and flown to Katmandu by way of Patna, arriving four days before me. With them had come Pasang Phutar (still a third one), a veteran mountain man who is both a close friend and relative of ours, and Lhakpa Tschering, an educated Sherpa who came as representative of our Sherpa Association.

But there was little time to talk of any of this on that crazy day when I myself reached Katmandu. After a few minutes I was pulled away from my family. I was taken out of the Jeep and put in a sort of big chariot, pulled by horses; and now many of the other climbers, whom I had not seen for some time, were there too, and Hunt and Hillary were also put in the chariot. Then we were moving into the city, and the crowds were thicker than ever. They threw rice and colored powder and coins, and the coins kept bouncing off my skull until I thought I was going to get a headache. But there was nothing I could do about it, because I could not look in all directions at once. Most of the time I just stood in the chariot smiling, with the palms of my hands together and the fingers upward, in the ancient Hindu greeting of *namaste*.

So many things were happening that it is hard to remember what came first and what afterwards. With most of us still in our dirty old expedition clothes, we were taken to the royal palace and welcomed by King Tribhuvana, who awarded me the *Nepal Tara* (Star Of Nepal), the highest decoration of the country, and gave two other medals to Hunt and Hillary. As with so many things at this time, the question of honors, and who received what, caused difficulty and misunderstanding. For at about the same time I was given one Nepalse award, and Hunt and Hillary another, lesser one, word came from England that the Queen had given them knighthoods, while I would simply receive the George Medal. The fuss that this caused was not only unfortunate, but foolish. Since winning its independence, the government of India, like that of the United States, has not permitted its citizens to accept foreign titles, and if anything, it would probably only have embarrassed both myself and my country if the Queen had offered such an honor. For me it was *kai chai na*—no matter. Would a title give me wings? And after I understood the reasons I in no way felt slighted or offended.

Politic—politics: suddenly they were making trouble everywhere. The Nepalese were wonderful to me. They gave me a welcome I could not forget in a hundred lifetimes. But in their effort to make me a hero they went too far; they almost ignored the British, instead of treating them as honored guests; and too many of them said foolish things and tried to twist the true facts for political reasons. There were all sorts of crazy stories around: that I had dragged Hillary to the top of Everest, that he had not got there at all, that I had practically climbed the whole mountain all by myself. And unfortunately there were the foolish statements I had been made to sign, without knowing what I was doing, when I was picked up by that wild crowd outside Katmandu. Finally the whole thing had got too much for Colonel Hunt. He lost his temper and implied that, far from being a hero, I wasn't even, technically, a very good climber. And this, of course, was like pouring kerosene on a fire.

Nepalese and Indian journalists kept after me all the time. People with political motives tried to get me to say things against the British, and because I was hurt at what Colonel Hunt had said, I, too, made a few statements that I later regretted. Luckily, though, there was much more good will than bad in our hearts. Neither the British nor I wanted to see our great adventure made into something small and mean. So on the twenty-second of June we met together in the office of the Prime Minister of Nepal and prepared a statement that we hoped would put an end to all the trouble. One copy was signed by me for Hillary, one by Hillary for me, and this second one, which I still have, reads:

> On May 29th Tenzing Sherpa and I left our high camp on Mount Evereyst for our attempt on the summit.
>
> As we climbed upwards to the south summit first one and then the other would take a turn leading.
>
> We crossed over the south summit and moved along the summit ridge. We reached the summit almost together.

We embraced each other, overjoyed at our success; then I took photographs of Tenzing holding aloft the flags of Great Britian, Nepal, the United Nations and India.

(signed) E. P. Hillary

Everything in the statement is true. Certainly nothing could be truer than that we reached the top *almost together*. And that is how the matter has been left until this time—when, for reasons I have already given, it seems right to me to tell all the details.

Beside the question of who reached the top first there was much talk and argument about my nationality. "What difference does it make?" I kept asking. "What do nationality and politics have to do with climbing a mountain?" But still the talk went on, and so I spoke about this too to the Prime Minister, Mr. Koirala. I said to him, "I love Nepal. I was born here, and it is my country. But for a long time now I have been living in India. My children have grown up there, and I must think of their education and livelihood." Mr. Koirala and the other ministers were kind and considerate. They did not, as some other had, try to put pressure on me, but only said that if I decided to stay in Nepal they would give me a house, along with other rewards and benefits; and they wished me luck and happiness, whatever my decision might be. I am still deeply grateful for their helpfulness when I was in a difficult situation. As I said then to the press: "I was born in the womb of Nepal and raised in the lap of India." I love both. And I feel I am the son of both.

We stayed in Katmandu for about a week. And every day there were new events, new celebrations—and new problems. This time we Sherpas slept, not in a garage, but in the Nepalese Government guest house; so there was no difficulty there. Or if there was, it was only in trying to keep out the crowds of people who wanted to swarm all over us. One evening there was a reception at the British Embassy. I was invited, but declined to go; and since this, like so many other things at the time, caused much loose talk, I shall explain the reason. It was that, the year before, when I was in Katmandu with the Swiss, I had had an unpleasant experience there. On a certain night there had been some sort of mixup in the expedition arrangements; I found myself with no place to sleep; and having stayed at the Embassy with Tilman in 1949, I went there and asked for shelter. It was a mistake, though. Colonel Proud, the First Secretary, turned me away. My feelings were badly hurt. And since Colonel Proud was now still at the Embassy I preferred not to accept its hospitality. This was the only reason I did not go that evening, and it was in no way intended as an unfriendly gesture to my comrades of Everest.

When I left Katmandu it was for Calcutta, in the private plane of King Tribhuvana. There was just myself and my family, with Lhapka Tschering, who was now acting as a sort of adviser to me. The others were going down to India in different ways. At Calcutta we were put up at Government House, and there was some excitement, more receptions, more *zindabad*. Among those who met us there were my good friend Mitra, whom I had wired to come down from Darjeeling, and one of the first things I did was to give him Raymond Lambert's red scarf and ask him to send it to Switzerland. [Tenzing and Lambert were close friends and members of the 1952 Swiss Everest Expedition. Together they reached 28,210 feet and, but for bad weather, would probably have made the first ascent of Everest that year.] Also while in Calcutta I told my story to the United Press, with whom I had now signed a contract. For a few days, at this time, it looked as if I would not be going to England after all, because I had decided it would not be right to go without Ang Lahmu and the girls, and the expedition had no money to take them. Meanwhile the London *Daily Express* offered me a big tour, with all expenses paid; but after thinking it over I refused, because I was afraid it would have some sort of political significance and after my experience in Nepal this was the one thing, more than anything else, that I wanted to keep away from. Instead, I went from Calcutta to New Delhi, where the rest of the expedition was gathered, still hoping that something could be worked out.

In Delhi it was the same as in Katmandu and Calcutta. Only more so. At the airport, when we arrived, there was a great welcome, with the biggest crowds I had seen in my life. Then we were driven to the Nepalese Embassy, where we were to stay, and that same evening there was a reception given by Pandit Nehru. This was a great moment for me—the moment Professor Tucci had spoken of long ago in Tibet and that thought of that night in my tent, high on Everest. And, in every way, it came up to what I had hoped and dreamed it might be. For, from the very first, Panditji [A term of affection and respect often applied to Nehru by Indians] was like a father to me. He was warm and kind, and, unlike so many others, was not thinking of what use he could make of me, but only of how he could help me and make me happy. The day after the reception he invited me to his office, and there he strongly advised me to go to London. There had already, he thought, been too much trouble and argument about the climb; Everest was better without politics; and he hoped everything possible would be done to heal any wounds that had been caused. With this I agreed with all my heart. And then, to make everything wonderful, he said it would be arranged that my wife and daughters could go to London with me.

Nor was this all Panditji did. Later he took me to his home, and since I had almost no clothes of my own, he opened his closets and began giving me his. He gave me coats, trousers, shirts, everything—because we are the same size they all fitted perfectly —and also some things that had belonged to his father and on which he placed great value. To Ang Lahmu he presented a fine pocketbook and a raincoat, saying with a smile that it rained a lot in London. And as still another gift for me there was a briefcase, so that I felt, "Now I am no longer a poor Sherpa at all, but a businessman or a diplomat." About the only thing to wear or carry he did not give me was one of his white Congress Party caps; for that would have had political meaning, and he completely agreed with me that I should stay out of politics.

While I was in Delhi there was also the question of a passport, which, in spite of all my traveling, would be the first I had ever had. As it turned out I was given not one, but two—one Indian and one Nepalese—and this was just the way I wanted it. Then, a few days later, we flew off toward the West. There were no other Sherpas with us, except Lhakpa Tschering, who was still acting as my adviser. The climbing Sherpas had not even come to Calcutta or Delhi but had gone straight home from Katmandu to Darjeeling. But most of the English expedition members were also aboard the plane, and besides Ang Lahmu and the girls there was also Mrs.— or now Lady—Hunt, who had flown out to meet her husband while we were still in Nepal. We flew in a BOAC plane, and our first stop was Karachi, where we stayed for an hour while another great crowd came out to see us. Then we went on to Baghdad, Cairo, and Rome, and I was at last seeing the world beyond India and Pakistan that I had dreamed of so often in the past.

In Rome we were welcomed by the Indian and British ambassadors, and then, because of engine trouble with the plane, we spend the night there. The next morning, when we boarded the plane again, Colonel Hunt looked upset about something, and soon I found out what it was. The newspapers had just published the first part of my story, which I had given to the United Press, and in it I had told something of the difficulties that had arisen during the expedition between the British and the Sherpas. As we flew north he came over and spoke to me, and we talked frankly about the things that had happened. I told him how hurt I had been at his statement to the press that I was not an experienced climber, and he in turn explained the problem he had had to face. Major Wylie had already spoken to me of these matters. He had pointed out how important it was that there be no ill will because of them, and I had agreed with him. And this I now said to Colonel Hunt. There *had* been certain difficulties during the expedition and afterward. There was no use denying it, and I had simply told the story from my own point of view, as honestly as I could. But this did not mean that I bore any grudge, or that I was trying to make an issue of these difficulties, as certain others had done for political purposes. Our talk was candid and friendly, and I think we both felt better for having had it.

After Rome, our next stop was Zurich. Though we stayed there only a short while, it was a wonderful time for me, for many of my old Swiss friends were at the airport to meet me. Best of all, Lambert was there, with a big embrace and a welcoming "Ca va bien," and

I told him about the final climb with Hillary and how I had been thinking of him when I stood on the summit. Then we flew on to London. Just before we landed Colonel Hunt asked if it was all right with me if he came out of the plane first, carrying a Union Jack attached to an ice-ax; and I said, "Of course it is all right." So that was the way it was, and soon all of us were out on the landing strip and in the middle of another great reception.

In London my family and I stayed at the Indian Services Club, and we were wonderfully looked after by the Indian Ambassador, Mr. B. G. Kher. Right after we arrived the other expedition members scattered all over England to visit their homes and family, so that I was almost the only one left in the city; but I was certainly not at a loss for things to do. Just meeting people and shaking hands seemed to take up most of the time, and in between there were newspaper interviews and posing for pictures and touring London and all kinds of public appearances. The English people were tremendously kind and considerate. Their welcome to me, a stranger from a far country, was every bit as warm as that to their own climbers, and I could not help comparing this to the rather indifferent reception the British had had from the crowds in Nepal. I went to so many places I could hardly keep track of them. I spoke on the radio. I appeared on television, before I had ever even seen a set. And the interviews went on and on. Finally there were so many of them, and I had been asked so often, over and over, how I had felt on the summit of Everest, that I began to get dizzy from it. "Look, I have a suggestion," I finally said to the newspapermen. "The next time, *you* climb Everest and let me be the reporter. When you come down I'll ask you one thousand and one times how you felt on top, and then you'll know how I felt—and how I'm feeling now."

We spent sixteen days in London, and they went by as if we were in a dream. The only bad thing that happened was that Pem Pem took sick soon after we arrived and had to spend most of the time in a hospital. But Ang Lahmu, Nima, and I got all around: to the theaters and movies and shops and sightseeing places. Once we went to the carnival and rode in the scenic railway, and I had a fine time with the ups and downs. In fact, it reminded me of skiing. But Ang Lahmu got so excited she kept pounding my hand with her fists, and when the ride was over she said, "What you trying to do—kill me?" Being a woman, she had her own best times in the shops, and soon we had a great collection of things to bring back to India. Also, people were all the time offering us presents, but, though I appreciated their kindness, I did not think we should accept too many. "Why not?" Ang Lahmu and Nima would say. "Because it's not right," I would tell them. And then there would be a family argument. I especially remember one day when we were at a photography store and the dealer offered us our choice of cameras as a gift. Nima right away picked out an expensive Rolleiflex, but I told her, "No, no, that isn't nice. You take a simpler one." Later, back in Darjeeling, she said to my friend Mitra, "Papa was mean. He wouldn't let me have a good camera." To which I answered, "It wasn't I who was mean. It was you who were greedy. That's the trouble with you females—you're always greedy."

Colonel Hunt invited us to come to his home in the country. Though we would have liked to go, we did not feel it right to leave London while Pem Pem was still sick; but we made two visits to Major Wylie and his wife, who lived close by. Also, I saw many old friends, such as Eric Shipton and Hugh Ruttledge, with whom I had fine talks about the old days. And I was deeply touched when Dr. N. D. Jacob, who had been so kind to me out in Chitral during the war years, made a journey of 500 miles just to see me. With all these things, the time passed very quickly. Sometimes, when I was not meeting people or being taken places, I would manage to go out on my own to look around the streets of London, and this I enjoyed greatly. For these walks I would wear Western clothes, in the hope I would not be recognized; and sometimes it worked. But for official events I wore mostly the Indian things that Pandit Nehru had given me in New Delhi.

After several days the other expedition members began to come back from their homes, and then came the biggest event of our London visit, which was our presentation to the Queen. As we drove to Buckingham Palace the streets were full of crowds, and I was very impressed by the British Guards with their red coats and big fur hats. Before meeting the Queen we went to a tea party on the palace lawn, and there was a great crowd there too; so much so that we were all pressed together and I felt that my insides might be squeezed out. But then I thought, "No, I shouldn't complain. At least I'm thin. But what's happening to poor Ang Lahmu—who isn't?" When the outdoor party was over we were taken into a big reception room in the palace, where we met the Queen and the Duke of Edinburgh. All the expedition members and their families were there, and the Queen and Duke presented us with medals and awards. Afterward there were refreshments, and for a minute I almost thought I was back on Everest again, because what I was drinking was—lemon juice! The Queen was very friendly and interested and asked me several questions about the climb, and also about my other expeditions. Colonel Hunt, who knows Hindustani, started to translate for me, but I found that I could understand and answer all right in English, and this pleased me very much.

After the reception there was a stag dinner, given for us by the Duke, and we were all wearing our decorations from here to there. Later, there was another reception. And the next day, and the day after, there were still more receptions, most of them given by various ambassadors. For a while that was all life seemed to be—one big reception—and I thought, "What would happen to me if this was *chang* I was drinking all the time, instead of just tea and lemon juice?"

At last the time came to leave London. The Hunts, the Wylies and many others came to see us off, and anyone who saw our good-byes would not have to be told that there was no ill feeling between us. The English people had been wonderful to me. The English climbers were fine men, and my friends. In spite of the minor difficulties, and the troublemakers who had tried to make them big, we had had a great and successful expedition. And if Colonel Hunt ever leads another expedition back to the Himalayas he will find me ready to help him in every way—even if it might not be possible for me to go along myself.

"Good-bye! Good luck! Happy landings!"

Then we were in the plane flying toward Switzerland; and the expedition was over at last, for now there were only myself and family and my adviser, Lhakpa Tschering. It had been arranged that we would spend two weeks in Switzerland on the return trip, as guests of the Swiss Foundation for Alpine Research, which had organized two expeditions in 1952, and when we arrived there was a big welcome and reunion all over again. But this time it was not to be just crowds and receptions and interviews. After only one night in Zürich I went off to the mountains with some of my old friends, and I had a chance not only to see, but climb, the famous Alps. Mr. Ernst Feuz, of the Swiss Foundation, and his wife made all the arrangements, traveled with us, and gave us a wonderful time.

First we went to the little mountain resort of Rosenlaui, where the well-known guide, Arnold Glatthard, runs a school of climbing, and there we went up a nice rock peak called the Semilistock. Then we went over to the Jungfrau, rode up to the hotel on the Jung-fraujoch on the mountain train, and the next morning climbed the peak itself. One of my companions was Raymond Lambert, and as we stood on top, looking out over the earth, I think perhaps the same thought was in both our minds: that with a little better weather, a little better luck, we could have done this together a year before—on the top of the world. These were the only real climbs there was time for, but I enjoyed them very much and liked the sound, firm rock of the Alpine peaks. One thing that especially impressed me was how similar the high Swiss valleys were to those of my old home in Solo Khumbu, though of course in the Alps the heights and distances are much smaller than in the Himalayas. And I was also interested to see how many people there were who went climbing—men and women, old and young, and even very small children.

Later we spent a day in Chamonix, across the French border. Here I met several members of the Lyons expedition to Nanda Devi, with whom I had climbed in 1951, and also Maurice Herzog, who had led the great ascent of Annapurna in 1950. He was a fine man, who had come through his hard experiences very well, and I much admired the way he drove his own car, even though he had lost all his fingers and toes. Unfortunately there was time only to look at Mont Blanc, not climb it. But I doubt if we could have fitted on to it if we had tried. On the day we were in Chamonix it was so crowded with climbers that it looked less like a mountain than a railway station.

So the two weeks passed, almost before they had seemed to begin. And then I had bid my friends good-bye and we were in a plane again, bound for home. . . . "Home," I thought. "What will it be like after all this time?" I had left Darjeeling on March first; now it was early August; and in those five months I had hardly for a minute stopped moving. I had reached the top of Everest. I had come down from Everest into a different world. I had traveled halfway across that world and been cheered by crowds and met prime ministers and queens. "Everything has changed for me," I thought. "And yet nothing has really changed, because inside I am still the same old Tenzing." . . . All right, I was going home now. But home to what? What would I do? What would happen to me? . . . First there would be more receptions, more interviews, more crowds, more *zindabad*. But then what?

I had climbed my mountain, but I must still live my life.

Descent of the Matterhorn

EDWARD WHYMPER

The last great unclimbed peak of the Alps, the Matterhorn, was ascended on July 11, 1865, bringing to a close the Golden Age of Alpine Climbing. Edward Whymper, one of the best-known names in mountaineering, was part of a large party that included Lord Francis Douglas, the Rev. Charles Hudson, Douglas Hadow, and guides Peter Croz, Old Peter Taugwalder, and Young Peter Taugwalder. Their glorious victory was immediately overshadowed by the infamous and tragic descent, which Whymper wrote of in Scrambles Amongst The Alps.

Hudson and I again consulted as to the best and safest arrangement of the party. We agreed that it would be best for Croz to go first, and Hadow second; Hudson who was almost equal to a born mountaineer in sureness of foot, wished to be third; Lord F. Douglas was placed next, and old Peter, the strongest of the remainder, after him. I suggested to Hudson that we should attach a rope to the rocks on our arrival at the difficult bit, and hold it as we descended, as an additional protection. He approved the idea, but it was not definitely settled that it should be done. The party was being arranged in the above order whilst I was sketching the summit, and they had finished, and were waiting for me to be tied in line, when someone remembered that our names had not been left in a bottle. They requested me to write them down, and moved off while it was being done.

A few minutes afterward I tied myself to young Peter, ran down after the others, and caught them just as they were commencing the descent of the difficult part. Great care was being taken. Only one man was moving at a time; when he was firmly planted the next advanced, and so on. They had not, however attached the additional rope to rocks, and nothing was said about it. The suggestion was not made for my own sake, and I am not sure that it even occurred to me again. For some little distance we two followed the others, detached from them, and should have continued to had not Lord Francis Douglas asked me, about 3 P.M., to tie on to old Peter, as he feared, he said, that Taugwalder would not be able to hold his ground if a slip occurred.

A few minutes later, a sharp-eyed lad ran into the Monte Rosa Hotel, to Seiler, saying he had seen an avalanche fall from the summit of the Matterhorn on to the Matterhorn Glacier. The boy was reproved for telling idle stories; he was right, nevertheless, and this was what he saw.

Michel Croz had laid aside his axe, and in order to give Mr. Hadow greater security, was absolutely taking hold of his legs and putting his feet, one by one, into their proper positions. As far as I know, no one was actually descending. I cannot speak with certainty, because the two leading men were partially hidden from my sight by an intervening mass of rock, but it is my belief, from the movements of their shoulders, that Croz, having done as I have said, was in the act of turning round, to go down a step or two himself; at this moment Mr. Hadow slipped, fell against him, and knocked him over. I heard one startled exclamation from Croz, then saw him and Mr. Hadow flying downward; in another moment Hudson was dragged from his steps, and Lord F. Douglas immediately after him. All this was the work of a moment. Immediately we heard Croz's exclamation, old Peter and I planted ourselves as firmly as the rocks would permit: the rope was taut between us, and the jerk came on us both as on one man. We held; but the rope broke midway between Taugwalder and Lord Francis Douglas. [Ropes, in Whymper's mountaineering era, were of twisted hemp and notoriously weak.] For a few seconds we saw our unfortunate companions sliding downward on their backs, and spreading out their hands, endeavoring to save themselves. They passed from our sight uninjured, disappeared one by one, and fell from precipice to precipice on to the Matterhorn Glacier below, a distance of nearly 4,000 feet in height. From the moment the rope broke it was impossible to help them.

So perished our comrades! For the space of half an hour we remained on the spot without moving a single step. The two men, paralyzed by terror, cried like infants, and trembled in such a manner as to threaten us with the fate of the others. Old Peter rent the air with exclamations of "Chamonix! Oh, what will Chamonix say?" He meant, Who would believe that Croz could fall? The young man did nothing but scream or sob, "We are lost! we are lost!" Fixed between the two, I could move neither up nor down. I begged young Peter to descend, but he dared not. Unless he did, we could not advance. Old Peter became alive to the danger, and swelled the cry, "We are lost! we are lost!" The father's fear was natural—he trembled for his son; the young man's fear was cowardly—he thought of self alone. At last old Peter summoned up courage, and changed his position to a rock to which he could fix the rope; the young man then descended, and we all stood together. Immediately we did so, I asked for the rope that had given way, and found, to my surprise—indeed to my horror—that it was the weakest of the three ropes. It was not brought, and should not have been employed, for the purpose for which it was used. It was old rope, and, compared with the others, was feeble. It was intended as a reserve, in case we had to leave much rope behind, attached to rocks. I saw at once that a serious question was involved, and made him give me the end. It had broken in mid-air, and it did not appear to have sustained previous injury.

For more than two hours afterward I thought almost every moment that the next would be my last; for the Taugwalders, utterly unnerved, were not only incapable of giving assistance, but were in such a state that a slip might have been expected from them at any moment. After a time, we were able to do that which should have been done at first, and fixed rope to firm rocks, in addition to being tied together. These ropes were cut from time to time, and were left behind. Even with their assurance the men were afraid to proceed, and several times old Peter turned with ashy face and faltering limbs, and said, with terrible emphasis, "*I cannot!*"

About 6 P.M. we arrived at the snow upon the ridge descending toward Zermatt, and all peril was over. We frequently looked, but in vain, for traces of our unfortunate companions; we bent over the ridge and cried to them, but no sound returned. Convinced at last that they were within neither sight nor hearing, we ceased from our useless efforts; and, too cast down for speech, silently gathered up our things, and the little effects of those who were lost, preparatory to continuing the descent. When, lo! a mighty arch appeared, rising above the Lyskamm high into the sky. Pale, colorless and noiseless, but perfectly sharp and defined, except where it was lost in the clouds, this unearthly apparition seemed like a vision from another world; and, almost appalled we watched with amazement the gradual development of two vast crosses, one on either side [a natural phenomenon created by sunlight on mist and sometimes referred to as a fog-bow.] If the Taugwalders had not been the first to perceive it, I should have doubted my senses. They thought it had some connection with the accident, and I, after a while, that it might bear some relation to ourselves. But our movements had no effect upon it. The spectral forms remained motionless. It was a fearful and wonderful sight; unique in my experience, and impressive beyond description, coming at such a moment.

I was ready to leave, and waiting for the others. They had recovered their appetites and the use of their tongues. They spoke in patois, which I did not understand. At length the son said in French, "Monsieur." "Yes." "We are poor men; we have lost our Herr; we shall not get paid; we can ill afford this." [They had been employed as guides by Lord F. Douglas, one of the victims.] "Stop!" I said, interrupting him, "that is nonsense; I shall pay you, of course, just as if your Herr were here." They talked together in their patois for a short time, and then the son spoke again. "We don't wish you to pay us. We wish you to write in the hotel book at Zermatt, and to your journals, that we have not been paid." "What nonsense are you talking? I don't understand you. What do you mean?" He proceeded—"Why, next year there will be many travelers at Zermatt, and we shall get more *voyageurs* [hikers who hired guides.]"

Who would answer such a proposition? I made them no reply in words, but they knew very well the indignation that I felt. They filled the cup of bitterness to overflowing, and I tore down the cliff madly and recklessly, in a way that caused them, more than once, to inquire if I wished to kill them. Night fell; and for an hour the descent was continued in the darkness. At half-past nine a resting place was found, and upon a wretched slab, barely large enough to hold the three, we passed six miserable hours. At daybreak the descent was resumed, and from the Hörnli ridge we ran down to the chalets of Buhl and on to Zermatt. Seiler met me at his door, and followed in silence to my room: "What is the matter?" "The Taugwalders and I have returned." He did not need more, and burst into tears; but lost no time in useless lamentations, and set to work to arouse the village. Ere long a score of men had started to ascend the Hohlicht heights, above Kalbermatt and Z'Mutt, which commanded the plateau of the Matterhorn Glacier. They returned after six hours, and reported that they had seen the bodies lying motionless in the snow. This was on Saturday and they proposed that we should leave on Sunday evening, so as to arrive upon the plateau at daybreak on Monday. Unwilling to lose the slightest chance, the Rev. J. M'Cormick and I resolved to start on Sunday morning. The Zermatt men, threatened with excommunication by their priests if they failed to attend the early mass, were unable to accompany us. To several of them, at least, this was a severe trial. Peter Perren declared with tears that nothing else would have prevented him from joining in the search for his old comrades. Englishmen came to our aid. The Rev. J. Robertson and Mr. J. Phillpotts offered themselves, and their guide, Franz Andermatten; another Englishman lent us Joseph Marie and Alexandre Lochmatter. Frédéric Payot and Jean Tairraz of Chamonix also volunteered.

We started at 2 A.M. on Sunday the 16th, and followed the route that we had taken on the previous Thursday as far as the Hörnli. From thence we went down to the right of the ridge, and mounted through the *séracs* of the Matterhorn Glacier. By 8:30 we had got to the plateau at the top of the glacier, and within sight of the corner in which we knew my companions must be. As we saw one weather-beaten man after another, turn deadly pale, and pass it on without a word to the next, we knew that all hope was gone. We approached. They had fallen below as they had fallen above—Croz a little in advance, Hadow near him, and Hudson some distance behind; but of Lord F. Douglas we could see nothing. We left them where they fell, buried in snow at the base of the grandest cliff of the most majestic mountain of the Alps.

All those who had fallen had been tied with the Manila, or with the second and equally strong rope, and, consequently, there had been only one link—that between old Peter and Lord Francis Douglas—where the weaker rope had been used. This had a very ugly look for Taugwalder, for it was not possible to suppose that the others would have sanctioned the employment of a rope so greatly inferior in strength when there were more than two hundred and fifty feet of the better qualities still remaining out of use. For the sake of the old guide (who bore a good reputation), and upon all other accounts, it was desirable that this matter should be cleared up; and after my examination before the court of inquiry which was instituted by the government was over, I handed in a number of questions which were framed so as to afford old Peter an opportunity to exculpating himself from the grave suspicions, which at once fell upon him. The questions, I was told, were put and answered; but the answers, although promised, have never reached me.

Meanwhile, the administration sent strict injunctions to recover the bodies, and upon the 19th of July twenty-one men of Zermatt accomplished that sad and dangerous task. Of the body of Lord Francis Douglas they, too, saw nothing; it was probably still arrested on the rocks above. The remains of Hudson and Hadow were interred upon the north side of the Zermatt church, in the presence of a reverent crowd of sympathizing friends. The body of Michel Croz lies upon the other side, under a simpler tomb; whose inscriptions bears honorable testimony to his rectitude, to his courage and to his devotion.

So the traditional inaccessibility of the Matterhorn was vanquished, and was replaced by legends of a more real character. Others will essay to scale its proud cliffs, but to none will it be the mountain that it was to its early explorers. Others may tread its summit-snows, but none will ever know the feelings of those who first gazed upon its marvelous panorama; and none, I trust, will ever be compelled to tell of joy turned into grief, and of laughter into mourning. It proved to be a stubborn foe; it resisted long, and gave many a hard blow; it was defeated at last with an ease that none could have anticipated, but, like a relentless enemy—conquered but not crushed—it took terrible vengeance. The time may come when the Matterhorn shall have passed away, and nothing save a heap of shapeless fragments, will mark the spot where the great mountain stood; for, atom by atom, inch by inch, and yard by yard, it yields to forces which nothing can withstand. That time is far distant; and, ages hence, generations unborn will gaze upon its awful precipices, and wonder at its unique form. However exalted may be their ideas, and however exaggerated their expectations, none will come to return disappointed!

The play is over, and the curtain is about to fall. Before we part, a word upon the graver teachings of the mountains. See yonder height! 'Tis far away—unbidden comes the word "Impossible!" "Not so," says the mountaineer. "The way is long, I know, it's difficult—it may be—dangerous. It's possible, I'm sure; I'll seek the way; take counsel of my brother mountaineers, and find how they have gained similar heights, and learned to avoid the dangers." He starts (all slumbering down below); the path is slippery—may be laborious too. Caution and perseverance gain the day—the height is reached! and those beneath cry, "Incredible; 'tis superhuman!"

We who go mountain-scrambling have constantly set before us the superiority of fixed purposes or perseverance to brute force. We know that each height, each step, must be gained by patient, laborious toil, and that wishing cannot take the place of working; we know that benefits of mutual aid; that many a difficulty must be encountered, and many an obstacle must be grappled with or turned, but we know that where there's a will there's a way; and we come back to our daily occupations better fitted to fight the battle of life, and to overcome the impediments which obstruct our paths, strengthened and cheered by the recollection of past labors, and by the memories of victories gained in other fields.

I have not made myself an advocate or an apologist for mountaineering, nor do I now intend to usurp the functions of a moralist; but my task would have been ill performed if it had been concluded without one reference to the more serious lessons of the mountaineer. We glory in the physical regeneration which is the product of our exertions; we exult over the grandeur of the scenes that are brought before our eyes, the splendours of sunrise and sunset, and the beauties of hill, dale, lake, wood and waterfall; but we value more highly the development of manliness, and the evolution, under combat with difficulties, of those noble qualities of human nature—courage, patience, endurance and fortitude.

Some hold these virtues in less estimation, and assign base and contemptible motives to those who indulge in our innocent sport.

"Be thou chaste as ice, as pure as snow, thou shalt not escape calumny."

Others, again, who are not detractors, find mountaineering, as a sport, to be wholly unintelligible. It is not greatly to be wondered at—we are not all constituted alike. Mountaineering is a pursuit essentially adapted to the young or vigorous, and not to the old or feeble. To the latter, toil may be no pleasure; and it is often said by such persons, "This man is making a toil of pleasure." Let the motto on the title-page be an answer, if an answer be required! [*"Toil and pleasure, in their natures opposite, are yet linked together in a kind of necessary connection"*—Livy.] Toil he must who goes mountaineering, but out of the toil comes strength (not merely muscular energy—more than that), an awakening of all the faculties; and from the strength arises pleasure. Then, again, it is often asked, in tones which seem to imply that the answer must, at least, be doubtful, "But does it repay you?" Well, we cannot estimate our enjoyment as you measure your wine, or weight your lead—it is real, nevertheless. If I could blot out every reminiscence or erase every memory, still I should say that my scrambles amongst the Alps have repaid me, for they have given me two of the best things a man can possess—health and friends.

The recollections of past pleasures cannot be effaced. Even now as I write they crowd up before me. First comes an endless series of pictures, magnificent in form, effect, and color. I see the great peaks, with clouded tops, seeming to mount up for ever and ever; I hear the music of the distant herds, the peasant's *jodel* and the solemn church bells; and I scent the fragrant breath of the pines: and after these have passed away, another train of thoughts succeeds—of those who have been upright, brave, and true; of kind hearts and bold deeds; and of courtesies received at stranger hands, trifles in themselves, but expressive of that good will toward men, which is the essence of charity.

Still, the last, sad memory hovers round, and sometimes drifts across like floating mist, cutting off sunshine and chilling the remembrance of happier times. There have been joys too great to be described in words, and there have been griefs upon which I have not dared to dwell; and with these in mind I say, Climb if you will, but remember that courage and strength are nought without prudence, and that a momentary negligence may destroy the happiness of a lifetime. Do nothing in haste; look well to each step; and from the beginning think what might be the end.

GLOSSARY

ABSEIL British term for **RAPPEL**.

ARETE A thin, sharp-crested ridge of snow or ice.

BELAY A system of using ropes and anchors fastened to a rock face to safeguard climbers from falls.

BERGSCHRUND A surface gap that forms between a glacier and higher snowfields, or between a glacier and a rock face, and which sometimes presents a major obstacle to climbers. See also **CREVASSE**.

BIVOUAC A night spent in the open on a mountain. Climbers carry necessary gear (stoves, shelter) when a bivouac is anticipated.

CAGOULE A lightweight, ankle-length, and windproof garment used by climbers for storm protection and as cover during nights on a mountain.

CARABINER A strong, metal snap link used to connect the climber's rope to the rock face.

CHIMNEY

A vertical fissure in a rock face that is wider than a crack but narrower than a gully. Chimneys often provide passage for climbers through otherwise impossibly steep or blank terrain.

CHOCK

An irregularly shaped metal piece with an attached wire or webbing loop that is jammed into a rock crack and attached to a climber's rope with a metal snaplink. See also **CARABINER**.

CRAMPONS

Metal spikes that fasten to climbers' boots and allow ascent of steep snow and ice.

CREVASSE

A crack in the surface of a glacier, which may be wide, deep, and dangerous. Climbers are usually able to cross crevasses either by jumping or on snowbridges. See also **SNOWBRIDGE**.

CWM

A deep, steep-walled, and usually snow-filled basin on a mountain.

DEADMAN

A lightweight alloy plate, also called a snow anchor, which when driven into the snow is used to safeguard ascending climbers. See also **BELAY**.

DIRECT AID

In this method of climbing, the rope, pitons and slings are used as climbing aids to overcome steep rock. See also **PITON, SLING**.

FIXED ROPE

A climbing rope that has been secured to the mountain and is used to assist in ascending or descending.

FREE-CLIMB

A method of climbing where the rope is used not to directly ascend, but only to arrest a fall.

HALF-BAG

A waist-length sleeping bag intended for use when sleeping on a mountain climb. See also **BIVOUAC**.

HEADWALL

The sheerest, often most difficult section of a cliff or mountain, and usually its uppermost.

JUMAR

The use of a one-way, metal locking device to ascend a rope. See also **PRUSICK**.

KARABINER

British term for **CARABINER**.

OVERHANG

A part of a rock or ice cliff that juts out beyond vertical and is difficult, if not impossible, to ascend.

PITONS

Metal spikes that are hammered into rocks and used to secure the climbing rope.

PRUSIK

A system for ascending a fastened rope, which uses a special knot (prusik) that "locks" on the fixed rope when weighted by the climber. See also **FIXED ROPE**.

RAPPEL

A method of sliding down a secured rope that is used by climbers to descend steep terrain.

SCREE

Unstable, stone-sized rock debris which gathers at the base of cliffs and crags, or in gullies and is tiring, and sometimes dangerous, to ascend. See also **TALUS**.

SERAC	A large pinnacle or tower of ice that is often unstable and dangerous to climbers passing underneath.
SHERPA	A race of people who have traditionally served as porters and climbing members to Himalayan expeditions.
SLING	A loop of nylon webbing used to safeguard climbers or when descending a cliff. See also **BELAY**, **RAPPEL**.
SNOWBRIDGE	A blockage of snow spanning a surface gap in a glacier, which, if strong enough, can be crossed by climbers. See also **CREVASSE**.
SPIKE	A pointed, projecting piece of rock, often used by climbers to attach a rope to the face for descending. See also **RAPPEL**.
SPINDRIFT	A fine and irritating wind-driven snow that seeps into insecurely fastened clothing and camp gear.
STAGE	In expeditionary mountaineering, the distance the climbers and their porters advance toward the mountain in one day.
STANCE	Any point on a steep rock or ice face where a climber can stand comfortably.
TALUS	Boulder-sized rock debris that gathers at the base of a cliff. See also **SCREE**.